Liberty and Education

This book takes the thinking of Quentin Skinner, Philip Pettit and J.G.A. Pocock on republican liberty and explores the way in which this idea of liberty can be used to illuminate educational practice. It argues that republican liberty is distinct from both positive and negative liberty, and its emphasis on liberty as non-dependency gives the concept of liberty a particularly critical role in contemporary society.

Each chapter formulates and expounds the idea that an empire of liberty requires the existence of what are termed 'liberty-bearing agents', and shows how education – with a particular emphasis on knowledge – is needed to foster the human powers that allow people to become liberty-bearing. It is also emphasised, however, that republican liberty is non-perfectionist and non-eudaimonic: the core values enshrined in an empire of liberty centre on non-dependency rather than the promulgation of a certain way of life. Drawing on prominent seventeenth-century contract theorists, the link between liberty and authority is explained, suggesting that appropriate authoritative structures need to underpin the provision of education, and especially schooling, if educational practice devoted to the pursuit of liberty is to flourish.

Liberty and Education will be of value to both educational theorists unfamiliar with republican theory, as well as republican theorists interested in how their theory might play out in education. It will also be of interest to researchers and students from the fields of politics and the philosophy of education.

Geoffrey Hinchliffe is Director of Academic Practice in the Centre for Staff and Educational Development, and an Honorary Lecturer in Education at the University of East Anglia, UK.

Routledge Research in Education

For a complete list of titles in this series, please visit www.routledge.com.

Liberty and Education

A civic republican approach

Geoffrey Hinchliffe

Routledge
Taylor & Francis Group

LONDON AND NEW YORK

First published 2015
by Routledge
2 Park Square, Milton Park, Abingdon, Oxfordshire OX14 4RN

and by Routledge
711 Third Avenue, New York, NY 10017

First issued in paperback 2016

Routledge is an imprint of the Taylor & Francis Group, an informa business

British Library Cataloguing in Publication Data
A catalogue record for this book is available from the British Library

Library of Congress Cataloging in Publication Data
Hinchliffe, Geoffrey.
Liberty and education: a civic republican approach /
Geoffrey Hinchliffe.
pages cm – (Routledge research in education)
1. Education – Philosophy. 2. Liberty – Philosophy.
3. Liberalism. 4. Republicanism. I. Title.
LB14.7.H555 2014
371.001 – dc23   2014007089

ISBN 13: 978-1-138-29087-7 (pbk)
ISBN 13: 978-0-415-73791-3 (hbk)

Typeset in Galliard
by Florence Production Ltd, Stoodleigh, Devon

To Mr Edwin Ho, NHS

Contents

Preface

The seeds of this book were sown in 2010 during a period of extended convalescence when I began to read the books and articles of Quentin Skinner. His ideas are the key inspiration for writing this book, although I alone am responsible for the particular path I have taken.

I am grateful for the support given to me by the University of East Anglia in Norwich, especially my colleagues in the Centre for Educational and Staff Development and also the School of Education. The latter, in particular, has strongly encouraged my researches and reading.

The Philosophy of Education Society for Great Britain financed some study leave without which I would still be trying to finish the book even now. It is always a pleasure to attend PESGB conferences and over the years I have been very lucky to make so many friends at these events. They give the right balance of critique and encouragement.

I need to thank my wife, Sally Ladbrooke, for her patience in helping me see this project through.

Frances Greenhalgh was kind enough to proof read for me and the final result would be much the poorer without her efforts.

Acknowledgements

Much of Chapter 6 ('Liberty and pedagogy') is based on the ideas in the following:

Hinchliffe, G. (2011) 'What is an educational experience?'. *Journal of Philosophy of Education*. 45 (3), pp. 417–431.

Chapter 9 ('Liberty and educational authority') is based on the following article:

Hinchliffe, G. (2013) 'On the need for well-founded educational authority in England'. *Oxford Review of Education*. 39 (6), pp. 811–827. [Online] available at: www.tandfonline.com.

Introduction

This book has two main aims. First of all, it aims to build on the concept of republican liberty, which has been developed by a number of philosophers and historians, primarily by J.G.A. Pocock (1975), Quentin Skinner (1998, 2002a, 2008a, 2008b) and Philip Pettit (1997, 2008). The second aim is to explore the relation between liberty and education and to show how for us living today the republican version of liberty requires a flourishing system of public education if liberties are to be sustained. Moreover, once a clear concept of liberty is in place then there is the basis for mounting a critique of educational practice and provision. Some reflections of this character can be found in Part II and Part III of the book, although critique of educational provision and practice is not its primary aim.

It is, I believe, Pocock and Skinner's salutatory achievement to have recovered the concept of liberty from the writings of philosophers and political actors, especially those from the early modern period – the Renaissance to the seventeenth century. In doing so they have shown how an historical perspective can go far beyond mere description and archive retrieval – they have furnished an account of conceptual discovery made all the more vibrant because it is illustrated with real, historical examples as opposed to those made-up examples, beloved by some philosophers as they sit in their study. Their account becomes all the more credible because it is rooted in human experience. By developing, in addition, an account of the way in which the republican conception was itself challenged at the very time it was being formulated, they are able to show how it has always been contestable and how the idea of liberty has changed and developed through argument and counter-argument, which often had, at the time, real significance in terms of the political ordering of, say, mid-seventeenth-century England. But in addition to all this, Skinner has not hesitated to enter – indeed, even to direct to some extent – areas of contemporary philosophical debate about freedom and liberty. His efforts in this respect have been amply refined and developed by Pettit who has provided both additional historical insight and further analytical treatment. Thus it is no accident that two recent full-length treatments of freedom by Ian Carter (1999) and Matthew H.

Kramer (2003) devote substantial portions of their books to discussing the ideas of Skinner and Pettit.

The claim is that republican liberty focuses on a type of constraint that has been neglected: that is, attention is paid to the extent to which my freedom is affected not only by interference but also, and especially, by domination. This modifies the account of negative liberty usually associated with Isaiah Berlin, in which liberty is characterised by the absence of constraints (Berlin, 1969) as opposed to positive liberty in which liberty consists of the realisation of selected human powers. Whereas with negative liberty I am free providing I am not being interfered with, the very threat of domination or subjugation is sufficient to impair my liberty when this is taken in the non-dominative sense. The paradigm case is that of the slave whose benevolent master affords him a far better life than that led by the impoverished freeman; yet the latter is not subjugated in the way that the slave is even if the master refrains from interfering in the slave's life. This kind of freedom – freedom from dependency – constitutes what is held to be a *republican* form of liberty because it is associated with the kind of liberty put forward by supporters of republics – whether the pre-Empire Roman republic, the Italian city states of the fifteenth century or the republican movement in England in the mid-seventeenth century. However, as Skinner is at pains to make clear, republican liberty must be differentiated from positive liberty: in particular, advocates of republican liberty do not advocate or argue for particular ends of life over and above that of the desire for liberty. In that respect, republican libertarians are as one with advocates of negative liberty: to use philosophical parlance to be elaborated in Chapter 2 of this book, they are strictly 'non-perfectionist'. There are two further implications of republican liberty, as I shall refer to it: first, that political authority should be constituted such that each person is free from domination and, second, that each has the resources or powers so that domination can be resisted. These two features are not independent of each other, for though arrangements in civil society must be such that no individual is subjugated yet it is only through conditions established by the state that individuals can develop resources to resist subjugation, whether individually or collectively.

Thus, an account of liberty needs also some account of those human powers that make their *free* exercise so important. As we shall see, this does not entail that liberty simply consists in the exercise of appropriate powers: those powers also need to be under the self-direction of an agent, often in co-operation with others. This also involves an acknowledgement of responsibility for actions and beliefs: to undertake an action freely implies, other things being equal, that I am responsible for that action (again, often in co-operation with others). In addition, it will be a crucial feature of my account of liberty that each recognises the other as what I term a liberty-bearing agent. That is precisely what the master of the master–slave relation (no matter how benevolent) does not do. Indeed, non-interference need not be based on any recognition at all of an agent as liberty-bearing, but may proceed from strategic reasons: this gives one's negative liberty a somewhat precarious basis. Finally, I will give an account of the relation between liberty and authority. For if liberty is construed as being normatively situated then relations between liberty-bearing agents must be mediated by authoritative structures that support and sustain liberty. And I shall also argue that a crucial part of liberty is its exercise in such that those structures need to be maintained and kept intact. Otherwise one's liberty ends up dependent on the good will of others. That would be little different from the situation described by those republicans of the seventeenth century who objected that while the crown was perfectly willing to grant subjects their liberties, this was dependent on the King maintaining his good will towards them.

Although advocates of republican liberty have provided us with what might be termed an essential historico-philosophical analysis, there has been little written on the application of republican liberty to contemporary political and social arrangements. It is sometimes thought that it is just here that the republican argument is at its weakest: given that in much of the world negative liberties are reasonably secure (to varying degrees), ridicule is heaped on the idea that republicans now wish us to cultivate civic virtue and earnestly participate in politics at all levels (see, for example, Robert Goodin who concludes his brief analysis of republican liberty in this vein with the statement 'we were right to have a look and we were right to reject' (2003)). My concern, however, is not so much the need to develop civic virtue (although I will be arguing for the necessity of some degree of political participation). Rather, my concern is with the prevalence of domination and dependency in contemporary societies, including (and especially) those in the so-called developed world. This is where the second aim of this book comes in: to show how the perspective of republican liberty can be used to inform and develop different and hopefully pertinent ways of thinking about education. It is perfectly true, of course, that domination and dependency – if not downright servitude – exist in many domestic situations and in the workplace generally. Indeed, a person can well find themselves enjoying a full range of political liberties and also be treated in the home as 'liberty-bearing' only to find that, each day as they enter their workplace premises, the very last thing that their employer cares for is their liberty. This can include high-earners too. But the focus in this book will be on education because of its critical importance in the role of maintaining our liberties.

I mentioned above that an analysis of liberty needs to include some account of the development of human powers and one of the purposes of education is to assist in this. Thus, part of my attention will be paid to the curriculum and what form it needs to take for the maintenance of our liberties. However, rather than conceiving knowledge in terms of a propositional content I explore the idea of a 'space of reasons' and the role of judgement. This, I believe, gives a much more dynamic foundation to thinking about curriculum issues. Furthermore, participating in the space of reasons is something that is fitting particularly for persons that are conceived to be carriers of liberty, or liberty-bearing agents. Their freedom is manifested in the giving of and asking for reasons.

But the reach of education goes further than curriculum. For one thing, in all developed states education is compulsory at least up to the age of 16; yet from the standpoint of liberty, what possible justification does the state possess in taking children out of their homes irrespective of what their parents might want for them? If this is to be justified at all then it must be in terms of educational authority. The lack of any substantive *authority* to educate is an enduring feature of the education scene, certainly in England, and therefore I wish not only to provide a philosophical basis for educational authority but also to make some more practical proposals as well. My analysis also has implications for those who educate because when teachers are considered as the bearers of a certain kind of liberty that emphasises non-dependency this gives substantive normative grounds for developing a kind of professionalism that is far removed from the tendency to see teaching as another species of service provision. Teachers, I will argue, are more than hired hands who must do the bidding of government, employers or parents. Respect for the teaching profession is, I submit, one of the key components of any society that proclaims itself a lover of liberty. This, of course, gives teachers immense responsibility not least of which is the development of children and students as liberty-bearing persons. However, in the current situation the position of teachers sometimes approaches that of subaltern status in so far as they are mere providers of a learning service, the nature of which is determined by politicians, parents and employers.

The book is in four parts. The first part develops and hopefully strengthens the analysis of republican liberty and includes a sketch of the idea of 'human powers' needed to defend liberty. The second part explores how the development of reason, judgement and knowledge can be placed at the service of liberty. The third part explores the relation between liberty and authority, taking educational authority as a case study. This includes some reflection on the role of educational authority in England, a country in which education has become, over the last thirty years, highly centralised. The fourth part explores the relevance of the ideas of Antonio Gramsci.

A brief word on terminology is needed. Like many who write on this subject, I can see no hard and fast distinction between 'liberty' and 'freedom'. Their meanings are co-extensive. Nonetheless I prefer on the whole, but by no means exclusively, the term 'liberty'. The reason for this is partly because the term 'liberty' has a certain historical provenance that connotes the idea of a political-social context, which happens to be the prime focus of this work (as opposed to personal liberty and privacy). In addition, I prefer the use of the term 'liberty' in part because of the way in which freedom has been commandeered by enthusiasts of the free market – the so-called 'neo-liberals'. They tend to use the term 'freedom' to denote absence of interference (especially by government) and the availability of choice. My argument against them is that their version of freedom is too restrictive and too easily sanctions dependency, at least in the economic sphere. Moreover, the desire of the more extreme free-marketeers to turn everyone into a customer and entrepreneur is itself a threat to freedom. Where I use the term 'liberty' I will be specifically referring to republican liberty unless the context suggests otherwise. Finally, in using the term 'republican' it should not be thought that I have any particular interest in undermining the British monarchy or of fostering any allegiance to the Republican Party in the USA.

Part I

Liberty and dependency

Chapter 1

Republican liberty and the free state

The value of an historical approach

The most accessible historical account of republican liberty is to be found in Quentin Skinner's short book, *Liberty before Liberalism* (1998). I propose to use this chapter partly to summarise Skinner's central contentions, but also to explore further some of the issues he raises. But why employ an historical approach in the first place? This may seem odd to those – there are many – who freely acknowledge the value of historical study but are less sure that such an endeavour has any central bearing on the problems we face today. Writings from fifteenth-century Florence or seventeenth-century England almost always reflect much smaller, highly stratified societies that were geographically compact, it may be said; but to take ideas from such different times risks putting forward theses for our own times that may be initially interesting but ultimately rather absurd.[1] Such a position may be held without taking anything away from the scholarship that has informed our understanding of the ideas of the early modern period.[2]

Such a perspective arises easily from what is now a commonplace, namely that ideas can only be understood in the 'context of the times'. What was perhaps at one time a salutary reminder against making quick and facile judgements concerning actions and beliefs that at first sight seem incomprehensible has surely turned into something else: the making of those actions and beliefs the prisoners of the past. The corollary is that we become mere prisoners of our own present, unable to learn anything unless the problems and concerns of the past are framed in the language and conceptual apparatus of the present. It is then only a short step to what might be called the condescension of posterity according to which certain civic attitudes or certain religious beliefs, for example, have been 'outgrown'. What this condescension fails to achieve is any kind of historical imagination that enables us to think of our present circumstances thus: human beings once did differently to what we do now. It prevents us from using the light of historical perspective to shine critically on our own beliefs and actions. More than that, it does not allow us to conceptualise possibilities that were once themselves lived and experienced and may be of use to us now. We may, of course, decide we have no desire to return 'to the past' but it may also dawn on us that *things don't need to be as they are*. But deprived of a past that is seemingly useless, emancipatory alternatives are then found in the realm of science fiction and fantasy and, above all, in new technologies.

Yet there is even more than this to be gained for taking history seriously. Employing what might be called a genealogy of concepts, we are able to see how concepts were used in earlier times and how they differed from what at first glance is the same concept today. Moreover, we can interrogate the contested nature of, say, 'liberty' in order to understand its trajectory over a period. We can then understand that the meanings we use (and those dimensions of meaning that are forgotten) are the result of accretions over time in which some usages are buried. Thus – for example – a concept that is in common use and which for many has a settled meaning may turn out to have a rather interesting past and, indeed, a richness of use that simply escapes us unless we are prepared to do a bit of digging. Such is the case with the concept of liberty.

This historical approach is adopted by one of Europe's most committed adherents to liberty. For one of the most striking features of Machiavelli's *Discourses*, in which he uses the writings of Livy to reflect on the politics of his own times, is that although there is much said about the subject of liberty, all of Machiavelli's reflections are set in the context of discussions about actual cities and states. Machiavelli is able to use history to ground his exploration of liberty in real examples. Definitions or conceptualisations about the meaning of liberty per se are apparently avoided, in favour of examples and evidence on the one hand and conclusions and judgements on the other. For example, we are told fairly early on that discord is to be welcomed: 'To me those who condemn the quarrels between the nobles and the plebs, seem to be cavilling at the very things that were the cause of Rome's retaining her freedom' (Machiavelli, 1960: 113). He goes on to explain that, drawing on the experience of Rome between the expulsion of the Tarquins and the rise of the Gracchi, disorder tended to result in 'laws and institutions whereby the liberties of the public benefitted' (114). He agrees that at first sight the scenes witnessed were apparently 'almost barbaric' – for example, 'how the senate decried the people, how men ran helter-skelter about the streets, how shops were closed', but goes on to conclude that the 'demands of a free populace are very seldom harmful to liberty, for they are due either to the populace being oppressed or to the suspicion that it is going to be oppressed' (115). Thus, Machiavelli uses historical example to illustrate the internal dynamic of the progress of liberty and to draw the conclusion that disorder is not necessarily harmful to the preservation of liberty.

Machiavelli seems to have been aware that the kinds of things he wanted to say would not always be welcome to his readers – hence the dedication to two citizens who he thought would understand the point of what he was doing (see the greeting to his fellow citizens, Zanobi Buondelmonte and Cosimo Rucellai: 93). In the preface this is made more explicit for he wishes to rectify 'the lack of a proper appreciation of history, owing to people failing to realise the significance of what they read'. His methodology is therefore what might be termed 'evidence-grounded' and as such he is happy to draw conclusions in conformity with what the evidence is saying, even if this may be unpalatable. There are numerous examples of this but one more will suffice. Machiavelli is discussing the way in which liberty and a republic can be undermined by certain social types of persons. One example is the gentry – those persons 'who live in idleness on the abundant revenue derived from their estates without having anything to do either with their cultivation or with other forms of labour essential to life. Such men are a pest in any republic.' (246).

He concludes that only a monarch can control them because of the forces required. If, however, one wishes to set up a self-governing republic, 'no-one can succeed unless he first gets rid of the lot' (247). The *Discourses*, then, is an attempt to give an account of those factors (social, political, judicial and moral), which promote not merely the idea of a self-governing republic but also the reality of one as well. The effect of the historically based methodology is the implicit, tacit acknowledgement of the entity 'republic', which is then made explicit through examples and evidence. Machiavelli, it seems, has no need to give an analytical exegesis of what constitutes a republic because this form of government has existed for (even when Machiavelli wrote) nearly 2000 years. Yet, historically speaking, republics were to prove a fragile, vulnerable form of government. In addition to the assumption of power by the Medici in Machiavelli's beloved Florence throughout much of the fifteenth century, during which republican forms of self-government were progressively undermined,[3] in 1494 the nemesis of the Renaissance city state arrived. This took the form of the arrival of the huge armies of Charles VIII of France and was succeeded in the next century by a series of invasions that extinguished Machiavelli's hopes.[4] Whereas the city states of Northern Italy had been able to repel the invader in the thirteenth century, this was now beyond them. The nation state now became the fundamental and most significant political reality which endures still, today. Hence, also, a natural tendency to view Machiavelli's writings today with interest – even with admiration of their brilliance – but essentially of mere antiquarian value nonetheless.

The concept of a free state

In some respects, Quentin Skinner adopts a similar methodology to that of Machiavelli and, indeed, the focus is the same – the self-governing republic. For like Machiavelli, Skinner uses historical examples (including ones from Roman antiquity) in order to identify and reflect upon an idea, shifting and changing its complexion in the course of its historical trajectory. But whereas Machiavelli had before him a real, living example of a republic (one admittedly never less than fragile), for Skinner the idea – the concept of a republic – is seemingly buried in historical trends and events. The suggestion is that the idea of liberty not only has a historical dimension, but that it is inscribed within political structures. Liberty cannot be theorised about and cannot even be given practical or prudential determinations apart from those structures. But what Machiavelli was able to take for granted, to some degree, now must be clearly identified and delineated. Skinner suggests, therefore, that liberty – freedom – can only flourish within a *free state*. Skinner traces this idea back to the Roman Republic in which some of the central elements of such a state are to be found. The basic concept can be found in Livy, who, having recounted in Book 1 of his *History*, recounted how the first kings were expelled, then starts Book 2 thus:

> My task from now on will be to trace the history in peace and war of a free nation, governed by annually elected officers of state and subject not to the caprice of individual men but to the overriding authority of the law (*imperia legum*).[5]

Through the course of his *History*, Livy then develops the elements of *libertas*, including the exercise of government through authority, so that even if the people did not actually govern, their authority and approval was needed. In addition, Livy traces the idea of equality before the law (*aequa libertas*) so that gradually, over time, neither social status nor past achievements could place a person beyond the law.[6] Skinner, building on these basic elements, also identifies another key element of *libertas* – the absence of servitude, the idea that one is self-directed as opposed to being in the power of another and so directed by him. Persons in servitude are *obnoxius* – perpetually subject to or liable to harm or punishment (Skinner, 1998: 42–46). The condition of servitude can apply either to states and peoples or to individuals.

We are unaccustomed to liberty or freedom being ascribed to corporate entities, but it is nevertheless appropriate to do so in a twofold sense. First, a state is free if it is not subjugated by another – in this sense, the thirteen states in North America that emerged independent from Britain in the eighteenth century were 'free states'. Richard Price, in his *Two Tracts* written in 1778, argued that in some ways state subjugation was worse than personal slavery:

> Between one state and another there is none of that fellow-feeling that takes place between persons in private life. Being detached bodies that never see each other, and residing perhaps in different parts of the globe, the state that governs cannot be a witness to the sufferings occasioned by its oppressions.
>
> (Price, 1991: 30–31)

Historically, it is unsurprising that the concept of a free state has never taken root in British political culture, since its history from the early nineteenth century through until 1960 (at least) has been one in which it has played the role of subjugator 'in different parts of the globe'. And although Price spoke about subjugation in terms of the sufferings of the subjugated, a constant theme of republican writings since Livy is that benign treatment reduces not one jot the fact of servitude. So long as the British Empire flourished, no state or peoples under its tutelage could be free, no matter how generous and kind its rulers might have (sometimes) been.

The conclusion to be drawn is that it is not only a subjugated state that is unfree; the state that is doing the subjugation is not free either. It is not free simply because it is assuming the role of mastery, which Hegel explored in the well-known passage on Master and Slave in his *Phenomenology of Spirit*. In considering their relation at the level of consciousness, Hegel explores the position of the master: seemingly independent and free, his position is compromised in that the only recognition he can attain is from someone dependent:

> the object in which the lord has achieved his lordship has in reality turned out to be something quite different from an independent consciousness. What now really confronts him is not an independent consciousness but a dependent one . . . his truth is in reality the unessential consciousness.
> (Hegel, 1977: 116–117)

This passage partly reflects the idea that if one's position as free and independent is only possible through inflicting subservience on others then the value of that recognition is affected unfavourably owing to the nature of its source – for Hegel, someone in bondage. The wider point that Hegel is making is that freedom depends on its recognition by another who is also free: that my freedom is absolutely and wholly dependent on its recognition by another because the main threat to freedom comes not from nature (which merely limits what we are *able* to do or not do but not our freedom as such), but from other human beings. Unless others are prepared to recognise me as a person who has the status of 'free person' then my claims to be free are as nothing. And, of course, as Hegel points out in his inimitably abstract manner: 'the movement is simply the double movement of two self-consciousnesses' (112), so that freedom involves, at its core, a *dialectic of recognition*. The freedom of each is dependent on recognition from the other; but this recognition has to be freely given – it must be the recognition, not of someone in bondage but of someone who is an 'independent consciousness'. In order, therefore, to avail myself of her recognition I myself must recognise the other as free. That is the only way in which her recognition of me can be freely given. And we should add at this most fundamental level of what might be called the logic of freedom, there is an inherent and basic equality in respect of those undertaking recognition. For even if the recognition of myself came from another not in my subjugation but from another who is perceived as being less worthy than myself, then again,

I would not be receiving the recognition I need because in that circumstance the value of my own freedom would be called into question.

The emancipatory dimension in the dialectic of recognition is sometimes disputed. For example, Orlando Patterson in his *Slavery and Social Death* has suggested that the master has no need of recognition from the slave: '. . . the master could and usually did achieve the recognition he needed from other free persons, including masters' (Patterson, 1982: 99). The culture of slavery enables masters to receive recognition not from slaves – who after all have suffered a 'social death' – but from other masters, and this is all they need. Yet as Patterson himself points out, 'freedom can mean nothing positive to the master, only control is meaningful' (98), whereas in a culture of liberty, the very thought of being able to control others is something base and ignoble. The recognition that one seeks in this case is the recognition of a free person, and the point is that masters are unfree to the extent that they cannot enjoy relations with others on the basis of liberty. The master may get recognition but only as a controller of destinies, not as someone who shares in those destinies.

Thus, it is that the logic of freedom has, inscribed in its very heart, a dialectic of recognition. Dominating others may enable me to enjoy the fruits of their labour but it does not give me, according to Hegel, what I really crave: recognition as a free person. Hegel's account of recognition is given at what could be seen as a primordial level, at the level of consciousness. But his account can surely be translated into a normative context and even a political context. We can see now, more clearly, why it is that a state that assumes the role of mastery cannot itself be wholly free. For its freedom to subjugate comes from superior power of arms and resources whereas, if it was seriously interested in its freedom, the idea of subjugating any other people would not even be considered as a possibility for it. Those thirteen newly freed colonies in North America – even leaving aside the subjugated Afro-American peoples in their midst – had their status as free states compromised owing to their depredations of the land, goods and persons of the native Americans. Even as late as 1890, a mere 27 years before their entry into World War I, the 7th Cavalry Regiment succeeded in killing at least 150 Lakota Sioux, many of them women and children, at Wounded Knee in the final action against the indigenous population in the American Indian War.

On this strict criteria of what counts as a free state (namely, that it refrains from oppressing other peoples) the Roman Republic itself hardly had an unblemished record since even before the Republic collapsed it had already subjugated large parts of North Africa and the Eastern Mediterranean, albeit with differing degrees of severity. Of course, it may be that there are those who are not cut out for freedom, who prefer servitude:

> The result was that in place of distaste for the Latin language came a passion to command it. In the same way, our national dress came into favour and the toga was everywhere to be seen. And so the Britons were gradually led

on to the amenities that make vice agreeable – arcades, baths and sumptuous banquets. They spoke of such novelties as 'civilisation', when really they were only a feature of their enslavement.

(Tacitus, 1948: 72)

These remarks of Tacitus in his work on Agricola, one of the early Roman governors of Briton, give us one point of view: the Britons themselves, unfortunately, had no such eloquent spokesperson of their own.

The other feature that Quentin Skinner identifies as an essential element of free state, already alluded to, is the absence of servitude *within* the state (Skinner, 1998: 50–53). For seventeenth-century republicans it was not the exercise of the King's veto on legislation (the so-called 'Negative Voice') proposed in Parliament that they objected to, but its very existence. Thus the Nineteen Propositions, which Parliament proposed in order to assert Parliamentary authority,[7] were defended by Henry Parker in his 1642 pamphlet *Observations upon some of his Majesties late Answers and Expresses*[8] in these terms:

Power is originally inherent in the people, and it is nothing else but that might and vigour which such or such a society of men contains in itself, and when by such or such a law of common consent and agreement it is derived into such and such hands, God confirms that law. And so man is the free and voluntary author, the law is the instrument, and God is the establisher of both.

(Haller, 1934: 167)

Having established the relation between a free people, the instrument of law and God's role in establishing both of these, Parker goes on to assert:

It is not just nor possible for any nation so to enslave itself and to resign its own interest to the will of one lord, as that that lord may destroy it without injury, and yet to have no right to preserve itself.

(168)

And having established the general principle of the need to resist 'the will of one lord' he then moves to the specifics of the case, with Charles I clearly in his sights:

If kings [who] be so inclinable to follow private advice rather than public, and to prefer that which closes with their natural impotent ambition before that which crosses the same, are without all limits, then they may destroy their best subjects at pleasure, and all charters and laws of public safety and freedom are void, and God hath not left human nature any means of sufficient preservation. But, on the contrary, if there be any benefit in laws to limit princes when they are seduced by *privadoes* and will not hearken to the Great Council of the land, doubtless there must be some court to judge of that seducement and some authority to enforce that judgment, and that court and authority must be the Parliament or some higher tribunal. There can be no more certain crisis of seducement than of preferring private advice before public.

(196)

As Michael Braddick explains, Parker was something more than a private individual himself: a Parliamentarian who was secretary to the Committee of Safety established in 1642, his views were read and listened to (Braddick, 2009: 196). No-one reading this pamphlet would be in any doubt as to exactly whom it was who was being seduced by 'privadoes'.

The aim of these seventeenth-century republicans (Milton prominent among them) was to focus on constitutional mechanisms that permitted the exercise of a prerogative or discretionary powers, the effect of which confirmed the dominion of the exerciser of those powers without reference to liberties, interests or beliefs to those affected by them. A free state could not be accounted 'free' if it had pockets of dominion within it, particularly so where they were sanctioned by constitutional procedure, common law or precedent.[9] Moreover, a free state cannot be accounted free simply by virtue of democratic forms of government. From the standpoint of the one in servitude it makes no difference whether this is sanctioned by one person or through a majority vote. The experience of the Rump Parliament and the Interregnum tended to re-enforce the view among republicans that sharing of powers was required in order to escape democratic tyranny (Skinner, 1998: 32–35).

A free state therefore can be seen as animated by a dialectic of recognition in a twofold sense: the relation between states is one that is free of domination, and at the same time within such a state the relation between persons is free of dominion as well. Moreover the cultural impulses of one tends to enforce the other because the cultural values established in a culture of recognition *within* a state are likely to make persons uncomfortable with the thought that domination is acceptable *between* states.

The challenge of Hobbes to republican liberty

However, in addition to the idea of a free state there needs to be a clear, unambiguous conception of the liberty-bearing nature of each and every individual in such a state. In some respects, it was Hobbes (the arch opponent of republicanism) who clearly delineated the basic conditions of liberty. In the first place, a person must be seen as the author of his or her own actions, and in the second place a person is capable of authorising another:

A person is he, whose words or actions are considered, either as his own, or as representing the words or actions of another man . . . when they are considered as his owne, then is he called a Naturall Person: And when they are considered as representing the words and actions of another then is he a Feigned or Artificial Person.

Of Persons Artificiall, some have their words and actions owned by those whom they represent, And then the person is the Actor; and he that owneth his words and actions, is the Author.

(Hobbes, 1991: 111–112)

The terms 'natural' and 'artificial' merely reflect the difference between the source of authority and those authorised to act on behalf of those who have authorised them. This tells us much of what we need to know about the structure of liberty: namely, an action is either directly owned by a person or she has authorised another to act on her behalf. And providing, we can add, that the authority is validated – that is to say, that the person *acknowledges* those words spoken by the 'person artificiall' are indeed authorised by her. By the same token, the person in authority acknowledges that the source of that authority lies in another. In this way, the relation of authority reflects the basis of liberty as mutual recognition. Part of what it is to be a free person is that I can authorise others to act on my behalf (but not on their own behalf) and this authorising capacity is symptomatic of my liberty. The point is crucial: for I may authorise a person to place my own life in jeopardy without for one moment sacrificing my own liberty.[10] Indeed, I may authorise laws that I myself subsequently break without undergoing any change in my liberty-bearing status. For I authorise what is permissible and impermissible, not predict what I myself will do at some future point.

It will come as little surprise to learn that, for Machiavelli, liberty was not an originary state of the human condition: his historically based methodology led him to view liberty in terms not of natural liberty but of civil liberty.[11] If, as I have argued, liberty is inextricably linked to both recognition and authorisation then liberty can never be natural, that is to say, originary: liberty is intrinsically normative. That is how it was viewed by Roman and Renaissance writers. However, Quentin Skinner argues that the crucial step from ancient, 'neo-roman' republican liberty to modern, negative liberty was made by Hobbes[12] for whom liberty was signalled by 'the absence of externall Impediments' (Hobbes, 1991: 91). The difficulty with this approach, from a republican standpoint, is that one's originary freedom is compromised the moment one enters a normative order. Even a law that constrains me – irrespective of whether I have authorised it or not – impairs my liberty. This is the precise opposite of the Republican view in which liberty can *only* be created and sustained within a normative order that recognises persons as liberty-bearing. The whole point of Hobbes' analysis was that in a state of nature, liberty was *un-recognised*.

This point was noticed by James Harrington who was under no illusions whatsoever as to the threat posed by Hobbes (referred to by Harrington merely as 'the Leviathan'). His *Commonwealth of Oceana* was published 5 years after Hobbes' great work, in 1656, and it is difficult not to suppose that Harrington had that work propped open as he was writing his own book. Although Harrington, in general, was unable to rival Hobbes for conciseness of thought and economy of expression (few can) he nevertheless understood just what was at stake. For example, early on in the *Commonwealth* he takes up Hobbes' notorious mocking of republicanism where, in the *Leviathan*, he draws the reader's attention to the words LIBERTAS above the portal of the city of Lucca and then goes on to observe that nobody can infer that the citizen of that city had any more liberty than one who lived in Constantinople. On Hobbes' reading of liberty as negative (i.e. where freedom = absence of constraints) the logic is impeccable. But Harrington makes the following observation:

> For to say that a Lucchese hath no more liberty or immunity from the laws of Lucca than a Turk hath from those of Constantinople, and to say that a Lucchese hath no more liberty or immunity *by* the laws of Lucca than a Turk hath by those of Constantinople, are pretty different speeches. The first may be said of all governments alike, the second scarce of any two: much less of these, seeing it is known that whereas the greatest bashaw is a tenant as well of his head as of his estate, at the will of his lord, the meanest Lucchese that hath land is a freeholder of both, and not to be controlled but by the law.
>
> (Harrington, 1992: 20)

Harrington is making both an adversarial point (the bashaw is a mere tenant of his own head) and a deeper one: that it is *by* the laws that we are free. Our freedom is created and maintained through the law. Harrington rams the point home by continuing: 'and that framed by every private man unto no other end (or they may thank themselves) than to protect the liberty of every private man, which by that means comes to be the liberty of the commonwealth' (20).

Note that a free state is one in which 'every private man' is free and is so because he has authorised laws explicitly designed to 'protect the liberty' of each. And if, perchance, in those conditions laws are made which do not protect liberty then they only have themselves to blame. The five little words in parentheses are most important here: the fate of each is in their own hands. Freedom means accepting the consequences of getting it wrong.

Harrington was right to be fearful of Hobbes' analysis for other reasons as well. When Hobbes explains the nature of the covenant that creates the commonwealth, he speaks of separate persons – a 'multitude' – agreeing to confer authority on the sovereign through which the multitude is transformed into 'one person' so that the sovereign 'may use the strength and means of them all, as he shall think expedient, for their peace and common defence'

(Hobbes, 1991: 121). The transfer of authority is absolute: the multitude have transformed themselves into *subjects*. What is more, from a republican stand-point they have, each and every one of them, authorised the servitude to which they are subject! It is a perverse use of authority that strips me of the uncertain liberties that I used to have in exchange for peace and security. Of course, as Hobbes points out, where the 'Law is Silent' one is free.[13] But then so, of course, is the slave: he or she is free to roam, at their master's pleasure. And since the law is subject to the sovereign's pleasure, from a republican stand-point there is no difference between servitude that has been authorised and servitude that has not. After all, the sovereign could determine what books could be read[14] and could, in effect, determine the boundaries and scope of one's negative liberty, which could be as wide or as narrow as he pleased. The fact that the sovereign could also be an assembly rather than one person makes no difference at all. As part of the Leviathan, persons are designated subjects, not free.

Harrington also bravely considers Hobbes' barb against those who wish to be ruled by an 'empire of laws', namely that they forget the 'easie truth that Covenants being but words and breath have no force to oblige, contain, constrain, or protect any man, but what it has from the publique Sword' (123). Harrington considers this but instead of directly challenging Hobbes head-on, loses himself in a discussion – digression even – over what it takes to maintain the armed resources of a militia (see Harrington, 1992: 13). Fortunately, a powerful reply to Hobbes' challenge does come from Locke. The question is one of motivation; Hobbes is maintaining that subjects will only come by appropriate motivations if there is a sword at the ready. Locke, however, takes the discussion to a different level, as follows:

> For Law, in its true Notion, is not so much the Limitation as the direction of a free and intelligent agent to his proper interest, and prescribes no further than is for the general Good of those under that Law. Could they be happier without it, the Law, as an useless thing would of itself vanish; and that ill deserves the name of Confinement which hedges us in only from Bogs and Precipices. So that, however it may be mistaken, the end of law is not to abolish or restrain, but to preserve and enlarge Freedom: For in all states of created beings capable of Laws, where there is no Law, there is no Freedom.
>
> (Locke, 1960: 347–348,
> para 57)

The difference from Hobbes is that for Locke, free persons who are under the law can use the law to 'preserve and enlarge freedom' whereas for *subjects*, law's function is only to restrain. Free persons have a different relation to the law so that the sword is needed only as a last resort.

The republican free state as a non-eudaimonic order

Even though from a republican standpoint Hobbes' analysis of political relations ends up in the wrong place (namely, servitude) the journey taken in getting there is full of interest. In particular, that the form of the state is artificial, mirrors the role of civic liberty as opposed to natural liberty, except that for Hobbes the hypothetical act of covenanting leads not to the role of citizenship but that of subject. There is, therefore, in this artificial normative order that takes the form of an 'empire of law', no area in which the writ of the law does not run: there is no 'outside the law'. Even our privacy is *within* the law as a 'protected' area. Nevertheless, Hobbes seems indisputably 'modern'. First of all, as we have noted, Quentin Skinner has shown[15] how the concept of negative liberty was developed by Hobbes partly in order to repudiate the idea of republican liberty that was gaining ground in England, in order to advance the conception of political obligation elaborated in his *Leviathan*. And it was liberty in its negative formulation that gradually prevailed over the eighteenth and nineteenth centuries.[16] In addition, Richard Tuck (1979, 1993)[17] has also shown how the seventeenth-century rights-based theorists Grotius, Hobbes and Puffendorf rejected not only the concept of republican liberty but also the whole structure of Aristotelian thinking that went with it. This meant also that the whole discourse of civic virtue, citizenship and civic participation was rejected too. It also included a rejection of any kind of perfectionist, eudaimonic discourse that aims at perfecting the human good through civic life. Are, then, republicans committed to a pre-modern view of civic life?

The Aristotelian assumptions regarding eudaimonia (well-being or happiness, or more generally, human flourishing) take as their starting point the idea that there is a final end to human purposes, for the sake of which activities are undertaken. This end is the human good that characteristically involves rational activity, which engages not only the theoretical dimension of reasoning but also its practical dimension that is orientated to action (praxis) and as such engages the emotions through the cultivation of dispositions or virtue.[18] The moral theory of the *Nicomachean Ethics* starts to take on a wider political significance when it is placed within a civic setting. For it is one of the key assumptions of Aristotle that a person's moral and ethical capabilities, the development of which constitutes human flourishing, can only be given full expression within a socio-political setting because the moral life is one that is shared. This is the basis of the common good, the furtherance of which is the end of political activity: 'the end and purpose of a polis is the good life and the institutions of social life are a means to that end', which is described as a 'perfect and self-sufficient existence'.[19]

On one interpretation, the republican ideal is essentially Aristotelian in character because the virtues required for human flourishing within a *polis* are also those required for maintaining and developing civic liberty. Our liberties therefore *consist* in exercising citizenship and participation in governance at different levels. This approach certainly represents one strand of thinking in the republican tradition. However, not all Aristotelians are republicans. For example, the tradition of 'communitarianism' established by Alisdair MacIntyre (1981) shows only weak associations with republicanism simply because MacIntyre's concerns are more ethical than political. Nevertheless, there are a range of republican theorists who would endorse a broadly Aristotelian approach.[20] However, although this certainly represents a strand of thinking in the republican tradition it ranges from the relatively mild suggestions from Michael Sandel on the salutary effects of civic participation (1996: 330) to the full blown theory of praxis (action) associated with Hannah Arendt who maintained that we can only achieve full humanity through active civic participation (1958, especially the sections on the *vita activa*).

There are two problems with the Aristotelian approach to republicanism. The first is that it is not clear how the claims of liberty and the claims for the need for human flourishing can be squared unless it is proposed that we are only free *through* human flourishing. This starts to look like another version of positive liberty (see Berlin, 1969) and it is not at all clear whether the republican approach would either need, or indeed want, to endorse this approach. To put it bluntly, republicans endorse the freedom *not* to flourish because the notion of self-determination, which does indeed underpin the republican ideal of liberty, implies that one takes the consequences of one's actions – which may include a deep desire not to have anything directly or indirectly to do with flourishing.[21] The second problem is that it is not at all clear that, historically, republicans were that much influenced by Aristotelianism. This is broadly Quentin Skinner's position, and he has argued that there is a significant strand in the tradition of republicanism in which a 'roman' or 'neo-roman' influence stemming from the Codex of Roman law can be traced in the growth of republican thinking in Medieval and Renaissance Italy (Skinner, 2002b: 13). It is the republicanism of Machiavelli that belongs to this tradition, which in fact owes little to Aristotelian thinking. In this, he was at one with Hobbes.

However, none of this implies that such thinking can be merely discounted. For one thing, in a free state political activity *is* important, whether or not it involves human flourishing. Moreover, the concept of *phronesis*[22] gives us a way of conceptualising that might be called the practico-theoretical economy of political activity. In addition – and this is most important – the fact that the purpose of political life is not for flourishing (but rather the maintenance of liberty) does not mean that in non-political spheres of social life the concept of flourishing can be of great service.

But if republicanism eschews what I have termed, perhaps clumsily, a 'non-eudaimonic order', it may nevertheless make use of civic virtue and civic participation in a different way: namely as a *means* to the preservation and maintenance of liberty. This might be termed instrumental virtue: if one is going to successfully hold on to one's liberty and avoid dominion then one had better, for prudential reasons, develop a desire for participation and the appropriate dispositions (virtues) as well – a desire to take risks, a willingness to stand in front of a crowd, having the courage to be found wrong and having to back down as a result, in full public glare. Civic action is not for the fainthearted, but it is necessary all the same.[23] This is the view that Quentin Skinner proposed in an earlier article on Machiavelli: 'He merely argues that the performance of public services, and the cultivation of virtues needed to perform them, both prove on examination to be instrumentally necessary to the avoidance of coercion and servitude' (Skinner, 1984: 217). These virtues include modesty, a degree of moderation in one's speech and demeanour, courage, persistence and especially the willingness to take risks and not to be frightened of 'tumults'.

But the difficulty with 'instrumental republicanism' is that the virtues needed cannot be just instrumental: one cannot adopt dispositions when it suits one and drop them when it does not. They need to become a way of life, a part of one's identity, otherwise the temptation to stay at home or to socialise with friends (rather than attend political meetings) will be too strong. Yet, however one construes one's responsibilities, in a free state these seem to require a degree of civic action. Therein lies the advantage of the Hobbesian state: one can cheerfully withdraw from public life – but only because one has, from a republican standpoint, willingly signed up to one's own servitude.

Are we, then, obliged to embrace a eudaimonic life after all? Are we, perforce, obliged to conceive of our own good in terms of relentless civic activity? There is one construal of eudaimonia that may provide a more palatable answer. First of all, one stretches the term 'rational activity' so that it includes a range of activities – including ones that involve pleasurable, non-ratiocinative activity, and expressive of creative activities. The next step is to disavow the idea that eudaimonia consists of a single goal (e.g. the goal of an ethical life suffused with virtue) for the sake of which everything is done. Finally we say that happiness – the good life – consists of a range of ends all of which are differing kinds of rational activity, broadly construed. These activities then become constituents of the final end, some (but not all) of which will include civic activity.[24] I am not entirely convinced that such a view of eudaimonia is quite what Aristotle had in mind[25] but what could be called an inclusive view of eudaimonia does provide a social ethic that is appropriate for a free state.

Yet these reflections merely throw into relief a much deeper and older question, namely which is the best life – the *vita activa* or the *vita contemplativa*? The inclusive notion of eudaimonia merely provides a re-statement of the problem rather than a solution. For we can readily concede that both the contemplative, private life and the life devoted to civic activity are worthwhile: but the inclusive view does nothing to help us decide between them. These matters, interestingly enough, were even debated in the Florentine republic: for example, Hans Baron noted that Coluccio Salutati, the chancellor of Florence during the crisis of 1402 (when that republic was in great danger of succumbing to the Caesar-like ambitions of Giangalleazzo Visconti, the head of state of Milan), was distinctly ambivalent about the merits of the two contrasting ways of living.[26] In a survey of Baron's analysis of this matter, and also taking into account the views of a range of scholars on how best to interpret the seeming fluctuations in Salutati's thinking, J.G.A. Pocock suggests, rather convincingly, that this issue was neither resolved in 1400 and, by implication, nor can it be fully resolved today: 'that ambivalence as between civic and contemplative values was inherent in the humanist mind' (Pocock, 1975: 66). There is, then, a dialectic between the two sets of values that is driven not only by differing conceptions of eudaimonia but also by *fortuna*. For chance, fate, can be guaranteed to wreck the best laid and philosophically determined plans of us all: sometimes we have no choice but to engage in politics, whether we like it or not. That being the case, we are best served by a cast of mind that is inclined to see the virtue and merit in the politically active life.

Conclusion

I have tried to show that an historical perspective in thinking about the idea of liberty helps us to identify some of its key elements. For example, we need to locate liberty within the idea of a free state, a state that avoids domination both within its borders and in its relations with other states. If liberty is considered purely in its negative form then the idea of a free state becomes less important since negative liberty may exist surrounded by pools of domination. But I have also tried to elaborate the idea of a non-perfectionist liberty as well. This is important since if republican liberty is given a communitarian interpretation then it may look as though the exercise of liberty must take the form of participation at the level of community. Yet I have also insisted that liberty, if it means anything, requires an environment in which people can live a life of non-participation, in which they obey the law, pay their taxes and are left alone. How can these competing views be reconciled? Part of the answer is to recognise that this tension is part of what liberty requires. In order to defend my liberty I may well have to take part in community affairs and participate even if this is not my first choice and even if I am somewhat suspicious of those who seem overly enthusiastic about 'joining in'. In the well-known phrase of Philip Pettit, liberty requires 'resilience' if it is to survive – and especially if domination is to be resisted – and this make the grounds of political participation prudential (Pettit, 1997: 24–25). However, it was also noted that the maintenance of liberty depends on recognition. This recognition needs translating into appropriate authority structures – something that will be examined in more detail in Part III.

The next two chapters will develop a more analytical treatment of the idea of liberty and dependency, without abandoning the historical perspective.

Notes

1 For example, Robert Goodin (2003), who gently mocks the pretensions of civic virtue and active citizenship.
2 The breadth and detail of the scholarship on the history of ideas in the Renaissance and early modern period since World War II is truly dazzling, ranging from (for

example) Hans Baron (1966), Nicolai Rubenstein (1968) and Eugenio Garin (1965) to the more recent writings of Skinner (1978) and Pocock (1975), which draw substantially on the pioneering work of these, and many other, indefatigable scholars.

3 See J.R. Hale (1977) for an account.

4 See Mallett and Shaw (2012).

5 See the beginning of Book 2, chapter 1 in Livy (1960).

6 See Chaim Wirszubski (1950: 9–15).

7 For an account, see Braddick (2009: 182–196)

8 A full copy of the pamphlet can be found in Haller (1934).

9 James Harrington (1992) understood this: 'If setting up for liberty you impose yokes, he (God) will destroy you'. He goes on to give Rome the benefit of the doubt: 'If you have subdued a nation that is capable of liberty, you shall make them a present of it, as did Flaminius unto Greece' (229).

10 'Neither the Sergeant, that could command a Soldier to march up to the mouth of a Canon, or stand in a Breach, where he is almost sure to perish, can command that Soldier to give him one penny of his money' (Locke, 1960: 407, para 139).

11 See Pettit (1997: 43–45) for a discussion of the eighteenth-century origins of this distinction.

12 See Skinner (*passim*) e.g. 1998: 79–80; 2003a: 15–17.

13 See Hobbes (1991: 152).

14 'It is annexed to the Sovereign to be judge of what opinions and doctrines are averse ... and who shall examine the Doctrines of all books before they are published' (Hobbes, 1991: 124).

15 Especially in his book *Hobbes and Republican Liberty* (2008b).

16 See Ghosh (2008), Skinner (2003a) and Skinner (2008c).

17 Tuck (1993) argues, interestingly, that as interest in the worthy Cicero declined in the sixteenth century, interest in the more cynical, world-weary Tacitus rose in the seventeenth century.

18 See Aristotle (1980: Book 1, especially 1094a1–1094b11 and 1096b27–1097a14) for the key moves in eudaimonic theory.

19 See Aristotle (1946: Book 3, chapter ix, para 13).

20 For a longer discussion, see Peterson (2011: 57–97).

21 I discuss this further in Chapter 2.

22 See Aristotle (1980: Book VI).

23 This is sometimes called 'instrumental republicanism' – see Peterson (2011: 61).

24 This view of the Aristotelian final end is argued by J.L. Ackrill (1980: 15–33).

25 Ackrill's view is disputed by Anthony Kenny (1977).

26 See Baron (1966): 106–118.

The value of liberty

The analysis of liberty offered here is normative – that is, a concept rooted in norms that signify actions and modes of living, which are seen to be valuable or less valuable. Moreover, for reasons to be explained shortly, it is a concept that must also be situated within laws, rules and conventions that are authoritative. The implication of this is that any particular concept of liberty that is offered for consideration is going to be normative as well. The republican concept of liberty is just such a concept: it does not pretend to be neutral. But this approach – which may seem fairly obvious – has been called into question by some philosophers. For example, Hillel Steiner has suggested that 'it is not the job of philosophers to legislate on which linguistic (much less, moral) intuitions we may hold nor, therefore, on what conception of liberty we should employ' (1994: 6). This seems odd if only that the philosophers that we read – with profit – on the subject of freedom and liberty have no compunction whatsoever in offering us what they take to be significant theories which, if adopted, have a direct effect on the kind of social and political arrangements we should adopt. When we read Hegel or Berlin, Hobbes or Locke, Machiavelli or Rousseau that is precisely what we get. If Steiner's suggestion is pursued we are instead offered endless mundane examples of people being locked in rooms or otherwise preventing (or 'unpreventing') each other from undertaking ordinary, routine activities that could equally well have been undertaken under any regime, libertarian or fascist. Sometimes this approach is taken to absurd lengths. For example, Matthew Kramer has argued that technically we may be free even in the most constrained of circumstances: a person in a prison cell whose walls are enclosing on him is always free to let himself be pressed by the wall 'as if he were a lifeless object' (2003: 18–20). The idea, apparently, is that even if this person is overall unfree he still has this particular 'freedom' left to him. But of course, this particular freedom is utterly worthless – yet adopting a non-normative methodology prevents one from seeing that. Indeed, it takes a particular, almost perverse, effort of will to come up with such an example, abstracted as it is from experience. The desire to furnish a concept of freedom unblemished by history, a freedom plucked out of the lifeworld, is one motivated by the supposition that there is a pure, unadulterated concept that gives the essence of what freedom is.

Persons as liberty-bearing agents

Much of the contemporary discussion of liberty is influenced by Isaiah Berlin's essay *Two Concepts of Liberty* and his subsequent considered reflections (Berlin, 1969). Even now, over 50 years on, Berlin's words still resonate and give us pause for thought. Liberty, he says, is 'the absence of obstacles to possible choices and activities' (Berlin, 1969: xxxix) and this is not to be confused with self-mastery; rather, liberty consists of that social space within which I am free to be active, to be lazy, to be good or bad and suffer the consequences. This space is not logically dependent on self-government – and although a democratic regime is less likely to threaten this space than tyranny, this cannot be assured: 'Everything is what it is: liberty is liberty, not equality or fairness or justice or human happiness or a quiet conscience' (125). Berlin calls this negative liberty and it seems to me that any theory of liberty worth its name needs to hold on, if not to the specific arguments Berlin puts forward, then at least to some of the ideal that inspires them. What ideal is this? One may think of the aims of the allies in World War II as fighting against fascism, fighting for democracy or fighting for moral decency, and all of this would be true. But one could also think of those aims in very simple terms, which no fascist could countenance: the right to be left alone. The freedom *not* to join either the Hitler Youth or the Boy Scouts; the freedom not to participate in organised sports at school; the freedom not be rung by one's boss on his cell phone at weekends. Any theory of liberty that does not encompass this kind of freedom is, I suggest, suspect. Whatever the responsibilities of liberty might entail, room has to be made for this ideal.

When Berlin discusses positive freedom he initially starts by acknowledging a different kind of ideal: 'I wish to be the instrument of my own, not of other men's acts of will', which, he says, 'derives from the wish on the part of the individual to be his own master' (131). But then Berlin very quickly moves the argument so that the desire not to be the instrument of other men's wills turns into something different: it is a 'freedom which consists in being one's own master . . .', which turns into a 'metaphor of self-mastery' (132). It is then a short step from identifying 'self-mastery' with a higher self (e.g. based on reason) in the name of which my 'lower self' (base desires, irrational wants) can be coerced. This then leads swiftly to the grotesque scenario in which coercion in the name of self-realisation is something that my true self *has itself willed*. The crucial step is from the desire to be the instrument of my own will (not someone else's) to that of self-mastery. But the desire to be responsible for one's own actions – and that is what being 'an instrument of my own will' amounts to – is not the same as self-mastery. For I may indeed be an instrument of my own will and yet fail to master anything, least of all myself. Indeed, I may freely acknowledge that self-mastery is an impossible, unattainable and even undesirable aim and yet still prefer that I be held responsible for my actions. Thus I suggest that the initial element of positive liberty – the desire that I be an instrument of my own will and not of someone else's – is an idea central to any concept of liberty. To associate that particular desire with positive liberty and all its disreputable implications is mistaken.

In subsequent reflections on his essay, Berlin distinguished between liberty and the conditions of liberty (liii) and then, rather interestingly, suggests that differences of status resulting from private schooling are an example of social conditions that adversely affect the exercise of liberties. It is clear from this remark, as well as others, that Berlin is well aware of the need to address the conditions of liberty if its exercise is to flourish. But for all that, the concept of liberty remains for him, as it were, an empty space, as if the very space of non-interference that surrounds the individual were reflected in the concept itself. In his fear of advocating any elements that might suggest positive liberty he has ended up with a concept of liberty – negative liberty – which although containing one essential element of liberty – absence of constraints – is not fully complete either.

My suggestion, then, is that if we take liberty to include the absence of obstacles to possible choices and activities then, within the space in which a person acts, the ascription of responsibility (namely the idea that one is an instrument of one's own will) to that person is not additional to the concept of liberty and does not form a part of the conditions of liberty, but is one element of liberty itself.[1] The ascription of liberty is not merely to that of a 'space' but to an *actor*. John Charvet, in criticising the concept of negative liberty, suggested that on Berlin's proposal: 'one can be free only in so far as one *does not act*' (1993: 7). This judgement seems fair to the extent that if liberty is only seen as an opportunity concept, denoting the space of possibilities, it fails to pick out what is at the centre of that space, namely an agent. This is a different point to the well-known suggestion of Gerald MacCallum (1967), that freedom must always be analysed in a tripartite way in terms of the freedom of a person to do something in the absence of constraints (freedom 'of', 'to', 'from'). Rather, Charvet draws our attention to what it is for a person to undertake a *free* act. After all, MacCallum's analysis could apply to the actions of slaves, i.e. to persons who cannot be said to be 'free' at all. Charvet suggests that 'we need the idea that the determination of the world to be *x* rather than *y* is something brought about by the agent through the actualisation of his power of choosing', which implies, he goes on to say, that the agent is *responsible* for his choice. This goes beyond the idea of responsibility in the ordinary sense of the word. A slave may be held responsible by his master for a whole range of tasks and it is quite likely that the slave feels no injustice if he is held to account. But what the slave cannot do is determine that the world be '*x* rather than *y*' because his world is determined for him. It does not matter that my attempts to determine the world be successful – they may well end up in failure or, as is more usual, at best partial success. What counts is that I have a perspective on the world and that I am entitled to undertake my beings and doings in accordance with that perspective *and take the consequences*. It does not matter if in another person's eyes that perspective is unwholesome: it is up to me to change that perspective if the consequences suggest that I should. Thus I am not merely responsible for my actions in the straightforward sense that applies even to a slave, but I also have ownership of my beliefs as well as those actions that flow from those beliefs.

The best way I can think of to capture this idea is to say that we should see agents as liberty-bearing. Thus agents are not simply free in terms of MacCallum's analysis but they have this additional status as free persons, as bearers of liberty. This status is not something that can be accorded outside of an appropriate normative order. Moreover, it is something much more than mere negative liberty. As we have seen, it is true that negative liberty is an essential component of being a bearer of liberty. Nevertheless there are many cultures and societies today that permit degrees of negative liberty and yet where citizens are not seen as liberty-bearing. And even in societies where citizens are viewed in this way it is comparatively rare for this dimension of agency to be recognised across all activities that are undertaken. In fact, Isaiah Berlin himself has expressed the idea of a liberty-bearing agent in terms with which no advocate of republican liberty could disagree:

> The fundamental sense of freedom is freedom from chains, from imprisonment, from enslavement by others . . . to struggle for personal freedom is to seek to curb interference, exploitation and enslavement by men *whose ends are theirs, not one's own*.[2]
>
> (Berlin, 1969: lvi, emphasis added)

Freedom and un-freedom

As we have seen in Chapter 1, it is Quentin Skinner's contention that the concept of negative liberty is essentially Hobbsian in its theoretical provenance. In a development of his thinking presented in a lecture in honour of Berlin, Skinner suggests that there is an historic third concept of liberty (2002a). Thus he does not take the path of many of Berlin's critics and insists that there are not two concepts of liberty but only one. On the contrary, Skinner is inclined to agree with Berlin, namely that there *are* two separate concepts of liberty (2002a: 238). In the case of positive liberty, he suggests that it is not so much the desire for self-mastery as the fulfilment of self-realisation that makes one free: the realisation of one's own inner nature or potentiality or, as T.H. Green puts it, 'Freedom is the natural term by which a man describes to himself the state in which he shall have realised his ideal of himself' (1927: 17–18). Green wishes to argue that negative liberty by itself (and Green was using this term in pretty much the same way in the late nineteenth century as Berlin took it up many years later in the mid-twentieth century) provides no lasting satisfaction and is simply the essential precondition for the realisation of one's own essential rational nature. Skinner's objection to this line of thinking follows Berlin in so far as he objects to its prescriptive nature, suggesting that there are many different ends that we can pursue (2002a: 243).

What Skinner further suggests, however, is that negative liberty is inadequate as well because it is possible to live in a state of dependency even if one is not being interfered with. The mere awareness of dependency can create a situation in which persons behave in such an anticipatory, proactive way that the need for exercising any constraint on them never seriously arises. And we are all familiar with situations in which persons (sometimes ourselves) avoid saying certain things and take care not to stand out or draw attention to ourselves because to do so may invite the disapprobation of those in authority and those, especially, who can make things worse for us should they so wish (Skinner, 2002: 257). A further corollary of this kind of servitude is that innovatory acts or acts of courage become rarer and Skinner cites the impact of the works of Tacitus and Sallust on early modern republicans as they sought to draw parallels between the servile flattery of the Senate towards some of the Roman Emperors and the behaviour of courtiers in the reigns of James I and Charles II (260–261). Hence the claim that there is a historic third concept of liberty that includes absence of interference but also specifically includes absence of dependency.

What emerges from this analysis is a clear view of what *un-freedom* amounts to. First of all, there is a tendency towards developing a disposition of servility, of an acknowledgement of one's subordinate status. The prevailing characteristic here is one of acceptance: one accepts that the main purposes and events in one's life are determined by another and one also accepts that changes in one's regime resultant upon the changing will of one's master are entirely legitimate and acceptable. Even if one complains one does so in the sure understanding that one is there to do another's bidding and that is an end to it: even the servant does not take his own complaints seriously. In a later article Skinner suggests that, drawing on the writings of Richard Price, freedom consists of 'being able to do or forbear according to your own will or desires' (2008a: 89; Price, 1991: 26, 76). Those who live in a mode of servility have given up their ability 'to do or forbear' assuming they ever experienced it in the first place. Or rather, this ability is severely constrained because the main lines of one's life are determined by someone else. Moreover, the tight circle within which one can do and forbear is itself also determined by another. This means that in all respects except trivial ones I am entirely dependent on the will of another – my health, shelter and all my beings and doings. It matters not one jot if my master is a kindly soul or not: I am un-free.

But there is also another mode of un-freedom. I refer to that tendency – even if one does not regard oneself as servile – to play safe, to keep out of the way, to be careful that attention is not brought to oneself. Typically, there is a fear of challenging those decisions that one believes are misguided because to do so risks immediate exposure and all the adverse consequences that will ensue. Often this is in institutional or organisational contexts where the expectation is that one will be obedient and that the only way of dealing with decisions that one believes to be misguided is to keep quiet. If one raises doubts with an immediate line manager then that is the very most one can do. And finally there is even an unwillingness not only to challenge decisions but the very value-set that motivates them. One may be unhappy with the ends that the organisation serves and yet one is not just powerless but fearful of doing anything about it, often with good reason (e.g. the likelihood of instant dismissal). All things considered, it is just better to keep quiet. Although historically, republicans have tended to emphasise the former mode of un-freedom – the life of servility and all the dispositions of servitude that go with it – it seems to me that the second mode of un-freedom is more salient in present times. It is the fear of speaking out, of speaking one's mind: the fear of public exposure – the fear of public gaze. One retreats, as a result, into a private realm where one's beings and doings are of no interest to others and of no consequence either. One may even convince oneself that in the comfort of this private realm it is there that happiness is to be found: and if one is able to trade off happiness for freedom then what is wrong with that?

The responses to these two modes of un-freedom – servility and the fear of public gaze – constitute different ways of dealing with the fact that one can no longer 'forbear and do as one wills'. They are different ways of *not* being a liberty-bearing person. By contrast, citizens who are imprisoned for falling foul of laws and deprived of their civil liberties may still preserve 'their underlying status as free-men' (Skinner 2008a: 88). This applies not only to the freedom-fighter but also the criminal. The latter is responsible not only for his specific misdeeds but also for the set of behaviours and dispositions that led him to acts of criminality and it is because of this that he is liberty-bearing too.

Critiques of republican liberty

It may seem as if there is nothing that can be said about dependency that can't be expressed using the vocabulary of interference – the vocabulary of negative liberty. Moreover, since from the standpoint of liberty neither interference nor dependency are desirable, what difference should it make? The answer is: a great deal. For if it really is the case that liberty can only be impaired through interference then the implication is that there is only one kind of liberty worth pursuing, namely negative liberty. The whole republican tradition of liberty that Skinner, among many others, has been attempting to revive would be essentially of only historical, if not antiquarian, interest.

These thoughts are salient in considering the viewpoints of two of the more sophisticated critics of republican liberty. One of these has offered us the useful concept of opportunities exercised 'conjunctively'. For example, if I am confronted with the choice between my money or my life, then while I may still be technically free to choose one or the other I am no longer free to live my life in conjunction with keeping my money as well (Kramer, 2008: 34). Pursuing this analysis, Kramer goes on to suggest that if K can only engage in x, y and z through deferential behaviour s then K is no longer in a situation where he could engage in x, y and z while also having the choice *not* to engage in s (35), and that this follows 'straightforwardly from the doctrine of negative liberty'. One possible thought here is that we do not have to make any judgement as to the kind of activity involved. So if K is perfectly happy to engage in s-type activities then that is fine for K; but if by chance he doesn't then K is un-free. Whereas the standpoint of republican liberty here is quite unequivocal: if K doesn't mind engaging in s-type activities (currying favour and so on) then K is un-free whether he knows it or not. And if K does engage in s-type activities and hates every minute of it but can't see any alternative to it then his objective situation is still the same, except for the important difference that K now knows exactly what is going on.

However, I suspect that Kramer wishes to make a different kind of point because in an earlier work (2003: 33) he suggests that a person's freedom is desire-independent so that in judging the extent to which someone is free we look at the opportunities available and not just at what a person wants to do. Berlin made a similar point in his reflections on the 'Two Concepts' when he pointed out that if desires were a relevant factor I could make myself free in a constrained situation by the simple expedient of curbing my desires (Berlin, 1969: xxxviii–xxxix).

The chief aim of Kramer is to show how a person's 'overall' freedom is determined by combinations of opportunities available to him. Thus if a person suffers from two types of constraint, one being straightforward interference of some kind and the other being deferential behaviour she has to adopt in order to avoid further interferences, then Kramer is quite content to include and recognise deferential behaviour as arising from certain constraints. He has no wish, in other words, to deny that Skinner's analysis has brought to our attention certain types of constraints that hitherto have not received full attention. But because Kramer's attention is focussed on opportunities, constraints and interferences his gaze does not take into account the *status* of the person involved. For as soon as someone is obliged, as she sees it, to undertake deferential behaviour in order to avoid making things worse for her then she is no longer recognised as a liberty-bearing agent. So if we go back to the example of the well-treated slave who engages in deference to oil the wheels of her life in order to take full advantage of all the opportunities her master provides for her then, compared to the free-woman who is far less well off, the slave is more free: she can do more with her life. Yet the slave is in servitude and it is *that* which is the most significant feature of her situation – she may have more opportunities but she is not recognised as a free person, as liberty-bearing.[3]

Ian Carter has suggested that providing judgements are 'equivalent' in terms of what a person is free/not free to do, it matters little whether we reach this judgement from the standpoint of negative liberty or republican liberty (Carter, 2008: 59). But again, like Kramer, he focuses on the range of opportunities and constraints in order to make a judgement as to how free a person is. For it makes all the difference in the world as to whether K is *recognised* as a liberty-bearing person. If he is not then he is ripe for being treated as subordinate and dependent. The need for recognition to be built into the very understanding of what liberty is follows from the analysis of it as arising out of a normative order. The moment we abandon the stance of negative liberty then liberty immediately becomes relational in which a condition of my being free is that I am recognised as a liberty-bearing agent. The problem with K is that his liberty is not recognised and so if K happens to manage to get by without currying favour then this is down to chance rather than to any structural features of his situation. On the other hand, as soon as K is recognised as liberty-bearing then his situation changes dramatically. It may be that he still undertakes x, y and z, just as before. But the reasons for his doing so have changed because now K has to be *persuaded* that x, y and z are good things to do and, moreover, K's point of view has to be taken account of without there being any hint of a suggestion that K might care to indulge in s-type, i.e. deferential, activities.

The value of liberty

But why should we value a liberty-bearing life in the first place? Sometimes the value of liberty is thought to consist in the distinctiveness of the autonomous life. Thus Joseph Raz argues for the role of self-creation and the creation of value: 'a life is a normative creation, a creation of new values and reasons . . . personal autonomy is the ideal of free and self-conscious self-creation' (Raz, 1986: 387–389). Furthermore, such an individual is aware of options and capable of discrimination and 'does not drift through life' (391). But proponents of republican liberty are perfectly comfortable with the thought that someone may drift through life, providing they are not servile. To say that someone is liberty-bearing need not imply that they are required to lead a purposeful life, the main lines of which have been carefully considered and deliberated over. It is quite possible that one could live a life that is reactive in its nature, a life in which I manage to react to all the various events that beset me without ever having any overall plan, goal or purpose. Such a life may not be an autonomous life but it could still be the life of a free person. We may want to criticise such a person for 'not taking control of their life', but what we are criticising is merely one way of leading a life of liberty. If autonomy implies self-rule, I may be acutely aware that I have achieved no such thing in the course of my life and I may even have cause to regret that. Nevertheless, provided I have not been subjected to dependency then at least my life is one that has been lived freely. Of course, there might be reasons for supposing that the ideal of autonomy advocated by Raz has many merits and within the realm of civil society (for example, in schools and universities, in the world of art and creativity) this ideal could be pursued. But republican liberty is essentially a *political* concept and is therefore to be distinguished from conceptions of what is the best way of life. Another way of putting this is to say, as we have already mentioned in Chapter 1, that the concept of republican liberty is strictly non-perfectionist: it has not inscribed within it any explicit or implicit *ends* that must be pursued if one is to fulfil one's human destiny. These include the ends of autonomy, if that is construed along the lines outlined by Raz.

For some, living a life of liberty is living a distinctive life, a life that is stamped with one's own individuality. Such a Nietszchean ideal is strongly attractive, particularly the idea of self-sculpting so that one manages to elude the easy categories that some are only too quick to bestow on each other. This is, indeed, a recognisable trope of the twenty-first century and occupies a powerful place not only in high culture but also in popular culture. In itself, however, it has nothing whatsoever to do with liberty despite the attractions that individuals who exemplify such a life may have for us. The reason is that the supreme idea of self-worth involved owes nothing to the recognition of others as liberty-bearing, or being recognised by others as such. Indeed, the attractions of this way of life often involve setting oneself as apart and aloof from others, made all the more easy through the acquisition of wealth. The pursuit of individuality need not, of course, undermine liberty and may even enhance the worth of liberty, but only if the individual is prepared to recognise others as liberty-bearing as opposed to being mere members of the herd. The desire to be different from others is a powerful motive for embracing liberty, but it is not the same as liberty.

It is sometimes thought that liberty must involve a life that is chosen, a life that is the product of choices. The idea here is that a free person is responsible for the choices she makes, all the way down. For example, Christians are responsible for their faith because they have chosen it and it is open to them at any time to reject it. Michael Sandel has explored this and related issues in his *Democracy's Discontent*. He argues that such a view supposes that the self can be separated out from all substantive elements that make its identity so that the self is, in effect, 'unencumbered'. This leads to the view that

> the case for religious liberty derives not from the moral importance of religion but from the need to protect individual autonomy . . . government should be neutral towards religion . . . and respect people's capacity to choose their own values and ends.
>
> (Sandel, 1996: 66)

But as Sandel points out in matters of religion, ends are often not always chosen but merely adopted or received. While some believers may undergo mid-life conversion, others may have had a Christian or other religious identity for as long as they can remember. It is a mistake to suppose that a free life requires the maximisation of choices and options and that ways of life that are not explicitly 'chosen' somehow compromise our freedom. Views that prioritise the role of autonomy in freedom are led to the position that somehow everything I do must be in some way the outcome of choice. But this is to place absurd demands on persons and discredits the idea of freedom by being too unrealistic. In any case, the view that we are the product of our choices runs the risk of a regress: if X is a set of ideas that determines choices a, b and c then X itself must have to be chosen according to certain criteria; but then these criteria themselves must be chosen, and so on.

What matters, from a standpoint of liberty, is not so much whether a life consists of choice but whether dependency is avoided. It is true that an impoverishment of choice and opportunities can sometimes be a sign of dependency, but this does not necessarily follow. For example, economies emerging from Western Europe following World War II had little in the way of consumer choice but, in comparison with depredations recently experienced by the citizenry, these inconveniences were a price worth paying for the restoration of liberty. At the same time, the enjoyment of a range of choices is quite compatible with dependency, particularly where choices are controlled or manipulated by corporate bodies. This matters little if I am at liberty simply to ignore all the choices offered me but this stance becomes more difficult if the choices are of the provision of healthcare or housing.

It could be argued, with some justification, that it is mistaken to interpret autonomy in terms of a life that is choice-driven in the way described above. It is enough that it involves 'the capability and inclination to reason for oneself, and to shape one's life on the basis of the deliverances of reason' (Callan, 1997: 58). The idea here is that at least some of my actions are driven by what might be termed 'categorical' considerations rather than a choice-calculus. For example, a person may feel inclined to devote much of their time to caring for an elderly parent not so much out of choice but because they felt they had no real choice: the alternatives were either practically unrealistic or morally objectionable (e.g. the thought of consigning the parent to a care home was something never to be entertained). The thought that goes into determining the decision is one of deliberating and thinking through the implications of one's 'choice' rather than considering alternatives.[4] This idea has some similarities with that of the 'strong evaluator', developed by Charles Taylor. He explains that whereas 'weak evaluation' is only concerned with the evaluation of the best means to attain pre-given ends (e.g. ends delivered through desires, or ends provided or prescribed by others), strong evaluation seeks to shape and modify existing ends and values (Taylor, 1985a: 15–44). Persons need to be strong evaluators if their lives are to have shape and their purposes interwoven into their values. A strong evaluator is prepared to face up to thinking about what ends in life are worth having; the implication here is that 'weak' evaluators are weak just because, in their focus on means, they allow themselves to be buffeted about by those with a stronger purpose.

The temptation is to suppose that 'liberty-bearing' must involve autonomy in the sense of being a strong evaluator and that in an empire of liberty each will be strong in her evaluation. It is just this link that I want to contest. It seems to me that the ideal of autonomy – i.e. the person who lives by the deliverances of reason – is precisely a eudaimonic[5] ideal carrying with it the counsel of perfection. It may indeed be not only a worthy ideal but a thoroughly sensible one too, but it is not entailed by the idea of liberty and to be liberty-bearing does not entail autonomy. For example, while the ideal of strong evaluation is a powerful one, it is possible to be guided by intuitive considerations in which one makes a decision and then works out the consequences. Alternatively one may be swayed by aesthetic or hedonistic considerations, neither of which pay much more than scant regard to the deliverances of reason. By all appearances one would have all the characteristics of a weak evaluator, swayed by what seems to be insubstantial evidence and pure whim. Yet, providing one is prepared to take the consequences of one's whims, one is acting as a liberty-bearing person just as much as those for whom evaluating, deliberating and judging are burdensome necessities. Suppose one lives one's life not so much dictated by aesthetics but in a way that sets out to be light and superficial. Arguably, I need to be very lucky indeed not to be ever faced by the adverse consequences of such a life and my hoping that they will never happen may show just how superficial I am. Nevertheless, if we take liberty seriously then we must accept that not everyone will want to be strong evaluators.

Conclusion

If there is one thing that is much worse than a life lived superficially then it is one that finds me dependent on the will of others either at a personal or a corporate level. This threat, and this alone, may be enough to persuade me that a life lived by superficial whim may ill equip me for resisting dependency. If in order to do this I must become a strong evaluator then so be it: but for me, it must always remain a second choice. For the value of liberty consists not only in the fashioning of a life that is recognisably my own and not determined for me: it also lies in my willingness to take responsibility for the life I have lived. In this sense there is a certain courage attached to liberty that those who only experience dependency are less familiar with: coping with risk, knowing that even attempts to live a safe, predictable life, can be undone by *fortuna*. If we are able to focus on the chief value of liberty as consisting in responsibility for actions coupled with non-dependency and an absence of servitude then we can also see the kind of life that is chosen is only of secondary importance, from the standpoint of liberty. But at the same time, if we are to protect our liberty then we must develop human powers equal to the task – this is the subject of the next chapter.

Notes

1   This is also the view of Philip Pettit – see Pettit (2001: 18–25) where he suggests that the concept of freedom has the idea of responsibility inscribed within it.

2   Charles Larmore, in a reading of Philip Pettit's *Republicanism* suggests that the underlying concern with non-domination is the moral idea of respect for persons (Larmore, 2001: 241). But although the idea of a person as 'liberty-bearing' includes the idea of respect, the concept of liberty-bearing has a political dimension that goes beyond respect for persons. For reasons that will become clear in subsequent chapters, republican ideas are not *reducible* to moral concepts.

3   At this point there may be those who will suggest that it is far better to be a slave with lots of opportunities than a free person with very few – it is just a question of trade-off. I make two responses to this: first, the impoverished freeman is not reliant on anyone's goodwill. Once one has experienced freedom one would not just want to 'trade it off'. Second, the free person can live according to their own beliefs and order their world as best they can in accordance with these and that can be considerably more significant in terms of liberty than the chance to grab random opportunities. In any case, it is valuable to contrast liberty with the 'worth of liberty' (Rawls, 1972: 204). Impoverishment certainly diminishes its worth and there may come a point when basic essentials become more important than liberty – this was clearly recognised by Berlin (1969: xlvi).

4   Categorical decisions usually seem to be right for the agent involved: they align her self-identity with a perspective on the world. Sometimes we may want to concur (e.g. the Nazi-resisters in Europe in the 1940s) but not always: for example, a categorical decision could be to send the aged parent to a care home and contribute to the bill oneself. These, and related matters, are interestingly discussed by Eamonn Callan (1997: 52–59).

5   *Eudaimonia* – the Greek philosophical term referring to well-being or happiness. According to Aristotle this is the 'final end' towards which our actions are directed, that is, that for the sake of which we undertake actions. The basic argument is elaborated in his *Nicomachean Ethics* (1980: Book 1). The argument in this book is not designed to undermine eudaimonic ideals as such but merely to show that they are not the same as ideals related to liberty.

Chapter 3

Liberty and human powers

We have seen how the idea of liberty implies that the agents of liberty are seen as liberty-bearing. In this chapter I will first of all explore how the exercise of liberty can be restricted through the creation of ties of dependency. I will then show how liberty is based on what I term two basic normative powers and show the relationship between liberty and powers. Finally I will discuss one or two aspects of capability theory.

The nature of domination

Historically, the role and nature of dependency is fairly clear. In the literature of republican liberty it refers to the way in which the master–servant relation is replicated in political form. This idea is aptly conveyed by a lament attributed to Brutus by Quintilian, as the former contemplated the rise of Caesar: 'For it is better to command no-one than to be slave to anyone, for we may live honourably without command, but in slavery there is no endurance of life'.[1] And in letters to Cicero, Brutus also complained that 'to endure submission and to suffer insults is worse than exile, worse even than death', particularly so where 'safety depends on the good will of anybody' (quoted in Wirszubski, 1950: 90). However, it may be thought that the anger of a Roman aristocrat in his resistance to domination and the effrontery of his tormentors cannot be replicated at will for Western Europe in the twenty-first century. It was Brutus' overdeveloped sense of his own honour that led to his downfall, not a concern with *libertas*. Moreover, Brutus presumably had a fine understanding of just what slavery and submission amounted to since slavery was an integral feature of Rome both during and after the Republic. Therefore the attempt by republican enthusiasts to convince us moderns that we also run the risk of domination in the way that Brutus feared 2000 years ago seems far-fetched, to say the least.

And of course, there is something in that observation: we are not dominated over the entirety of our lives and so the comparison with slavery is inflated. The problem we face, it might be said, is not so much that of domination as that of interference. This objection, however, is merely to restate the criticisms of republican liberty by Matthew Kramer and Ian Carter noted in the last chapter: that statements about domination can be re-cast as statements about inter- ference. As was noted, it is only possible to do this at the cost of ignoring the conception of individuals as liberty-bearing persons. Further, when persons are understood in these terms then the difference between interference and domination becomes clear and stark.

Interference, I suggest, may be unwelcome but it is capable of justification. It need not be justified in terms of the interests of the individual interfered with: reasons may be given that are other-regarding. The reasons for interference need not be cast in terms that satisfy the claims of liberty: as Berlin himself noted many times, there are values and goods that at particular times may override the claims of liberty – in the interests of fairness, public decency and even simply on the grounds of public convenience. There are two further features about interference. First of all, it is not accompanied by a *denial* of the liberty-bearing status of the person interfered with: the justification of interference will either be in terms that suggest that the abrogation of a particular liberty is much exaggerated, or it is suggested that the particular liberty counts for little (e.g. being compelled by authorities to drive on the left) or – less frequently – it may be claimed that a particular liberty be sacrificed in the name of some greater good (e.g. the infringement of a liberty to enjoy a rural view is compensated for by the energy the wind turbines will generate). Justifications of interference will be, and usually are, subject to dispute and argumentation. Even where the act of interference is finally authorised by an appropriate public body, and even if this is backed up by the courts, it is often the case that questions of interference are never fully accepted. Philip Pettit has suggested that interference can be justified 'if it tracks the interests and ideas of the person involved' (1997: 55), but we should note that the 'person involved' may take a quite different view. Interference can be justified, but only, I suggest, on a case-by-case basis.

The case of domination is quite different. It constitutes the systematic direction of a person's actions, backed by sanctions such that the liberty-bearing status of that person is ignored for all practical purposes. Pettit suggests that domination involves arbitrary interference (1997: 53) but there is nothing whatsoever arbitrary about what I term systematic domination. In its extreme form it is backed by the most brutal sanctions and not only are the liberties of the subjected ignored but even their basic moral rights. In less extreme cases – the cases I am concerned with here – the sanctions concern loss of status and livelihood. Pettit's concern with arbitrary domination perhaps alludes to the way in which, in one historic version of domination, persons were subject to the vacillating will of a ruler – sometimes kind, sometimes cruel, but never predictable (61). But I suggest that contemporary modes of domination that take this form tend to be in domestic settings in which the will of one person (usually male) dominates the home and the private lives of all those under the same roof.

Other forms of domination, however, are predominantly institutional. Sometimes, as Pettit suggests, the domination can be fairly blatant – for example, through manipulation – this includes 'the shaping of people's beliefs, agenda fixing and the rigging of outcomes' (53). He goes on to refine this analysis further by suggesting that direction takes on a specific form through the reduction, removal or replacement of choices and also through the setting of the terms and conditions of an action. Where the latter occurs there is then no need to interfere any further (see Pettit, 2008: 111).

Several features are worth noticing at this point. First, this domination is the outcome of a set of institutional arrangements that have been intended by certain individuals. By contrast, it could be that one's choices are restricted through changed economic circumstances. Although there might be persons who are responsible for such circumstances it would not follow that one is in a relation of dependency and domination. There has to be *intentional* domination, namely the intention to restrict someone's actions and for this to have been done with purposive intent. Second, those who are dominated are systematically deprived of a voice with which they can express their own concerns and exercise tangible influence on processes and events. They are, in short, treated as if they are all – at best – weak evaluators. Discussion with the dominated therefore revolves around the best means to execute pre-determined ends. Often, even discussion over the best means is curtailed or ruled out. Typically this means that the dominated have a restricted area for discretion. Third – and this is most important – the *motives* of the dominators may be fine and very worthy. They may act for the professed good of those they are intent on dominating or they may act for the good of others (or even both). Indeed, it could happen that the motives of the dominators are so fine and pure that everyone (both dominators and dominated) are quite blind to what is actually going on. The fourth point is that those who are dominated typically are required to account for their actions on a regular basis through meetings, procedural monitoring and detailed planning (all of which must be accessible, on request, by the dominators).

Thus, some organisations may be characterised by a culture of domination that operates at all levels and which may have arisen as a response to political or commercial pressures. Domination is therefore associated with layers of management so that those doing the dominating are often, in their turn, dominated by a higher tier. At this stage, it might be objected that what I am describing is merely the form of modern bureaucracy, identified by Max Weber at the beginning of the twentieth century (Weber, 1948: 196–240). Institutional domination is merely the rationalisation of procedures through instrumental reasoning taking procedural form. The structures of so-called 'domination' are merely an organised and reasonable response to providing goods and services upon which we all, at one time or another, depend. The operatives and service providers within such structures are treated fairly (they are not slaves and they are not in servitude) and safeguards are provided in order to protect staff against arbitrary decisions. My response is twofold. First of all, to the extent that institutional structures undermine and disregard the status of liberty-bearing persons then their legitimacy is questionable. The second is that their legitimacy can only be established through a process of authorisation, which is itself based on the recognition of persons as liberty-bearing. This means that authorisation to give and accept instructions is clearly and publicly defined. Moreover, there is a clear scope identified beyond which the writ of command does not run. Domination occurs when channels of authorisation are circumvented or ignored, when reputations are undermined and when unofficial links of communication are opened without accountability. Domination also occurs when the connivance of some is sought at the expense of others, often with the prospect of reward or advancement dangled or hinted as a possibility. Finally, channels of authorisation are circumvented to such an extent that alternative systems of patronage and personal dependency are established so that those few who try to rely on official authorised channels of communication end up ignorant of what is actually going on. This then generates climates of uncertainty, which further increase relations of dependency as each seeks out patrons with whom confidences can be exchanged and prospects confirmed. But these private exchanges merely confirm an active fear of speaking out so that the suppression of individual voice is accomplished in large part by the individuals themselves. We might characterise the status of persons enmeshed in these kind of environments as that of *subaltern*.

It is important to notice that the power and abilities of subalterns are not simply comprehensively suppressed and diminished. On the contrary, organisations mobilise, orchestrate and direct a range of human powers – powers which, in different circumstances, could be used in the exercise of liberty. Human powers can also be used to resist depredations of liberty and to contest subaltern status. For while it is rare in western democracies for persons to live in complete servitude, it is common for them to inhabit a subaltern status whether in the home or the workplace, a status that mocks and undermines their liberty-bearing status. Some analysis of human powers is therefore required.

Liberty and human powers

Persons capable of exercising liberty must have, at least potentially, particular powers. One way of construing these is to be found in the well-known passage of Hobbes:

> The power of a man . . . is his present means to obtain some future apparent good; and is either 'original' or 'instrumental'. 'Natural power' is the eminence of the faculties of the body or mind . . . liberality, nobility. 'Instrumental' are those powers which, acquired by these or by fortune are means and instruments to acquire more.
>
> (Hobbes, 1991: 62)

There are two things worth noticing about this view of human powers. The first is that it is decidedly strategic in conception: powers are means to an end – the end being 'some future apparent good', which is left open. It is down to the agent to determine what this good consists of: it could be material wealth, but it could just as easily be public honour. In contrast to a strategic view of powers is what might be termed a developmental perspective, which relates the development of powers to some version of what constitutes human flourishing. Unsurprisingly, Hobbes has no interest in canvassing any ideas redolent of Aristotelianism and so he leaves it absolutely open as to just what constitutes the 'future good' sought for. Nevertheless, he is very generous in what he allows to be counted as a power: it includes eloquence, affability and even 'forme': 'Forme is power because being a promise of a good, it recommendeth men to the favour of women and strangers' (63). Thus even what might be termed the social graces are seen as 'powers' because they enable persons to obtain some future good through the ability to influence and persuade others. So although Hobbes gives a list of powers, this list is by no means exhaustive and this brings me to the second feature of Hobbes' concept of human powers: the definition is non-prescriptive so that precisely what quality or activity may fall under a power is left open. As Hobbes himself says, 'nobility is a power' – but not in all places and not always.

C.B. Macpherson argues that Hobbes worked with a descriptive concept of power and contrasts this with an ethical, developmental concept of power, which involves man's abilities to develop his capacities – Macpherson gives a list of these including rational understanding, friendship and emotional activities among others (see Macpherson, 1971: 52–54). But there is no need to adopt a list-approach to human powers. Hobbes is correct in advocating a view of human powers that is non-prescriptive for the simple, practical reason that any survey of specific powers will always be provisional and will always be dependent on culture and history. But is Macpherson right about having a developmental perspective on powers as opposed to Hobbes' strategic view? This would seem to commit us to the view that powers are needed in the furtherance of human flourishing of which rational understanding, friendship and so on are constituents. On the one hand, therefore, we have the Macpherson view of powers as linked to human flourishing and we have already had reason to distinguish eudaimonistic ends from liberty as such. On the other hand, we have the Hobbesian view in which powers are essentially instrumental and strategic, where the connection with liberty is at best contingent. But in this study we are assuming the end to be investigated is neither an 'apparent future good' nor some version of human flourishing, but liberty itself.

As far as liberty is concerned, there are only two powers that really count: the power of self-determination and the power to co-operate with others. The first power, as we have seen in the last chapter, is what liberty itself entails for each person said to be liberty-bearing, adding the proviso, once more, that from the standpoint of liberty it matters not if a woman or man seeks to be a vagabond, an entrepreneur, a priest or a hermit or has no ambition or aim in life whatsoever. The second power – that of being able to co-operate with others – arises immediately when we recognise that we must seek to live our lives with others who are also liberty-bearing and who wish, as far as possible, to determine their own lives too (even the hermit relies on others co-operating to leave him alone). The modes of self-determination and co-operation will vary – possibly markedly and surprisingly so – from place to place and from time to time. But it should be noted that organisations characterised by a culture of domination will invariably attempt to inhibit and curtail *both* of these powers for the simple reason that, in such organisations, liberty counts for little or nothing. For if we ask what a person is deprived of and what is not recognised when his liberty is denied it is precisely the power to determine one's own life in co-operation with others. These, then are the two basic powers: the power of self-determination and the power to co-operate with others.

Although powers are related to liberty, they need to be distinguished from liberty. Hobbes makes the distinction between someone unable to leave a room because of constraints on his movement (e.g. he is in chains) and someone who is 'fastened to his bed by sickness'.[2] He defines a free man as someone who 'in those things which by his strength and wit he is able to do is not hindered to do what he has a will to do' (Hobbes, 1991: Ch 21; 146). This view is endorsed by Quentin Skinner: 'To be unfree is to have been rendered incapable of exercising an ability I possess. But the blind man has not in this way been disempowered; he is simply not in the possession of the relevant ability' (Skinner, 2002a: 246). But the distinction is not always apparent as far as the English language is concerned. Taking the example of a disabled person who has recently lost the use of his limbs, he might say: 'I am no longer able to walk unaided'. Or he might say: 'I am no longer free to walk unaided'. A person may say 'I am able to leave the room' or 'I am free to leave the room' and mean exactly the same thing in each case. But despite the similar use of the words 'able' and 'free', the distinction between powers – or abilities – and freedom is of great importance.

To see why this is so, let us consider, briefly, some of those powers that Hobbes refers to and which Macpherson calls capacities: the power to run, jump, work, think, play and procreate. It should be noticed that persons who are keen to put others in a state of dependency may also be very keen to develop their powers – the power to work to task all day, for example. Indeed, the development of powers (or capacities or abilities) is entirely neutral as far as the purposes for which they can be employed are concerned: they are the kind of powers that can be harnessed for the good of the bearer or the good of her master, or for the benefit of others. The key point is that powers can be developed without any reference whatsoever to liberty. These may include more sophisticated powers – for example, the ability to plan, control and evaluate a project. Of course, if one does value liberty then there are some powers that one needs more than others – e.g. the power to think and to communicate.

But thinking and communication are perfectly consistent with living a life that is determined by someone else, a life of servitude or the life of a subaltern.

Even the basic power of self-determination is not the same as freedom, even though we have already argued that it is the essential premise of freedom. A person who is unable to undertake his or her own self-determination lacks the power for free action. For example, a person in a coma no longer has that particular power. Interestingly, however, we would still want to say that the person was liberty-bearing and as much as possible her treatment should reflect this. For she was self-determining before she went in to the coma and if she comes out of it she will be self-determining once more. The power of self-determination and the power to co-operate with others can be seen as *normative* powers without which the concept of liberty and liberty-bearing agents is incomprehensible. These can be contrasted with those contingent powers or capacities that are needed in pursuit of our goals, whatever they may be. If persons are recognised only in terms of their capacities to the neglect of recognition of the two basic normative powers then liberty is immediately called into question. The section in this book that addresses education, knowledge and curriculum explores the development of capacities within the context of the development of the two normative powers. For example, the ability to reach judgements, taking into account and responding to the arguments of others, is a process that combines these two powers. Because of the existence of a multiplicity of liberty-bearing persons, self-determination is never enough: I can determine my ends through the co-operation of others. Learning to exercise liberty involves learning to recognise others as liberty-bearing through the differing exercise of capacities.

Capability theory

We need powers to exercise our liberty and to make use of the opportunities our liberty enables us to pursue. Charles Taylor, however, has suggested that liberty is either an 'exercise' concept or an 'opportunity' concept, but not both at the same time. He argues thus:

> Doctrines of positive freedom are concerned with a view of freedom which involves essentially the exercising of control over one's life. On this view one is free only to the extent that one has effectively determined oneself and the shape of one's life. The concept of freedom here is an exercise concept. By contrast, negative theories of freedom can rely simply on an opportunity concept, where being free is a matter of what we can do, of what it is open to us to do, whether or not we do anything to exercise those options.
>
> (Taylor, 1985b: 213)

Taylor then goes on to develop the implications of the exercise concept, which he favours, into a full-blown theory of positive freedom consisting of self-realisation. In particular, freedom is inhibited if we experience some of our desires as 'fetters, because we can experience them as not ours because we experience them as incorporating a quite erroneous appreciation of our situation' (225). Taylor is arguing, in effect, that freedom involves the exercise of some powers and not others – particularly the powers associated with strong evaluation. But although liberty certainly implies the exercise of powers that assist in self-determination, the prescription of *which* powers takes us beyond a theory of liberty into moral theory. So even if what Taylor recommends is perfectly correct and he describes well the need to overcome certain rogue desires if I am to perceive myself as fully self-determining, this is not a theory of liberty even if the words used are those of freedom. Taylor is putting forward a view that was earlier proposed by Spinoza:

> So I call a man altogether free in so far as he is guided by reason, because it is to that extent that he is determined to action by causes that can be adequately understood solely through his own nature.
>
> (Spinoza, 2000: 42)

For Spinoza, freedom consists in the exercise of the power (*potentia*) of reason and if one fails to exercise that power one cannot be called free. But of course, self-determination can take many forms, some of which may have very little to do with reason on any common understanding of that word: persons may be motivated by aesthetic or otherworldly beliefs. Nevertheless, they are still free and they are still liberty-bearing persons.

However, it may well be thought that the concepts of exercise and opportunity are both needed for a theory of liberty. We need to be able to determine more accurately the role of powers in the exercise of liberty and yet acknowledge that we need opportunities to exercise them. These may extend to certain actions or to fulfilling certain preferences – the accomplishment of which can be identified, evaluated and measured. But opportunity also extends to the development of those powers themselves. Part of what freedom involves is the opportunity both to exercise and develop our human powers. For it is through those powers that we are able to determine ourselves and our lives, in co-operation with others. Hence the interest of capability theory that addresses these matters, first put forward by Amartya Sen.

When he first theorised the concept of capability Sen suggested (in the context of asking questions about social re-distribution) that perhaps we should focus not so much on goods and resources as what people could actually *do* (Sen, 1982: 365–367). This idea was further theorised by Sen in terms of 'functionings' or modes of being and doing. The idea is that a capability can enable a range of possible functionings (Sen, 1999: 74–75). A 'capability set' is therefore, according to Sen, a combination of functionings. The key point here is that there is no one-to-one correlation between capability and functions – capabilities enable a range of functionings. It follows that the development of capabilities has an empowering dimension: capabilities enable persons to do more with their lives in terms of potential functionings. For Sen, the concept of capability therefore includes a normative dimension that goes beyond standard human capital theories: a capability set becomes an index of freedom and well-being.

Once we have the idea of combining the power of self-determination with other powers, further questions arise concerning the exercise of those powers. A social space opens up, which designates the *opportunities* for exercising powers that are different from the powers themselves. For I may have certain powers but be unable to exercise them in a way that exemplifies my basic power of self-determination. Capability is an 'opportunity' concept but directed at the exercise of powers. The concept therefore appears to combine what Taylor had taken to be two distinct concepts. The term 'capability' has now become part of the lexicon of social philosophy, but it can be misleading since it has nothing directly to do with competencies, abilities or attributes of persons since the whole point of Sen's approach is to focus on opportunities for functioning rather than on particular individual abilities or skills. But whether we refer to capabilities, substantive freedoms or the exercise of social powers, the capability theory only makes sense against the background of the basic power of self-determination. This is made clear by Sen's insistence that functionings are only admissible if they are ones such that the bearer has reason to value them (Sen, 2009: 231). In this way, capability theory avoids charges of patronisation since the arbiter of what counts as adequate functioning lies with the agent herself.

Sen also insists that the 'process' aspect to freedom needs to be acknowledged – that is, functioning does not merely consist of the opportunity to secure desired outcomes, rather that these outcomes themselves may consist in deliberating, judging and choosing (228–229). Thus there is a difference between functionings. Some may consist of goods and use-values that contribute well-being – for example, the capability of having adequate leisure time or the capability of being able to feed one's family. But other functionings may be far more difficult to quantify, such as the capability for judgement and deliberation. Although these kind of functionings may enhance well-being they do so in a way that involves the idea of not just choosing but of exercising one's self-determination. There is therefore a way of interpreting capabilities that sees them as not only contributing to but as exemplifying the *liberty-bearing* status of an agent. What is required for this is the opportunity to develop and exercise a range of powers – whether or not they lead to the acquisition of use-values and goods. Thus, functionings may consist of personal *accomplishments*, which in the end may be more significant for individuals involved than the securing of tangible use-values. For example, literacy programmes for adults who hitherto had struggled to read and write may contribute directly to their ability to lead a life that is more self-determined than it was before. The same could be said of the acquisition of technical skills and knowledge and broader-based knowledge derived from the humanities. As we shall see in more detail later on, these kinds of accomplishments may themselves be provided in a narrow way that ends up restricting functionings. Literacy programmes that only target functional literary tasks may help students to write business letters, but not to read poetry and literature from their own culture. Technical knowledge may be provided for in a way that has a narrow skills focus directed at specific tasks. In neither case is much done for the exercise of human powers. We could therefore see capability theory as a critical tool that enables us to judge whether liberties are being enhanced across a range of activities. Capability theory enables us to link liberty on the one hand and human powers on the other through the question: what functionings are going on that didn't happen before and to what extent do they enhance the liberty-bearing status of an agent?

If we read capability theory as having an explicit focus on the development of human powers (and not just use-values) does it fall to the charge of 'athleticism' posed by Gerry Cohen? According to him, on the capabilities view we are not free unless we strive to better ourselves (Cohen, 1993: 24). We end up with a performance-based, sporting view of freedom. I am free to develop my sporting prowess, but I'm not free to sit at home on the sofa. Sen, not unnaturally, countered that the development of capability laid down possibilities for individuals, not prescription (Sen, 1993: 43–44). Could Cohen's charge be pressed further? If capability theory is read as a theory of well-being and well-being is held to consist of valuable functionings then the charge would be more serious. But read as an opportunity theory the charge is less serious. Yet it remains the case that in much of the literature of capability theory the kind of functionings written about are primarily ones drawn from a development context. The functionings of loafing about, chatting or just 'going for a stroll' tend not to be made much of. Even if the theory itself is not athletic, some of its proponents seem very much in earnest, which gives rise to the suspicions that Cohen entertained.[3]

However, there is a different way of viewing capabilities and that is in theorising (with implications for policy) a way in which human powers can be developed that increase resilience to domination. Moreover, it could be argued that this resilience is all the better for focussing on those powers that are directly related to modes of self-determination. Another way of seeing this is to suppose that the best way of resisting dominance and the resultant fall into subaltern status is to keep on exercising liberties themselves. The development of capabilities is a way of doing this, particularly if these are developed in co-operation with others. We have seen the Cohen perspective exercising its influence before, for example in the observation that the ends of liberty need not be eudaimonic or perfectionist. But we may also be inclined to think that in the face of depredations of liberty and the continuing risk of falling into subaltern status, such concerns are the least of our worries.

Conclusion

The link between liberty and education is twofold and stems from the role that human powers play on the one hand and authority on the other in the maintenance if liberty. Any theory of liberty (this even includes negative liberty) rests on a tacit or explicit recognition of the role of self-determination. The reason why we value liberty, why it is important to us, is because human beings wish to shape their own destinies, in co-operation with others who are similarly self-determined. This thought naturally leads to asking what powers we have – mental, physical, emotional – that enable this self-determination to take place. If we care about liberty, therefore, we have a strong interest in the development of these powers, in such a way that the development *itself* reflects self-determination. In other words, the development of human powers cannot take place in conditions of servitude or semi-servitude: this is exactly how slaves are treated, even if they are slaves destined to perform complex and difficult tasks for their masters. The development of human powers must reflect the fact that persons are already liberty-bearing persons. This includes children: one cannot prepare young people for a life of liberty without recognising them as free in the first place. Hence the connection between human powers and education: for while the exercise of those powers is certainly a matter for liberty, their development is one of the key responsibilities of a free state. In Part II we will look more closely at the relation between human powers and education in terms of implications for the curriculum.

Notes

1 From Quintilian (1920). Quoted from Wirszubski (1950: 90) who dates this statement to around 53BC.
2 See Hobbes (1991: chapter 21, 146).
3 For example, Martha Nussbaum gives a list of ten desirable capabilities – see Nussbaum (2000: 70–77).

Liberty, education and the space of reasons

Chapter 4

An epistemological perspective on knowledge, learning and education

It may be thought that a theory of liberty is quite independent of epistemological stance. And indeed, there is no necessary connection between the two: for example, Gottlob Frege adopted a fairly orthodox, authoritarian, pro-Bismark political stance that led him to disdain democracy; Russell (and later, Ayer) adopted a much more libertarian approach to both morals and politics, which presumably would have appalled Frege. Yet all three philosophers embraced broadly the same analytical, empiricist-influenced epistemological perspective. But as this section will try to show, there are some epistemological perspectives that provide more favourable and fertile ground for the development of liberty than others, even though there is no *necessary* connection between the two. For example, for reasons to be explained, an idealist perspective is less likely to help the cause of republican liberty – and I include in the orbit of idealism contemporary constructivist approaches and also those that are inclined to assign priority to the concept of a practice. By contrast, I will maintain that epistemologies that adopt a broadly 'realist' perspective are more likely to be helpful to the cause of liberty.

In this chapter I develop an epistemological perspective that establishes the central role that knowledge plays in education. I do this through first of all elaborating John McDowell's ideas on the 'space of reasons'. I then use this concept to re-interpret and develop the concept of the 'forms of knowledge' associated with Paul Hirst. I then show how one of the key features of the space of reasons – the making of judgements – is also a key feature of knowledge production and learning. Finally, I elaborate on the nature of judgements by taking some features of Robert Brandom's account of inferentialism. In the following chapter, and subsequent ones, I will try to show the relevance and importance of what I term an epistemological perspective for liberty itself.

We can interpret the idea of the 'space of reasons' as the domain in which liberty-bearing persons conduct themselves and interact with each other. Education can therefore be seen as preparation for living in the space of reasons. The asking and giving of reasons exemplifies, in practice, how people recognise each other as free beings. By contrast, those in dependency do not ask for reasons and those in the role of mastery do not feel obliged to give them. Hence, an understanding of the space of reasons and its philosophical basis is important for seeing just how liberty-bearing persons can enact their self-determination in co-operation with others.

Second nature and the space of reasons

We have seen how an account of human powers is necessary so that the bearers of liberty maintain their resilience in the face of threats. The development of human powers is not a part of liberty as such: we have already emphasised that the concept of liberty does not enjoin agents to pursue some ends rather than others or to develop some powers rather than others. Nevertheless, without human powers talk of liberty would be redundant and therefore an epistemological perspective needs, if possible, to incorporate into an interpretation of knowing an account of relevant human powers. Such an account, it is suggested, is provided by John McDowell, first set out in his *Mind and World* (1994, henceforward referred to as *MW*).

McDowell's exposition is wide-ranging, but the force of his argument is lost unless its different strands are held together. His starting point is Kant's well-known remark that 'thoughts without content are empty, intuitions without concepts are blind' (Kant, 1929: 93), which McDowell thinks underpins what he sees as a pernicious, oscillating dualism. On the one side is, borrowing from Wilfred Sellars, the 'Myth of the Given' (Sellars, 1956: 298–299) and on the other side is a coherentism that McDowell attributes to Davidson (see Davidson, 2001). The problem with relying on the 'given' is that it is not clear how the relation between sense experience and concept can be considered as one of genuine justification since unalloyed, bare sense data is simply 'other' to conceptual thought. Hence, we are obliged to veer towards Davidson's view that the only thing that can count for holding a belief is another belief. Yet this approach, McDowell thinks, condemns us to a 'frictionless spinning in a void' (*MW*: 11) and we are recoiled back to the myth of the given in order to find some kind of constraint or underpinning to our beliefs. Davidson's solution to this (that the relation of belief to the world must be causal) is certainly an explanation of our beliefs (or conceptual scheme) but is not a *justification* of them: for I cannot justify those beliefs in terms that make sense from the standpoint of those beliefs, according to McDowell.

McDowell's proposed solution is in two stages. First, he insists that receptivity at its most basic, passive level is always conceptual: there must indeed be constraint on beliefs but this constraint need not be outside what is thinkable. Moreover, this 'thinkable content' is linked to a wider repertoire of content without which individual bits of receptivity could not be experienced as anything intelligible (*MW*, Lecture 2). But it is the second stage of the solution that moves the whole argument up a gear. McDowell proposes that humankind has a 'second nature' in which sensory processes and other experiences that we share with the natural world become saturated with conceptual meaning. This formation and acculturation is analogous to the development of ethical dispositions and practical reasoning so that what McDowell is proposing is an Aristotelian form of habituation, which extends beyond the ethical into the domain of the epistemological. That is to say, the way in which experience itself is formed is through a receptivity that is itself conceptualised. This habituation into the world, through the formation not only of dispositions but through the development of our very cognitive faculties suggests, McDowell thinks, that experience is never directly of the 'given' (for example, in the form of raw sense data) but is impregnated with what he terms 'conceptual content'.

I have mentioned in passing the analogy with an Aristotelian account of the development of virtues but, interestingly, McDowell draws on two further historical accounts of this habituation to the world. One suggestion is that it is possible to interpret the account of *praxis* in the writings of the early Marx in terms of a second nature that arises out of human activity itself (*MW*: 117–119). Indeed, when Marx criticises traditional materialism for supposing that the world is experienced passively, 'in the form of an object or perception', as opposed to being the product of 'sensuous, human activity',[1] then there is indeed a close parallel to the criticism McDowell makes of traditional empiricism, which stands accused of falling victim to the myth of the given. The conceptualising of receptivity plays the same role for McDowell as conceiving human activity in terms of praxis did for Marx: it is not just that the world is transformed through human activity but the way in which that world is *experienced* is also transformed. If this is the case then the theory of alienation itself could be recast and re-interpreted as nothing less than the alienation from the flourishing of this second nature. This could arise through the brutalisation of social and working conditions that reduce a person to enjoy only the animal functions of eating, drinking and procreating (*MW*: 118).

Further, McDowell also appeals to the concept of *Bildung*: second nature is also a function of upbringing and self-formation (*MW*: 87–88). What this suggests is that the development of second nature is not only the inevitable by-product of linguistic practices, but is also something that can be purposefully shaped and nurtured. And this development may not only occur at the level of belief but also through what might be termed the aestheticisation of experience. Thus, the natural world may be experienced not so much as a wilderness but as an object of beauty and care in that it is subject to and depends on humankind for its own flourishing. Or again, persons may be educated into hearing sounds (e.g. birdsong) as calming and restful rather than being a possible food source, while other kinds of sound may be learnt to be treated as an unwelcome intrusion. The sculpting of the antennae of experiencing – the cognitive and emotional process through which content is drawn in and interpreted – is something that can be purposefully crafted. It is not that experiences – in terms of their content – are somehow neutrally drawn in and then subject to an internal processing that varies depending on what kind of personal dispositions and character a person has developed. Rather the very mode of experiencing itself – i.e. the character of the experience – is subject to cultural and educative formation. Second nature is not a black box, internal to each of us, marked 'personal development'; rather it is manifest in all the different ways in which the process of experiencing itself takes place.

What all this means is that the 'space of reasons' becomes enlarged to encompass the whole domain of human activity. McDowell explains the idea of the space of reasons by linking it to freedom, as follows:

> The space of concepts is at least part of what Wilfred Sellars calls 'the space of reasons'. When Kant describes the understanding as a faculty of spontaneity, that reflects his view of the relation between reason and free-dom: rational necessitation is not just compatible with freedom but constitutive of it. In a slogan, the space of reasons is the space of freedom.
>
> (*MW*: 5)

The idea here is that the internal connection between rationality and freedom is not simply expressed through a self-imposed moral law by virtue of a Kantian categorical imperative. Building on Kant's insight into the relation between reason and freedom the idea of the space of reasons constitutes a more creative and supple way of thinking through that relation as, for instance, a domain that facilitates the giving and asking for reasons as a process of justification. The idea also assumes, moreover, that a possible inhibition of justification is a con-tingent feature of a society and that the realm of the normative need not be thought of as subject to social determinism.

The space of reasons can only be fully understood alongside and as part of the problems that arise if one too easily accepts the idea of the 'given':

> The idea of the Given is the idea that the space of reasons . . . is supposed to allow it to incorporate non-conceptual impacts from outside the realm of thought. But we cannot really understand the relations in virtue of which a judgement is warranted except as relations within the space of concepts: relations such as implication or probabilification, which hold between potential exercises of conceptual capacities. The attempt to extend the scope of justificatory relations outside the conceptual sphere cannot do what it is supposed to do.
>
> (*MW*: 7)

It is true that the *motive* behind the myth of given is salutary: the processes of justification ought to be subject to external constraint without which anything at all could be justified. But, McDowell suggests, we go about it the wrong way if we suppose that these constraints must be extra-conceptual. Their efficacy cannot be accounted for because no adequate account of the relation of conceptual to non-conceptual can be given.

Moreover, the supposition that the realm of experience derives from the extra-conceptual leads to further problems:

> Davidson thinks that experience can be nothing but an extra-conceptual impact on sensibility. So he concludes that experience must be outside the space of reasons. According to Davidson, experience is causally relevant to a subject's beliefs and judgements, but it has no bearing on their status as justified or warranted. Davidson says that 'nothing can count as a reason for holding a belief except another belief'. And he means in particular that experience cannot count as a reason for holding a belief . . . Davidson recoils from the Myth of the Given all the way to denying experience any justificatory role, and the coherentist upshot is a version of the conception of spontaneity as frictionless, the very thing that makes the idea of the Given attractive.
>
> (*MW*: 14)

Thus the idea of the space of reasons emerges as the realm in which justifications for beliefs are sought, from the standpoint of agents themselves. Hence, it is that 'experience' never comes without conceptual content: for example, in colour discrimination I understand the concept of 'red' as not-blue or green and that this understanding characterises colour experience as well so that there is not a two stage process of first, the onset of raw sense data followed by second, some internal processing of this data. Yet, McDowell is also insistent that this conceptualised experience does act as a constraint upon belief, which potentially can answer to worlds being 'thus and so' (*MW*: 26). On the one hand, the space of reasons constitutes the structure within which meanings and intelligibility emerge; on the other hand, it is not merely self-generating without any constraint. The space of reasons does not dissolve the dualism of mind and world: rather, it provides a way of thinking through that relationship.

In a later paper, McDowell links experience to judgement so that it is proposed that

> what we need and can have is the idea of a case of receptivity in operation that, even while being that, is an actualisation, together, of conceptual capacities whose active exercise, with the same togetherness, would be the making of a judgement.
>
> (McDowell, 2009b: 249)

If we construe judgement as making up one's mind about how things are – as coming to have a view of the world – then we can see that the process of judging is emblematic of what the space of reasons is about because, of course, my judgement may come to be questioned by others and, indeed, by myself. In judging I am proposing a view of the world which is quite different from merely *asserting* that things are thus and so. The space of reasons must be able to permit more than mere assertion and counter assertion if the process of justification is to be given room. Moreover, the process of judgement (as opposed to assertion) would not be possible without the possibility of constraints on what seems reasonable. And these constraints do not merely arise from the counter-judgements of others but also from their having a world in view that is the *same world* for each. For without this there would merely be so many conceptual schemes each with their own, separate world in view: the very essence, that is, of an epistemological frictionless spinning in a void.

It may be thought that a different view of McDowell's perspective is feasible. This could take the form of treating the justificatory character of the space of reasons as essentially naïve, a realm that in time will be replaced by a naturalist discourse that will be satisfied with descriptions of states of affairs (be they mental or non-mental) and causal explanations of them. Nature is best considered, on this view, as the 'disenchanted' realm of law, which is impervious to human design and intentionality. According to McDowell such a standpoint sets up two, contrasting (and ultimately futile) paths: first, that of 'bald naturalism' (which insists that our space of reasons be recast so that it coincides with the realm of law – see *MW* : 76–77) and 'rampant platonism' (in which the space of reasons is cut off from nature entirely and permitted to pursue its own, introverted and unfettered purposes – see *MW*: 77–78). The problem with bald naturalism is that its reductivist programme in effect writes spontaneity out of the relation between mind and world; the problem with rampant platonism is that spontaneity – the operations of the understanding, suitably structured – is treated as *sui generis* and nature treated as a mere side effect of its deliverances. McDowell's position can be seen as an attempt to think through the tensions between mind and world and at the same time resisting temptations to dissolve one of these two terms into the other.

What starts as an epistemological problem of the relation between mind and world is addressed not only through an alternate epistemology but also through an historicisation of knowing and belief in the account of second nature. No doubt there will be many who are impressed, but not convinced, by the sweep of this argument.[2] Does not second nature amount to a form of coherentism after all? After all, the suggestion that receptivity contains conceptual content may be said to concede to idealism everything it needs. The answer to this, from a McDowellian standpoint is that so long as the relation between mind and world has been adequately characterised then it matters not if it be called 'idealist'. What does not adequately characterise this relation is a position that licenses a perpetual oscillation between the myth of the given and an ungrounded coherentism. Or again, how does the realm of law sit with what we might call, following Marx, 'humanised nature'? McDowell is adamant that the realm of law, exemplifying, as it does, modernity itself, cannot be dis-invented – but is the realm of law one element of humanised nature or does it sit, unconnected, outside it? Here the answer would appear to be that the realm of law (for example, the world in view from the standpoint of physics) is itself a part of the space of reasons and cannot be prised apart from it.[3]

However, what particularly interests me are the possible connections between second nature and education. The clear implication of McDowell's argument is that education and learning take place in the space of reasons or what he often calls (echoing Kant) 'spontaneity' and this thought prompts a number of questions.

Does the development of second nature take place simply through participation in a language community or can it (or indeed, must it) be subject to further guidance, development, art and purpose? Presumably the nurturing of the space of reasons must surely be a purposeful endeavour: paradoxically, the development of the realm within which spontaneity flourishes cannot be left to chance. Yet the development of second nature should not be supposed to take on the character of extrinsic, instrumental purpose as if learning to live within the space of reasons is merely a goal that can be achieved through extra hard work and forward planning. This is not only because the process of learning and acquiring second nature is one of living a life but also because the constraints on the space of reasons – encountering a world that is 'thus and so' – ensures that the best laid plans and goals may be frustrated. The development of second nature is not a process that can be brought about by means of a comprehensive pedagogic strategy. The role of pedagogy must be conceived on more modest lines.

Would the extrusion of the realm of law from second nature imply that scientific approaches to learning are inherently misguided as an attempt, knowingly or not, to fashion human sensibility in ways of non-spontaneity? What McDowell calls 'bald naturalism' is a form of reductivism – whereby the space of reasons gets overwritten by natural law. We can see, once we reject bald naturalism, why the space of reasons must be *sui generis* (without lapsing into rampant platonism). The implication is that approaches to teaching and learning that are dictated by science (e.g. by forms of behaviourism) amount to bald naturalism. This implies that teaching and learning must employ the methods appropriate to the space of reasons – justification and judgement. Learning to live within the space of reasons cannot be brought about through causal means. Conversely, we could ask if the wrong kind of educational approach might produce a warped and deformed second nature and if so how it could be recognised as such. McDowell's remarks on Marx's concept of alienation point to a way of identifying second natures that have fallen into an alienated state, when taken together with some remarks of Hans-George Gadamer to which he draws our attention. According to McDowell, following Gadamer, animal life is structured by a natural environment such that an animal has to respond to the succession of problems and opportunities that are presented in such an environment through the biological imperative of self-survival (*MW*: 115, also Gadamer, 1989: 443–445). Thus, an alienated life is one that compels humankind to seek satisfaction in a way of living that is characteristic of a struggle for survival. This would be the case if social life itself is structured in such a way that the only way to live is by responding to an endless succession of problems (presented as 'challenges') and opportunities. In this way, the essential characteristics of the realm of the natural are replicated in the domain of the social. This alienation is complete if teaching and learning itself are purposefully structured and planned as a series of problems and opportunities. It should also be noted that when social life takes on the character of this kind of alienation then the prospects for liberty, in the republican sense, are bleak. For if a way of life is presented as this endless succession of problems to be overcome not only does life take on a futile character but dependency itself becomes a way of life. The principal form of conduct becomes that of responding to problems, again and again: self-direction takes the form of directing and motivating the self to ever greater challenges. And if, by chance, there are no problems to be solved, new ones can always be invented. It is a social environment hostile to liberty because one is never left alone and what is worse, one can never feel that one could leave oneself alone either.

Thus the idea of a second nature has a twofold dimension to it. First of all, it signifies the development of human beings with conceptual powers with an ability to formulate and respond to patterns of reasoning. While this certainly implies an initiation into linguistic practices it also requires a further initiation into the giving and asking for reasons within a justificatory framework. Hence the attractiveness, from this standpoint, of the idea of *Bildung*, which summons up the notion of the growth of self-formation through enculturation and education.[4] Just as *Bildung* emphasises the transformative qualities of acquiring a culture so the assumption of a 'second nature' transforms the individual who, through learning to live with others through the shared space of reasons, leaves behind that biological, naturalistic, first nature. The problem with bald naturalism is that it cannot quite bring itself to recognise that human beings are more than first nature beings. The other dimension of second nature is the fact that it is still engaged with the world in a twofold way. First, the stratum of 'first' nature is never left behind or cast off completely: human beings still are animal creatures who must sleep, eat and sometimes bleed, and for whom life is finite. Second, although the space of reasons cannot be rendered intelligible through natural-scientific means, this does not mean that it is *sui generis* in the sense that it is free from the constraints of the world. In particular, the space of reasons does not license the ability to believe whatever one happens to choose. There are epistemological constraints arising from the determinate character of the world (considered as both non-mental and mental). The space of reasons is a space that is grounded. For example, the formation of second nature permits individuals to formulate judgements that are answerable to criticisms and exemplify the self-directedness of the person making the judgement (see Backhurst, 2011: 75–76). But such judgements are not only answerable to other persons: judgements are also responses to the perceived determinate character of identifiable events, processes and states of affairs.

Knowledge and the space of reasons

If the purpose of education is to develop the capacity to act and judge within the space of reasons then what role does the acquisition of knowledge play? The seminal essay on the relation between knowledge and education by Paul Hirst, *Liberal Education and the Nature of Knowledge*, is still, in my view, very instructive. The essay is in four parts. The first part surveys the role of knowledge drawn from a reading of ancient philosophy that envisages the development of mind through knowledge, which both furnishes a knowing of reality in terms of truth and, through this process, also plays a central role in the development of the good life. Knowledge therefore plays, on this reading, both an epistemological and an ethical role. In the second part, Hirst considers certain modern (in fact, mid-twentieth century) proponents of the idea that the purpose of education is to cultivate certain attributes of mind (effective thinking, communication, ethical judgement). He makes quick work of showing that such attributes cannot be developed without disciplinary (subject) engagement in which is embedded what counts as effective thinking, good communication, etc. (Hirst, 1972: 90–95). In the fourth section, Hirst elaborates in more detail what he envisages to be a knowledge-led curriculum, of which the details need not concern us since over the passage of time new disciplines and sub-disciplines have emerged while others have receded.[5] It is the third part of the essay that is of most interest.

Hirst begins by disavowing the suggestion in the first part of the essay, namely that the relation between knowledge, mind and reality has a 'metaphysical' basis and initially goes on to suggest that the relation between mind and knowledge is rather 'logical', such that the achievement of knowledge 'necessitates' the development of mind (97). This thought, however, is not developed and Hirst then goes on to suggest that the focus of knowledge is rather 'experience, structured under some conceptual scheme' (97). 'Experience' is enumerated in terms of 'sense perceptions, emotions or different elements of the understanding', which it is suggested 'are intelligible only by virtue of the conceptual apparatus by which they are articulated.' This sounds as though Hirst, in separating out experiences as such from the conceptual apparatus through which they become known, is sailing perilously close to the muddy waters of the myth of the given. What emerges, however, is that forms of knowledge become coextensive with forms of experience. For, first, experiences can only be articulated through conceptual forms – they can only be recognised as experiences of such and such character because they are presented and articulated through a conceptual apparatus. Second, the system of concepts takes the form of publicly known and shared criteria for their application – it is this that allows experiences to be recognised, evaluated and compared. Third, this structuring of experience is not confined to traditional academic divisions of knowledge since 'the forms of knowledge are the basic articulations whereby the *whole* of experience has become intelligible to man' (98, my emphasis). The generation of knowledge – that conceptual apparatus through which experience becomes intelligible – pervades the whole experience of human kind. The clear implication is that experience is constituted through the forms of knowledge:

> it is by its terms that the life of man in every particular is structured and ordered . . . without its structure all other forms of consciousness, including for example, emotional experiences, or mental attitudes and beliefs would seem to be unintelligible.
>
> (98)

This thought is developed further under the fourth characteristic of Hirst's conception, namely that the experiences we undergo must not be thought of as primary or foundational but are themselves in part the product of meditation, evaluation and validation of those publicly specified criteria that identify and articulate experiences themselves (97–98).

Although Hirst postulated the concept 'forms of knowledge', it will be seen that this could just as well have been recast as 'forms of experience'. It is often supposed that Hirst proposed the forms of knowledge in terms of so-called 'propositional knowledge' – inert statements bundled into disciplinary domains that generations of children and students are obliged to learn, repeat and forget.[6] It is assumed, in other words, that the forms of knowledge are disconnected from experience, whereas in fact they arise from a certain understanding of the structuring of experience. I want to suggest, then, that to the extent that the 'forms of knowledge' characterise the articulation and intelligibility of experience then they inhabit the space of reasons and are pervaded by this space. Forms of knowledge can be seen as clusters within that space and exemplifying the character of that space, namely giving and justifying reasons. One of the problems, however, with Hirst's theory of knowledge is that he never quite differentiated between what McDowell terms the 'realm of law' on the one hand (i.e. the realm of causal explanation, fetishisation of which leads to bald naturalism), and the space of reasons, namely that justificatory realm in which experience of the world is made intelligible. If, then, the forms of knowledge are identified solely with the realm of law it is not difficult to see – indeed, it is perfectly understandable – why so many have had problems with it. Nevertheless, Hirst does make it clear that the forms do include (for example) moral knowledge and literary and aesthetic appreciation as well as the traditional disciplines in the sciences and mathematics.

However, apart from the space of reasons/realm of law distinction there is another feature, which plays an increasingly major role as McDowell's analysis has developed and which is also a crucial feature of the forms of knowledge, once viewed through the perspective of the space of reasons. This is the role played by judgement, namely the ability to constitute a state of affairs as having certain features and to evaluate their relative importance. Judgement is usually contextual so that the discrimination of a state of affairs (which, it should be noted can be mental or non mental or a combination of these) is situated within a wider understanding. When we refer to the forms of knowledge as under-pinning educational purposes then the ability to make judgements occupies a central place. Learning does not merely consist of the mastery of concepts and information: what we are looking for is the ability to make judgements. Understood in this way, learning becomes an active process that engages and challenges the learner in two distinct ways.

The first links judgement and responsibility and is described by McDowell in these terms:

> judging can be singled out as the paradigmatic mode of actualisation of conceptual capacities, the one in terms of which we should understand the very idea of conceptual capacities in the relevant sense. And judging, making up our minds what to think, is something for which we are in principle responsible – something we freely do, as opposed to something that merely happens in our lives ... and this freedom, exemplified in responsible acts of judging, is essentially a matter of being answerable to criticism in the light of rationally relevant considerations. So the realm of freedom, at least the freedom of judging, can be identified with the space of reasons.
>
> (McDowell, 2009a: 5–6; see also Backhurst, 2011: 75)

Roughly speaking there will be at least some of our beliefs for which we are not responsible in the sense that they are formed through the world's being 'thus and so'. But supervening on such beliefs are a complex of beliefs – judgements – for which we are responsible. Engagement with forms of know-ledge is therefore a risky endeavour since we are accountable for our judgements and being able to account for them is also what one has to do if one lives within a space of reasons. The kinds of judgements one makes, as far as learning is concerned, will range from the theoretical and the interpretative down to the severely practical. For example, the deliverance of a judgement may be a decision on which form of clinical treatment is most appropriate on the one hand, to a judgement that assesses the weight of responsibility accruing to Germany in terms of the causes of World War I. The learner, in acting and making judgements thereby becomes accountable. Viewing the forms of knowledge through the perspective of the space of reasons brings this out.

The second feature is the way in which subjective or agent-centred con-siderations must be laid aside. When Hirst speaks of knowledge that is subject to publicly specified criteria we can see that coming to be acquainted with such criteria helps us extrude personal considerations in reaching a judgment. That one is held personally accountable for making judgements in accordance with impersonal criteria takes some time – many years – in learning and if the beginnings of this are started in primary schooling it certainly takes the whole experience of education at all levels before the appropriate habituation is in place. But this also implies a willingness to challenge and revise public criteria in order to provide backing for controversial judgements. A good example of this is presented in a discussion of what constitutes good professional practice in teaching where it is suggested that the well-being of the teacher herself needs to be built into an understanding of practice; this presents a challenge to the view that practice can be evaluated in terms of technical competence alone (see Higgins, 2011).

In a brief article published in 1998, Hirst disavows the central thesis that he developed in the 1960s. He suggests that 'social practices and practical reason are the fundamental concerns of education, not propositional knowledge and theoretical reason' (Hirst, 1998: 19). The thinking behind this arises from a pragmatist turn of mind, in which it is held that 'reason operates most fundamentally in the satisfaction of physical, psychological and social needs and interest . . . what is rational is what is successful in experience' (18). In some ways, this new approach can be interpreted as having a perspective on knowledge that goes beyond the realm of law ('propositional knowledge' and theoretical reason) towards a more expansive view of the reach of the space of reasons, which does indeed reach into the realm of the practical. In part, this is what the idea of 'second nature' is all about. It follows, therefore, that the 'forms of knowledge' can indeed include what has traditionally been termed vocational knowledge. Moreover, it also implies that even traditional disciplines (history, bio-chemistry) may be taught in practical ways in such a manner as to encourage learners in the making of judgements. However, when Hirst now maintains that reason is to be placed at the service of needs and interests then here, I think, a step too far is being taken. For needs and interests themselves must be evaluated within the space of reasons in order to see what counts as a need or interest, in accordance with (as the Hirst of old would say) publicly specified criteria. Needs and interests must be identified and justified *within* the space of reasons. For example, a need arrives into that space already conceptualised as a particular need that requires justification. Moreover, through the activities that generate knowledge within the space of reasons new needs and interests may arise (or old ones modified); knowledge activities cannot be placed in service of needs and interests that they themselves may help to generate.

Working within the space of reasons

If working within the space of reasons involves justifying and being able to justify what one says, we need to be able to identify the kinds of activities that enable one to do this, and, in the context of this essay, activities that have an educational character. For McDowell, 'one comes to inhabit the space of reasons – to have conceptual capacities in the relevant sense – by acquiring a command of language' (McDowell, 2009b: 247). However, depending on what is meant by 'command of language', it may be that such a command is necessary to participate at all in the space of reasons but such command, in itself, does not enable one to enter into activities of a more justificatory nature. To do that, much more is needed. In particular, how does one develop those conceptual capacities that are needed?

One promising approach has been sketched out for us by Robert Brandom in his account of inferential reasoning.[7] Building on investigations undertaken by Wilfred Sellars (1953) into the nature of inference, Brandom distinguishes between formally valid inferences that require an enthymeme and material inferences that are valid through the connection of conceptual content. A formally valid inference relies on the truth of a conditional in order that the inference be valid. Thus, if it is the case that 'whenever it rains the streets will be wet' then if it happens to be raining today then the streets will indeed be wet. But Brandom suggests that there are other forms of inferring that do not require this kind of formal structure. He gives as an example the inference 'Pittsburgh is to the west of Philadelphia' from 'Philadelphia is to the east of Pittsburgh' (Brandom, 1994: 98). Brandom concludes that 'the material inferences codified in subjunctive conditionals are inferential involvements that are essential to the contents of the concepts used in science and everyday life. These are not logically valid inferences' (103). The idea is that endorsing certain inferences is a part of grasping and understanding a range of concepts. The example given above of a material inference may be seen to be valid by virtue of meaning, once one has grasped the relation between 'east' and 'west'. At the same time, one could also maintain that learning what 'east' and 'west' mean could be achieved precisely through the use of such an example, accompanied by looking at a map.[8]

But arguably not all inferences operate in the way of this example. As a different example, consider the idea of democracy as equivalent to 'rule by the majority'. Armed with this definition, one can certainly infer examples of non-democratic rule. But there will be grey areas – for example, the use of popular mandate to underwrite one-person rule, or examples in which the majority tyrannise a minority. At one point in his exposition, Brandom refers to 'practical inferences'[9] and I would suggest that many inferences are neither formally or materially valid, just because of the likelihood of counterexamples. Rather they have a practical efficacy once related to context. If one takes a concept such as the Reformation, there are a number of inferences that one can make or that become clear, once the concept has been grasped. Suppose the fundamental idea of Lutherism is taken to be that the relation between humankind and God is directly individual – namely, the idea of the 'priesthood of all believers'. It certainly follows from this that the authority of the traditional Church could be undermined (since there is less of a need for a mediating authority between man and God) and that the Bible should be written in the vernacular (since this would give people access to sacred texts without the need for reliance on interpreters). But none of this follows from the 'meaning' of the term 'Reformation'. It is just that, given a specific context, inferential links of the kind cited become plausible. They are also subject to counter example so that an important part of what 'being knowledgeable' entails is the ability to take part in discussions of what a concept implies and what it does not imply, taking into account contextual content.

I have mentioned the role of judgements working in the space of reasons and have suggested that the idea of 'forms of knowledge' be re-worked to accommodate the central role of making judgements. This requires some understanding of the relations between context, reasons and judgement. Suppose it is claimed that Henry VIII of England was a tyrant. The following reasons are adduced for this claim: a) he badly mistreated his wives, b) he conducted a Reformation, which was in effect imposed on unwilling subjects and c) he dissolved the monasteries. But if a different understanding of context is offered, the reasons become modified and a different judgement emerges. Thus, it could be said that the Tudor claim to the throne was weak[10] and a male heir was essential to the stability of the kingdom of England and, further, there was nothing to suggest at the time – from either the recent past or the more distant past – that the prospects of a female heir would be anything other than bleak. Given all this, it could be argued that Henry's conduct to his wives was motivated by a real and genuine concern that was not borne out of a tyrannical disposition. Further, it could be argued that since the Lutheran pressures were very real (even if these took some time to percolate down to the greater part of the population), Henry managed these rather well and succeeded in avoiding civil war (which beset a number of other European countries at the time). Much more could be said regarding Henry's reign, but the point is this: by re-working the context one yields a different set of reasons that could endorse the judgement that Henry was not a tyrant after all. Judgements are related to reasons through context so that disagreement over judgements may well prompt a revision of understanding of context.

Thus, agreement on judgements may ensue once the main outlines of the relevant context are settled. Judgements may be questioned not only as to their efficacy but also whether they are appropriate. Thus, in the example of Henry VIII, one may re-draw the context in terms of the changing nature of kingship in early modern England and conclude that the judgement that 'Henry was a tyrant' is not particularly interesting. But note that the only way of reaching this conclusion is not by pursuing the reasons for or against the tyrant question but by asking new questions that relate to context so that the latter is re-configured.

Jan Derry has helped to show us how the role of inferences 'provides a basis for a conception of knowledge and the process of acquiring it . . . it is necessary to 'make explicit' the connections and determinations that constitute a concept' (Derry, 2008: 60).[11] I have suggested that 'context' is made up of a multiplicity of concepts with inferential connections – the strength of which may be contested –and that the reasons which back a judgement are related to context. It is not that the context itself rests on a further evidential base that can somehow be identified independent of context. Nevertheless, there are nodal points of evidence that do intrude. Whatever we think about Henry mistreating his wives the fact is that two of them were beheaded. Judgements regarding the extent of global warming are complex and contestable, even though scientists might agree on the basic physics and also on the fact that the Arctic icecap is melting. These observations flow from McDowell's analysis of the space of reasons as constrained by features of how the world is. The building and shaping of context does not rest solely on inferential connections.

It should be noted that the capacity for judgement is internally related to an understanding of context. While one may, through experience, acquire the disposition of a judging temperament (for example, through the habit of discounting personal preferences) this in itself is no substitute for an engagement with content. Hence, there is no skill of 'judging' that can be transferable. If learning is to involve as one of its central features the making and contesting of judgements then there is no escaping the difficult process of building up and understanding appropriate contexts. In this respect, the early Hirst's central thesis that education comprises the pursuit of forms of knowledge still stands. Part of the difficulty in accepting the overall thrust of Hirst's ideas on the connection between knowledge and education is the tacit assumption that knowledge, to count as knowledge, must be orientated towards truth. But there is a better way of interpreting knowledge, which steers clear of more controversial claims as to whether claims to knowledge are also claims to truth. This view of matters has been explored by Catherine Elgin, who suggests that the pursuit of knowledge in educational contexts is better understood in terms of the pursuit of understanding. For unlike knowledge, understanding need not be validated in terms of truth. Rather, understanding admits of degrees may also be evidenced where what is thought to be 'true' is contested (see Elgin, 2007: 419–420). Moreover, it is through understanding (for example, understanding contexts) that judgements become possible. However, it should be noted that if we ask what it is that is to be understood then we are referred to different bodies of knowledge that themselves are composed of 'truths', some of which may, for all intents and purposes, be beyond dispute while others are fiercely contested. Bodies of knowledge are usually messy, uncertain and at their leading edge are composed of a series of problems, not a series of confirmed propositions.

Conclusion

The suggestion being put forward here is that the epistemological domain that is identified through the idea of a 'space of reasons' is also a space within which liberty can develop. Specifically, this involves the development of those human powers that are needed if liberty is to become resilient. But it is not merely a question of engaging in learning and developing specialisms within some corner of the forms of knowledge. It also includes the development of the powers of judgement, which themselves depend on an inferential understanding of appropriate context. It is through our ability to judge and take the risk of judging that our liberties can be protected. Conversely, situations of dependency require that those in subordinate or subaltern roles have the scope of making judgements restricted to what is merely personal or trivial. The risk of making judgements is too much and so, far from being habituated into the making of judgements, subordinates are habituated into the avoidance of judging. Or – what can be just as bad – judgements are made without the utilisation of knowledge and thus become empty complaints. In subsequent chapters some of the implications of this analysis will be further developed.

Notes

1　See Karl Marx's *Theses on Fuerbach* in Easton and Guddat (1967: 399–400).
2　See N.H. Smith's (ed.) *Reading MacDowell* (2002) for several critiques, e.g. that of Michael Friedman, 55–86.
3　See the discussion in MW: 82–84.
4　David Backhurst brings out very well the connection between second nature, *Bildung* and education – see Backhurst (2011: 14 and 149).
5　Originally, Hirst identified seven forms of knowledge were mathematics, the physical sciences, the human sciences, history, religion, literature and the fine arts, and philosophy and moral knowledge. In addition there were interdisciplinary 'fields' of knowledge.
6　See, for example, the comments of J. White (2009: 138) where it is suggested that Hirst's view of the curriculum rested on a conception of the value of knowledge as 'instrinsic'. See also chapter 3, *What is Education For?* by R. Marples, in Bailey (ed.) (2010: 38) in which the propositional character of Hirst's conception of knowledge is discussed.
7　Brandom's ambitious undertaking to show that inferential relations underpin meaning as such lies outside the scope of my investigations.
8　The influence of Brandom's work on inferentialism is influencing a growing number of those working in educational theory. See, for example, Winch (2013: 130–132) who argues that our understanding of propositional knowledge is deepened by envisaging it in terms of inferential links and the ability to make those links.
9　See Brandom (1994: 100) where he refers to a purported belief of an animal.
10　See Lucy Wooding (2009: 13) for an account of the tenuous basis of the Tudor dynasty based on the female line from Edward III and how this influenced the policy of both Henry VIII and his father, Henry VII.
11　See also Derry (2013: 229). In this article, Derry also stresses the role that inference plays in concept construction – see especially 231–232.

Chapter 5

Second nature, liberty and autonomy

Second nature and liberty

The idea of a 'second nature' has certain attractions for a view of liberty that prioritises civic-based liberty over natural liberty. For the normative context needed for civic liberty to develop is one that enables persons to develop their powers within a framework of recognition. Contrary to certain mythologies, man is not 'born free' and certainly the powers needed for the exercise of liberty to be efficacious are not powers that are given at birth. It may be protested that this is a mere truism; of course, it must be the case that babies and young children have their powers developed before they can take on the responsibilities of liberty-bearing agents. But the idea of second nature is not the development of natural powers and rational faculties as if these are to be regarded as so many muscles to be strengthened. Rather it involves introduction into the space of reasons so that individual faculties and dispositions are developed within that normative context. In particular, it involves the idea of discriminating receptions and communicating judgements. Nor does the idea of second nature involve merely the inculcation of social practices along the lines of learning rules and knowing how and when to apply them. There is an epistemological dimension to second nature that is not reducible to mere social practice. This involves the ability to discern the world as being 'thus and so' and to communicate that thought as a judgement. And there is no social practice that constitutes the 'practice of judging' – judgement cuts across all practices. Yet the process of asking for and responding to the giving of reasons is not something that can be left to chance, which is why the process of education has as its central feature the process of inference, of reasoning and of judgement. Thus the connection between second nature and educative process is not merely contingent since in learning to make judgements children and students are learning to participate in the space of reasons. What is important also, however, is the idea of an institution that is constituted so that this can be achieved: however education is structured, a non-response to reasons is not an option. In being educated I cannot pretend that an instruction has not been given or that a reason has not been asked for. Nor do I respond to an instruction merely because it is someone's will that I do so. Schools are – or should be – reason-giving environments and for some children this can be a liberation in itself if a domestic background is one in which commands are issued in an arbitrary fashion and in which home life is dictated by parental mood swings.

The idea of second nature can also be understood by contrasting it with the position that develops if one cleaves to a conceptual scheme that supplies its own criteria of validity with no external constraint – what McDowell describes as a 'frictionless spinning in a void'. For part of the process in developing second nature just is the recognition that there are constraints on what we think and believe and that we cannot just think or believe anything we want. The constraint here is not social but epistemological. From the standpoint of liberty this is important. For frictionless conceptual schemes may involve relations of dependency and if one is not able to point to an event or state of affairs as being 'thus and so' then the last bastion of resistance to dependency may be gone. For example, the system of apartheid in South Africa was a well worked-out conceptual scheme in which, from within that scheme, social disadvantage appeared to have a natural sanction. Black and coloured peoples were constricted in the type of judgements they were able to make and these were not perceived as mere social constraints but as supposed limited capabilities that inhered in people. One of the dangers of supposing that epistemological problems are susceptible to solution through the employment of conceptual schemes – and the attendant relativism this involves – is that relations of dependency may be licensed with no basis for resistance other than coming up with an alternate conceptual scheme. Realist epistemologies cannot guarantee the development of liberty but at least they can provide a perspective from which depredations of liberty cannot be merely conjured away by a mythologising conceptual scheme.

It may be protested that apartheid needs to be opposed not by 'facts' but by an alternative and more attractive conceptual scheme – a set of moral practices based on equal respect, for example. But such a set of practices needs to point to a set of facts as well – in this case, the fact that black people were, and are, no less intelligent than white people. In particular, all are capable of participating in the space of reasons. One of the huge advantages of establishing what might be termed the 'space of reasons perspective' is that it provides a standpoint from which different conceptual schemes – e.g. social moralities – can be evaluated. One of the basic tests is that of exclusion: if a morality can only flourish on the basis of systematically excluding persons from the space of reasons (which is precisely what apartheid did) then the foundation of one's liberties is simply swept away. What is interesting about a system such as apartheid is that the external constraint that was dismissed (namely the equal intelligence of members of different races) was precisely that which determined non-membership of the domain of space of reasons – alleged inferior intelligence and culture of black persons – and was used as a reason to deny admittance into that public space. Now, within the space of reasons there will be much discussion about what constitutes an 'external constraint' within any particular context – where it is assumed, however, that each person is a fully fledged member of that public space. But if the use of external constraints is to deny access to the space of reasons then one would need to start questioning the integrity of that space. This would not be only because some people are excluded from it: the implications go deeper. The restriction of the space of reasons in this way would mean that what counts as an external constraint is never fully recognised, just because of the reduction and deprivation of reason giving. Since it is through the giving and asking of reasons that what counts as an external constraint is recognised as such then there is a greater chance of that space being a deformed space – one that ends up as frictionless spinning – if some people are excluded from it. For the existence of external constraints – that the world is 'thus and so' – can only be realised through reason-giving activities – i.e. not through mere intuition that one must either accept or reject but through justification. So restricting access to the space of reasons is not just a moral question – though it certainly is that – it is one that reflects on the epistemological integrity of the domain.

The argument thus far is that liberty is more likely to flourish within a normative context of the space of reasons. But it does not follow, however, that 'rational necessitation is constitutive of freedom' so that 'we are free just to the extent that we respond appropriately to rational requirements' as David Backhurst has argued (Backhurst, 2011: 83). This idea has its provenance in German Idealism, which ties together freedom and rationality so that rationality becomes the constitutive basis of freedom. We are free to the extent that we respond to rational requirements. The difficulty with this view is threefold. First, it is unnecessary to make the link between freedom and rationality so strong if one takes the view (as argued throughout this book) that freedom is a relation between persons constituted through civic authority. One might well argue that without rational powers the concept of freedom would be worthless since the former provides the idea of self-direction and without this freedom would merely consist of the 'free' movement of an entity buffeted about by events and causes, an entity that would exist outside the space of reasons. But it does not follow that freedom only consists in the exercise of such powers. Second, if I am less than rational then presumably I am unfree. Whenever I do not act rationally then I am, at that point, lacking in freedom. Whereas I would argue that freedom may sometimes consist in acting irrationally (and taking the consequences). Thus, I may act utterly foolishly: my freedom consists in my willingness to accept responsibility for my foolishness. In any case, there are many actions and beliefs that may escape a complete analysis in terms of reasons (e.g. activities of an aesthetic character) but my freedom is not thereby impugned. Third, as we have already noted in Chapter 3, rational powers may be excellently exercised and evinced but I may not, on just that account be free: I may be in a state of dependency nonetheless.

Freedom, autonomy and education

Backhurst pursues the logic of this argument – the necessary link between freedom and rationality – in his consideration of the aims of education – in particular, in thinking of 'freedom as an educational ideal' (Backhurst, 2011: 75). This might seem at first sight as thoroughly consistent with the aim of promoting liberty but I wish to resist the temptation of making freedom an *aim* of education. Rather, the aims of education are more related to the development of those human powers that enable agents to exercise their freedoms and to resist potential and actual invasions of liberty. The reason for this is that liberty needs to be seen as constituted through authoritative structures as opposed to being an ideological goal as such. Thus, although the practice of education certainly needs to be informed by considerations pertaining to liberty (this is something we shall consider in more detail in the chapter on 'Liberty and pedagogy') it does not follow that liberty (or freedom or autonomy) should be made an overall educational aim as such.

The idea that autonomy should be an educational aim is long established (e.g. see Dearden, 1972) and some of the arguments have conveniently been summarised by Michael Hand. He distinguishes between what might be called political freedom (which he calls circumstantial autonomy) and personal freedom (which he terms dispositional autonomy). He points out that what he calls circumstantial autonomy cannot be imparted by education and therefore he concentrates on dispositional autonomy, which is described as 'a preference for relying on one's own judgement, to be independent-minded, free-spirited, disposed to do things one's own way' (Hand, 2006: 537). Hand points out that this trait may be undesirable on two counts: first, there are times when one should defer to another's knowledge, and second, there will be times when one ought to defer to another's authority. An educational system that encouraged as a dispositional trait persons to disregard both knowledge and authority would be absurd since it would not be to the benefit, however this could be construed, of the individuals involved. Rather, Hand suggests that we wish to encourage 'rational, well-balanced people willing and able to exercise judgement, rely on expert advice or submit to legitimate authority as the occasion demands' (539).

Hand's arguments have been challenged by Aharon Aviram and Avi Assor as follows:

> We need to educate for autonomy, among other things, since in our pluralistic information-saturated and relativistic era there are very few fundamental questions on which there is ongoing agreement among authorities, be it ethics, economics, managerial and business theories or medicine. Thus, by assuming that authorities can decide on the effective and the appropriate, Hand is relying on unstable foundations. Put in other words, this approach overlooks the huge difficulties in locating 'experts' who would know what is effective, appropriate or worthwhile.
>
> (Aviram and Assor, 2010: 116)

They then go on to suggest that 'it is up to the autonomous individual to decide who to follow' and that 'where there is a need to decide between acting autonomously or giving up one's autonomy' one should exercise independent judgement (116). The difficulty here is that the 'giving up of autonomy' is premised on independent judgement so that the individual always is able to decide whether to follow someone or not: she is the final arbiter of her destiny and as such has what might be termed 'epistemological independence'. It is just this perspective that McDowell's arguments in favour of the space of reasons challenge. For what is being suggested in this perspective is that each of us, in effect, have our own conceptual scheme, which we bring into play whenever we are faced with making a judgement. If a course of action that is suggested by another happens to fall in with our own particular conceptual scheme then there is no loss of autonomy at all, strictly speaking, since on the basis of that scheme we have decided to follow someone else's judgement. Our own personal conceptual scheme remains intact and it is only me who is entitled to revise it, should the need arise. But the idea of each of us having our own separate conceptual schemes really is nothing more than that frictionless spinning in a void that McDowell warns against. This is not the way to engage in the space of reasons. If reasons have a compelling force then they do so on their own account, not because they must first be tested against a conceptual scheme. Aviram and Assor are quite right to draw our attention to the 'pluralistic era' in which we live but the development of an endless multiplicity of private, autonomous conceptual schemes merely complicates and adds to this pluralism. Thus, if 'autonomy' is construed in terms of the development of individualised conceptual schemes then this cannot be the aim of education.

Interestingly, David Backhurst's interpretation of freedom ends up much closer to that of Hand rather than that of Aviram and Assor. He considers the view that 'education is charged with equipping individuals with the resources to form considered preferences and make unpressured choices about how to satisfy them' and suggests, instead, that education is better seen as developing 'the power to make up one's own mind what to think in the light of what there is reason to think and do' (Backhurst, 2011: 142). This point is significant because here the idea that freedom is essentially an opportunity concept is rejected in favour of a conception of freedom that centres on self-determination and the powers needed for this to happen in a world characterised in terms of the space of reasons. The choice-driven view of reason is defective because the agent may play no, or little, part in determining the range of choices available. Indeed, since the range of choices may be determined by others this may testify to my dependency rather than my freedom as such. Given that processes of education in themselves cannot influence availability of choice, the emphasis on autonomy as choice seems inappropriate. As Backhurst says, it may well be that reasoning and deliberation may point to one particular judgement in any case, so that a multiplicity of choices becomes irrelevant. It is perfectly true that if one lives in circumstances where there are very few choices available then this may be indicative of constraints and restrictions. But it does not follow that freedom therefore must be associated with a multiplicity of choices or, even less, the maximisation of choice. The nature of choices available may be far more important than how many there are and so the question before me is whether I have the internal resources and powers to deliberate and come to a judgement. In this way it may happen that, following reflection, all the available choices are rejected: this would indeed be an exemplification of liberty. The confusion of liberty with choice is easy to make because we naturally think of a state of *unfreedom* as one with no or little choice. But the converse does not follow: it does not entail that the enhancement of freedom must be accompanied by and driven by ever-widening choices. Thus it also follows that one way of giving the illusion of freedom is to maximise choice while doing little or nothing to develop powers of reasoning and deliberation: a society, for example, in which markets are encouraged to grow while expenditure on education is kept static or even reduced.

Mill and autonomy

It may be objected, however, that the arguments adduced so far against making the promotion of freedom and autonomy an aim or the even the principle aim of education have failed to do justice to the ideal of autonomy. This is what Aviram and Assor argue against Hand; that his somewhat workaday definition of autonomy simply fails to do justice to what is a rich tradition of thinking (Aviram and Assor, 2010: 117–119).

One particular source of influential thinking on autonomy can be found in Mill's *On Liberty*, in which many of the salient issues are raised and are applied to education and schooling. Although Mill does not mention the term 'autonomy' as such in his tract, nevertheless what he says about liberty – and especially individuality – are directly relevant to the issues raised by Hand, Aviram and Assor. As is well known, Mill starts by suggesting that there is a 'simple principle' that governs liberty, namely that:

> the sole end for which mankind are warranted, individually or collectively, in interfering with the liberty of action of any of their number, is self protection. That the only purpose for which power can be rightfully exercised over any member of a civilised community against his will, is to prevent harm to others. His own good, either physical or moral, is not a sufficient warrant.
>
> (Mill, 1991: 30)

It has been argued in Part I that one of the particular examples of 'harm to others' is that of domination, and that the scope of what counts as harm needs to include within it attempts either to dominate or to bring about the dependency of some on others where it is unwarranted. But one of Mill's concerns is to develop what might be called the ideal of liberty and it is this that I want to examine briefly here. For Mill is clearly aware that having asserted his 'simple principle' he needs not only to discuss what constitutes 'harm' but why 'liberty of action' (and, by extension, liberty of thought, as he makes very clear) is so important.

As will become clear it is reasonable to assume that what Mill means by liberty pretty much corresponds to what is often termed 'autonomy'. There are two aspects to his account of liberty. The first is concerned with the need for choice: 'The human faculties of perception, judgement, discriminative feeling, mental activity, and even moral preference, are exercised only in making a choice. He who does anything because it is custom makes no choice' (74).

Moreover, individuals often find it easier to subject themselves to the 'despotism of custom', which he sees as in 'unceasing antagonism' to the 'spirit of liberty' (86). Mill is under no doubt that it is often individuals themselves who fail to develop their autonomy and at one point he inveighs against persons for whom 'it does not occur to them to have any inclination except for what is customary' (77). If I merely defer to custom then I am consigning myself to a state of non-liberty simply because I do not exercise choice, even though there is nothing preventing me from doing so other than the feared disapprobation of my fellows if I do. For Mill, to be in thrall to custom is a form of dependency that is often self-induced and self-perpetuating, in contrast to a preferred state in which there is 'independence of action and disregard of custom' (83).

The second aspect of liberty concerns what might be termed 'free deliberation' – the idea that any proposal, thesis or recommendation must be subject to scrutiny so that a person is 'capable of rectifying his mistakes by discussion and experience. Not by experience alone. There must be discussion to show how experience is to be interpreted' (Mill, 1991: 40). And Mill goes on to argue that 'a person whose judgement is really deserving of confidence' is one who 'has kept his mind open to criticism of his opinions and conduct' (40). The idea here is that not only do human beings need to have the capacity for deliberation but that also the social environment should be conducive to free discussion and an exchange of views. Mill voices his concern that these conditions are not present in his own society: 'For it is this – it is the opinions men entertain, and the feelings they cherish, respecting those who disown the beliefs they deem important, which makes this country not a place of mental freedom' (50).

Thus, liberty requires both the exercise of choice and free deliberation so that an individual is able to think and act with independence of thought and action. As he makes clear in the fourth chapter of *On Liberty*, Mill is perfectly aware that 'no person is an entirely isolated being' (95) and that whatever I do or say will not be without effect on others nor free from the influence of others: the question is whether I can steer my own path, taking these influences into account.

But if we ask why liberty (or autonomy) is so important for Mill, then the answer is very clear:

> It is not by wearing down into uniformity all that is individual in themselves, but by cultivating it and calling it forth, within the limits imposed by the rights and interests of others, that human beings become a noble and beautiful object of contemplation . . . and by the same process human life also becomes rich, diversified and animating.
>
> (79)

Autonomy is not demanded because it better leads to an appreciation of a classical form that serves as a standard of taste and morals for any civilised human being; Mill is quite deliberately turning his back on received standards of taste (including those deriving from antiquity) in favour of the good of diversity and individuality. That is why comments such as those by John Gray, who suggests that Mill has an Aristotelian view of the way in which rationality and desire are fused into the development of character (see Gray, 1991: 201) need to be treated with great care, because Mill was emphatically not Aristotelian in the sense that he thought there could be discovered criteria as to what constituted the good life that could hold for all. Mill re-enforced this view by proclaiming the virtue of originality (80) and insisting that for a man, 'his own way of laying out his existence is best' (83). Finally, Mill perhaps rather optimistically thought that the growth of individuality assisted human progress in terms of cultural and moral development (86), but it is clear that for him, individuality was not a means to progress but an intrinsic part of it.

However, liberty is not the same as individuality, for individuality may flourish in all kinds of states of dependency. One might almost say that in a state of dependency at least one may have a degree of individuality to cling to even if one has lost one's liberty. At the same time, a state of liberty is perfectly consistent with a degree of uniformity of outlook and perspective. It is unclear that individuality has any more value than uniformity since the former may take trite and shallow forms while the latter may be committed to a comprehensive and deep-reaching moral or religious ideal. Alternatively, individuality could be construed as so many surface styles and dispositions to be enjoyed and applauded while each shares in a common acknowledged moral code that allows individuality to flourish without ever becoming reckless. By contrast, if individuality is construed along the lines of so many individualised conceptual schemes then the kind of free discussion and deliberation that Mill favours could be undermined if even the terms of discourse itself were disputed. Indeed, it would seem that Mill is committed to a degree of shared public discourse to make possible the free exchange of ideas that is needed, with the requisite understanding and comprehension of all those taking part.

In terms of aims of education, therefore, if it is difficult to see why individuality as such should be promoted and to the extent that autonomy, following Mill, is construed along the lines of individuality then it is difficult to see why autonomy should be promoted either. On the other hand, if autonomy is construed along the lines of 'capable of entering free discussion and deliberation' then this indeed could become an aim of education because it is a characteristic of participating in the space of reasons typified by the existence of public discourse. But this kind of autonomy has little to do with individuality and even less to do with the type of autonomy construed along the lines of a proliferation of conceptual schemes. It is, rather, the ability to reach understandings and make judgements as a result of an engagement with a body of knowledge and practices. To the extent that those judgements are rooted in a recognised context and network of inference there is nothing 'autonomous' about the process of reaching judgements and still less is that process 'individualised'.

Mill himself was of the firm view that education, just by its nature, encouraged uniformity and so was inherently illiberal, but the context makes clear that by 'education' he in fact means 'schooling'. He advocated a diverse provision of schooling in order to encourage the growth of individuality (119). But if we demur from the goal of promoting individuality as an *educational* aim (however much we might welcome and delight in personal foibles and eccentricities) then it is not clear that diversity of provision will necessarily of itself produce that engagement with knowledge and practices that is needed for well-founded judgement to develop. Diversity of educational provision may be valued for all sorts of reasons but of itself such diversity is not going to deliver the ability to make sound judgements.

Rousseau and autonomy

It is worth considering, briefly, one renowned attempt to make personal autonomy the chief purpose of education – I refer to Rousseau's *Emile*. In that most complex work, Rousseau sets himself the task of elucidating the principles (accompanied by many case studies and *vignettes*) of educating a child to become as self-sufficient as possible both in terms of the practical skills and knowledge needed to make a living on the one hand, and in terms of moral self-sufficiency on the other. In this way, a person could become free of dependency on others and, in particular, free of dependency on the corrupt and self-serving conventions that passed for morality, in Rousseau's eyes. There was, however, a paradox that Rousseau openly admitted: before achieving full autonomy, the pupil was entirely dependent on the tutor who skilfully orchestrated Emile's education through providing a succession of learning scenarios. This approach was based on a perspective of childhood, which is stated in the Preface to *Emile* as follows:

> We know nothing of childhood and with our mistaken notions the further we advance the further we go astray. The wisest writers devote themselves

to what a man ought to know without asking what a child is capable of learning. *They are always looking for the man in the child without considering what he is before he becomes a man.* It is the latter study to which I have applied myself the most; so that if my method is unrealistic and unsound at least one can profit from my observations. I may be greatly mistaken as to what ought to be done, but I think I have clearly perceived the material that is to be worked upon. Begin thus by making a more careful study of your pupils for it is clear that you know nothing about them. If you read this book with that end in view I think you will find that it is not entirely useless.

(Rousseau, 1979: 33, emphasis added)

Part of the lasting attraction of *Emile* stems from its thinking in which the writer does indeed strive to adopt the perspective of a child and the enduring belief that childhood above all is something to be enjoyed. Hence, along with encouragement to children to play, run and shout is a solemn injunction to tutors that the way to make a child miserable is to give in to all its wants 'since his desires grow constantly due to the ease of satisfying them' (87). We are asked 'to respect childhood and do not hurry to judge it' (107).

The method of achieving autonomy was to be through 'negative education': 'The first education ought to be purely negative. It consists not at all in teaching virtue or truth but in securing the heart from vice and error' (Rousseau, 1979: 93).[1] This was to be achieved by encouraging a child to be as self-sufficient as possible, dependent on things but not on man: 'Keep the child in dependence only on things. Never present to his undiscriminating will anything but physical obstacles or punishments which stem from the actions themselves and which he will recall on the proper occasion' (85). What this meant in terms of pedagogical practice was an *absence* of overt instruction:

In trying to persuade your pupils of the duty of obedience, you join to this alleged persuasion force or threats or, what is worse, flattery or promises. In this way . . . they pretend to be convinced by reason. They see quite well that obedience is advantageous and rebellion harmful. But since everything you insist on is unpleasant and, further, it is always irksome to do another's will, they arrange to do their own will covertly.

(90)

Moreover, if the 'force of reason' is associated in the child's mind with unease and pain, reason itself can become discredited, since it only takes the form of unwelcome instruction:

Since what is wanted is not to make a child out of a child but a doctor out of a child, fathers and master can never soon enough scold, correct, reprimand, flatter, threaten, promise and instruct . . . bringing reason to bear on unpleasant things only discredits it early to a mind not yet in a condition to understand it.

(94)

In its most positive and attractive formulations, *Emile* provides us with a way of envisaging the development of a 'second nature' that opens the pupil to living in the space of reasons. This is achieved not through instruction but providing scenarios in which the pupil does not answer questions put to him but generates his own questions. This is not facilitated through reading since 'the child who reads does not think, he only reads . . . he is not informing himself, he learns words'. Rather than imposing an instructional regime, the tutor should 'feed his curiosity but never hurry to satisfy it' and take the time to 'put questions within his reach but leave them to him to resolve'. In this way the pupil will not so much learn science as 'discover it' (168). The danger of an instructional regime is spelt out clearly: 'if you substitute in his mind authority for reason . . . he will be nothing more than the plaything of other's opinions' (168). Rousseau then suggests taking a child out at sunrise and to the same place at sunset, in order to formulate questions in the child's mind regarding astro-physics.

There is, admittedly, an ambiguity here because what Rousseau could be taken as saying is that learning best comes through untutored experience, as if the skill of the tutor rests in supplying as much unmediated experience as is possible for the child to absorb. Note that what precedes the learning is the experience of the sun setting and rising and when Rousseau earlier suggests that learning through observation, trial and error is more instructive then adducing proofs and reasoning (145) we may be led into thinking that what is being advocated is a form of experiential learning, especially when Rousseau insists that 'the true masters are experience and sentiment' (178), having inveighed against instruction based on scholarly didacticism, which may produce 'docile pupils' but also guarantees that they will be 'credulous and a dupe when grown up'. In Rousseau's favour, therefore, it may be argued that 'experience and sentiment' are suitable starting points for younger learners since only this will allow them to generate their own questions in their own way and at their own pace. The tutor does not so much frame the questions as frame the environment in which questions are to be raised. The plausibility of what later became termed an enquiry-based approach to learning stems directly from Rousseau's own injunction to 'respect childhood'.

Less successful, however are the descriptions of attempts to develop autonomy in the child. The reason is not far to seek and has often been noted (e.g. Charvet, 1974: 50–52). Rousseau is, time after time, obliged to set up scenarios in which the pupil learns for himself the dangers and hazards of life at the expense of being manipulated by the tutor. Rousseau, to his credit is disarmingly frank about this: 'Let him always believe he is the master, and let it always be you who are. There is no subjection so perfect as that which keeps the appearance of freedom. Thus the will itself is made captive' (Rousseau, 1979: 120).

The tutor goes to ever greater lengths in arranging situations in which, unbeknown to the child, outcomes desired by the tutor are secured without the child's co-operation and participation. For example, when Emile insists on going to town alone, the tutor agrees knowing full well that the child will be unable to cope, but then arranges for an assistant to follow the child and rescue him once he becomes distressed. In defence of Rousseau, it could be argued that maybe we should distinguish his pedagogical methodology from his philosophy of education; some of the methods may be a bit crude but since Rousseau is a pioneer in 'respecting childhood' we should not be too harsh. But that distinction is too quick: much of his philosophy is reflected and expressed through his pedagogy. It is because Rousseau takes autonomy seriously and because he wants his pupil to 'learn from things rather than men' that the pedagogy becomes suspect at this crucial point. In his deep desire to obtrude any appearance of *authority* the tutor is obliged, time after time, to manipulate his charge in an unseen, non-transparent manner. If the price of autonomy is persistent organised deception, then we might well feel the price is too high. It would be far easier for the liberties of the pupil to be prescribed within a teacher authority that is fully recognised, specified within the public domain of education.

Rousseau's *Emile* still has the power to shock and to drive points home. Reading it, one feels that even today there are many who would benefit greatly by it. Yet it is full of paradoxes. The writer of this 500 page tome proclaims on p. 181 'I hate books', and recommends just one for young charges, *Robinson Crusoe*, on account of the great utility to be found in its pages. The man who proclaims on the priority of 'experience and sentiment' seems strangely attached to pen and ink. If only he could have devised a way of enabling his readers to experience learning through discovery rather than reading Jean Jacques! But the most valuable feature of *Emile* is the way in which it takes seriously what is to all intents and purposes the development of 'second nature' and the formative experience of this process. In doing so he also raises interesting questions concerning how children are to become acquainted with the space of reasons and, moreover, provides some answers too. At the same time, Rousseau's attempts to develop autonomy through manipulative scenarios cast doubt on whether such an ambitious aim can be achieved without a sleight of hand. This is why I suggest that while educational pedagogies can certainly develop enquiry-based learning this is best done within the context of a teacher authority that is well-specified and has a clear public role. On the basis of this authority teachers could instruct and direct without the need for any dissimulation. These matters will be further pursued in Part III.

Conclusion

In this chapter I have developed further the idea of 'second nature' and have argued that this should not be confused with autonomy or 'individuality'. However, a warning needs to be sounded. If one was to ask what would be better – relations of dependency and subalternship or the flourishing of individuality and myriad conceptual schemes – then the answer has to be, undoubtedly, the latter. In casting doubt on the *value* of diversity as such and questioning whether an education system has in any sense the duty to foster such diversity it does not all follow that a culture of dependency is somehow better. Undoubtedly, a regime of liberty may be more likely to encourage widespread diversity and so much the better for it, many may think; my point is that liberty is not the same as diversity. The fact that I may choose to lead a mainstream, conventional life in terms of cultural preferences, tastes and style of living does not impugn, in any sense, my liberty.

Note

1   For an interesting discussion of negative education, see Timothy O'Hagan (1998: 63–65).

Chapter 6

Liberty and pedagogy

The idea of an educational experience

Education is often analysed in terms of process or outcomes. But here I wish to focus on the experience of education from the standpoint of the child or student who is having the experience. I want to see if there are characteristics of this experience that can be identified in such a way that we can say, with reasonable confidence, that the experience was both worthwhile *and* consistent with the liberties of those who are learning. What I further want to suggest is that a worthwhile educational experience will also be one in which the learners – children and students – are treated as liberty-bearing agents and who experience their education in this way. Even if the process of education takes place in a political environment that is oppressive or not conducive to liberty there may be something about that process itself that does at least promote the experience of what it is to be liberty-bearing. Thus here I wish to analyse this experience independent of results and outcomes, that is, independent of assessment (I will have a few words to say about assessment later on in this chapter). For even if no assessment has taken place at all, something has happened nonetheless: an experience has occurred and the child may even be able to communicate something of the nature of that experience later on. It may, of course, not be a particularly memorable or pleasing experience, but something has happened all the same.

As the chapter proceeds I shall try to develop a more philosophical under-standing of what I mean by a significant experience. But for the time being a few non-philosophical remarks are in order just to fix the starting point. First, I am referring to a significant or worthwhile experience and not just any experience. For example, one may derive great pleasure from reading a piece by, say, a parliamentary sketch writer; but the pleasure does not usually extend for long after one has finished. By contrast a significant experience is one that can be set in the context of life-activities. Of course, there are many degrees of significance and only a few, if any, experiences will turn out to be, of themselves, life transforming. More often than not a significant experience takes its place in the context of activities or practices in which one is engaged and so only affects a part of one's life. Moreover, a significant experience does not need to be remembered over a lifetime: its lessons can be absorbed and brought to bear on subsequent experiences, so though it may be forgotten it may still possess efficacy.

All this implies that a significant educational experience is one such that, if it is taken outside its educational context, may be compared to other, non-educational experiences. So a good seminar in philosophy *may* be a significant experience in the sense that the long walk I had last weekend in which I started to notice certain types of birdsong for the first time was a significant experience; or the lengthy conversation I had in the pub last night that turned out to be significant because it disabused me of a prejudice that had started to form in me, hitherto unnoticed. Of course, most (not all) experiences occur in context so I am far from asserting that the worthwhile experience is entirely discrete and context-free. Indeed, without the context, interpretation of the experience may be virtually meaningless. Nevertheless, we do sometimes consider different experiences and compare them, despite the fact that they each come with different contexts, and a significant educational experience, I am suggesting, could be included in this in this kind of informal exercise.

As I have already hinted, an educational experience need not be significant. It may turn out to have been a very poor one indeed and best forgotten. Thus dissatisfaction at school is typically characterised by children in terms of a succession of poor or indifferent experiences, from their point of view. It may even turn out that although children did indeed have a memorable experience it had nothing to do with what the teacher and school had aimed and planned for. In this case, what was undergone was not so much an indifferent experience but a completely different one from that intended by the teacher. Whether it was an *educational* experience is another question. But it may have been worthwhile and significant all the same.[1]

If we suppose, along with R.S. Peters, that the term 'educational' implies that 'something worthwhile has been transmitted' (or perhaps developed), which involves knowledge and understanding (see Peters, 1966: 25, 30), this does not, in itself, imply that the process of being educated as such has been composed of worthwhile experiences from the standpoint of the person undergoing that process. It may well be that both at the time and also on subsequent reflection one realises that very few of one's educational experiences have been worthwhile.[2] A significant educational experience in the sense I wish to explore is one that helps to make education as a worthwhile process actually feel worthwhile as experienced by the child or student.

I am assuming that an educational experience is one that has an identifiable beginning and an end and qualifies as a single experience under some appropriate description. For example, a course, unless it is a very short, is composed of a number of related experiences, but it is always possible to view the whole course as 'an experience'. There is an understandable tendency to make educational experiences fairly short and sharp (this greatly assists assessment) but many significant experiences may last days or weeks (as readers of *Bleak House* will testify). There are then, no fixed rules as to how long an experience can last but it must have some kind of identifiable end point. In practice, of course, the duration of educational experiences is not only determined by subject matter but by timetabling constraints and the like.

I will first of all briefly set out two fairly common types of educational experience: this will more firmly locate the terrain I wish to explore. The rest of this chapter will then be spent elaborating the particular type of experience with which I am concerned.

Two types of educational experience

The first example of educational experience is taken from the UK Department of Education (DfES) Key Stage 3 National Strategy document, *Pedagogy and Practice* (2004). Here I focus on Unit 2: Teaching models. If we look at what is termed the 'deductive teaching model' (11) we learn that this is concerned with the teaching of concepts and specifically with the attributes that a concept possesses, which must be understood if it is to be distinguished from other, related concepts. The example given concerns democracy: 'with a concept of democracy in a citizenship lesson, the concept rule might be that "Democracy is government of the people by the people"'. The document then outlines for teachers the steps by which these concept rules may be taught, as follows:

> The deductive teaching model has five phases which can be divided into episodes.
>
> • The teacher begins the lesson with the concept rule, or a statement of what the pupils will attempt to prove during the lesson.
> • The teacher provides some examples which show proof of the concept rule.
> • The teacher, through questioning of the pupils, identifies the critical attributes and the non-critical attributes which are essential and non-essential characteristics of the concept.
> • The teacher follows this by showing examples and non-examples of the same concept to the pupils.
> • The pupils must categorise the examples or non-examples (those which do *not* show essential characteristics of the concept rule) by explaining why they do or do not fit the concept rule being discussed.
>
> (DfES, 2004: 11)

Now, in many ways it is difficult to quarrel too much with this approach. It is systematic and purposeful. The process is allied to the objectives of the lesson. It is interactive and space is given for student activity. Yet despite all these merits, not least of which is that there is a sporting chance that the concept rule will be understood, we might feel a certain unease. For one thing, the entire process is directed – indeed, controlled – by the teacher. There seems little room for student voice that has not already been sanctioned within the process. There also seems little chance of exploring the concept in such a way that relates to student or child experience (though much depends here on the kind of examples used). There is little allowance for the emergence of what might be termed 'creative deviancy' – note that the 'pupils *must* categorise the examples by explaining why they do or do not fit'. The lesson seems to read as a series of tasks to be accomplished. To be sure, the tasks are thought through and relate to the objectives but it is not clear that there is any space here for any enjoyment or fun: there seems little opportunity to relax in this lesson. Right from the start, the teacher has an agenda to drive through – and everyone must play their part.

Now, I do not deny for one moment that such a lesson could turn out to be enjoyable: much here would depend on the teacher style, the rapport he or she has with the class and the richness of the examples discussed. Nevertheless, from the standpoint of the children, this experience is essentially teacher-driven and if a teacher taught like this for each lesson every day he or she will probably end up completely exhausted before the end of the school week. Moreover, such a learning experience, however worthwhile it might be and whatever might have been accomplished, is not one where the learner – the child or student – is being treated as a free agent. While, as I have conceded, such learning may be effective it is one in which, as far as the pedagogical relationship itself is concerned, the learner is in a state of dependency *vis-à-vis* the teacher. From the standpoint of liberty, it would be unsettling if the *whole* of the learner's pedagogical experience was of this type. Even if the learning was effective, if this was the only type of learning experienced by children their experience could turn into one that accustomed them to dependency. It could be argued that, as a matter of fact, pedagogical relationships do take the form of dependency, namely the dependency of those who do not know on those that do. It is just this that I want to contest, from the standpoint of liberty: if, sometimes, models of teaching such as the deductive teaching model are the best and most effective way of bringing about learning it does not follow that they should predominate.

For the second type of educational experience, I take as my example *The Art of Constructivist Teaching in the Primary School* by Nick Selley. Here we are told in no uncertain terms that, in contrast to orthodox transmission pedagogies, the constructivist approach allows that 'the learner always controls the sense she makes of an experience'. This would seem to put the learning experience firmly in the camp of liberty. However, what may seem to be a highly questionable epistemological stance (namely rampant subjectivism) is modified through the additional requirement that constructions and interpretations be validated: 'you are helping the child to build up the best version of his/her model and to test it against experience' (Selley, 1999: 24). This is achieved through conversation, questioning and investigation. However, as Selley himself concedes, the business of 'trying out one's own ideas' is not easy: scientific investigation, for example, requires that the student

> must know what the question is, must want to find a solution, must know a promising line of procedure, must know how to set up and manipulate the necessary apparatus and must expect to be allowed to extract meaning from the results.

And presumably, the more any of this is lacking the greater teacher intervention is required. Constructivism seems to place a considerable burden and responsibility on the child. What one might term a child- (or student-) driven educational experience is not so much the having of an experience but the directing and managing of it. This looks difficult, by any standards, because it seems to involve not only an activity but also the meta-activity *by the child* of monitoring, recording and communicating what is going on in the primary activity.

So, for example, in the constructivist teaching of history, the child must be able to demonstrate the construction or interpretation of evidence through 'a talk, a diagram, role play or a drawing . . . by examining this representation we are able to assess the validity or fairness of the construction regarding the available visible evidence of the past' (Copeland, 1998: 125). What concerns me here is not so much that these constructions may not be historically accurate; after all the historical understanding of the child is bound to be simplified or abbreviated and any serious misconceptions can always be corrected. It is that so much is expected of the child: just as the teacher ends up exhausted after intense teacher-driven learning, so it seems to me that children will end up burnt-out before the end of the week if they are subjected to a series of non-stop constructivist exercises across the curriculum.

Aside from these practical difficulties, the constructivist approach presents further problems. For it may be said that what may start off as an emancipatory ideal of self-formation is transformed into a pedagogy of self-management and self-discipline – what may be termed an *auto-pedagogy*. This kind of pedagogy is subtly different from emancipatory pedagogies (e.g. the methods associated with Rousseau). For through it one also embraces a whole identity: one cannot be a learner without bringing in the associated features of the reflective learner, teaching through facilitation, the emphasis on the transferability of learning and the importance of self-direction and self-management. One cannot be a learner unless one absorbs a whole discourse of pedagogy. To become a learner is to *learn* a pedagogy and thereby to acquire an identity of the 'learner'. Pedagogy isn't simply the means whereby a curriculum is delivered: a person has to live a whole ideology so that one must 'acquire the self-image of a lifelong learner' (Knapper and Cropley, 2000: 49). This auto-pedagogy (a pedagogy of the self, a pedagogy of coping) requires a self-monitoring and a self-surveillance that are to be developed as habitual dispositions.

On the one hand, it may be said that a person needs to develop, as part of those human powers needed for the exercise of liberty, the means of self-discipline and self-monitoring. On the other hand, in so far as a person acquires the *identity* of learner, they may also acquire the identity of an internalised dependency. This arises from the way in which pedagogical procedures do not merely comprise a set of methods that require compliance from an external source, but from procedures that are self-imposed. If one was to write a genealogy of deference in the form of a just-so story, one would start with an account of relations of domination and subordination defined through publicly recognised forms of behaviour associated with social roles. But once those particular kinds of social relations are superseded by relations that take a more democratic character, deference may still survive in the form of procedures, disciplines and self-constraints that still have the effect of ropes that tie even if these are unseen. The self now has its own methodologies of monitoring, evaluation and assessment and it is now *this process itself that becomes known as 'learning'*. The final stage in the genealogy of deference, then, is that the subject matter of learning is transformed into 'content'. This content itself then becomes indeterminate; the knowledge is acquired, used up and forgotten since the 'what' of learning becomes determined by pragmatic or operational requirements.[3] What remains of learning are the internalised procedures of a pedagogy that each individual – each 'lifelong learner' – carries around for the duration of their life.

Of course, constructivist pedagogies need not lead to auto-pedagogy; and the acquisition of the methods of such a pedagogy need not lead to an habitual deference of a learner who as a matter of course manages their own learning without really knowing what is learnt. Moreover, there will be times when a more constructivist approach seems appropriate because this gives the child the space and time to design and construct their own learning in their own way and at their own pace. Moreover it may well be appropriate that at times the teacher-driven approach is salutary for pupils and students. The complaint here is that if either of these approaches become the dominant mode of learning then the liberties of those who are learning may become imperilled. In particular, those learning are no longer treated as liberty-bearing agents. I therefore now wish to explore a different kind of learning experience that is neither teacher nor child nor learner-driven, and which does not take the role of a pedagogy performed on an agent, whether externally by an instructor or internally through her own means.

Dewey's concept of experience

In order to illuminate the kind of experience I have in mind, I will first of all turn to John Dewey's concept of aesthetic experience. He did not write on this systematically until the early 1930s when he was in his seventies. His working assumption is that aesthetic experiences are not special events that only happen to certain highly sensitive individuals in particular circumstances, but are much more widespread. This assumption is made good by the analysis of experience that he provides in *Art as Experience*. He is concerned, initially, in this important book, to distinguish those experiences with little connection with each other and which prompt opposing emotions and reflections from what he calls '*an* experience'. Here, he says, 'the material experienced runs its course to fulfilment' (Dewey, 1934: 35) and only then is it identified and integrated within the general stream of experience. He puts this point more cogently as follows: 'Such an experience is a whole and carries with it its own individualising quality and self-sufficiency. It is *an* experience' (35). Dewey's concern, then, is to try and say *how* we have an aesthetic experience by pointing out that although there may be a succession of events or experiences nevertheless there is a unity while at the same time the self-identity of each part is maintained. There is a 'flow', the sense of which he tries to capture through the word 'phases' and he contrasts this with Locke and Hume's analysis of experience in terms of impressions and ideas that are discrete and separate. The idea of 'phases' is that an experience may be composed of emotions, thoughts and activities that have a connection and continuity (though that connection may itself need to be explored and unfolded). This flow culminates in a consummation of a movement – a conclusion – which implies that the full meaning of an experience can only be grasped if the experience has also been undergone in all its phases. Dewey goes on to say that a quality pervades the experience which he characterises in terms of a property: 'we may find that one property rather than another was sufficiently dominant so that it characterises the experience as a whole' (37).

We can, I think, readily recognise this description as one that approximates to experiencing a work of art. Thus, we might say that *Guernica* conveys a certain quality of experience, which is quite different from, say, Monet's different versions of *Water Lilies*, painted when he lived at Giverny. However, Dewey wishes to extend this thought to claiming that, for example, thinking has a certain aesthetic quality when it takes the form of a movement of an idea, a 'movement of anticipation and cumulation, one that finally comes to completion . . . and has a satisfying emotional quality because it possesses internal integration and fulfilment reached through ordered and organised movement' (38). With 'an' experience it is the whole process that is experienced and not just the outcome. Thus moral actions need not be experienced solely on the plane of duty but may also have an aesthetic character when they have a unity reaching a conclusion. Dewey maintains that the enemies of the aesthetic are neither the practical nor the intellectual, but the 'humdrum . . . and submission to convention . . . both coerced submission and slackness of loose ends are deviations in opposite directions from the unity of an experience' (40). He is suggesting, then, that the aesthetic is an *integral* experience and that this type of experience is by no means confined to the conventionally aesthetic.

Dewey goes on to identify further elements that characterise this integral experience. First, he states that struggle and conflict may be enjoyed as a feature of developing an experience: it is not necessary for the experience to be passive, as when one surveys works of art in a museum. He develops this idea further by suggesting that for any integral experience there is an element of 'undergoing', of suffering even: this ensues because an experience involves taking in something and may be 'more than placing something on the top of consciousness over what was previously known. It involves reconstruction which may be painful' (41). An integral experience therefore requires an engagement with materials, ideas or processes and cannot be unduly hurried because there is a time appropriate to its unfolding. It cannot be cut up or divided into small parts or 'chunks' without compromising its unity. It cannot be appropriated, directed or managed without the risk of directly undermining the very quality that constitutes the experience's particular value. Whether this appropriation be by somebody else (e.g. a teacher) or myself (in the capacity of someone keen to manage their own learning) something of the experience may be lost because it has not been properly 'undergone'. There is a balance to be struck between doing and undergoing, a balance too often neglected in favour of doing:

> Zeal for doing, lust for action, leaves many a person, especially in this hurried and impatient human environment in which we live, with experience of an almost incredible paucity, all on the surface. No one experience has a chance to complete itself because something else is entered upon so speedily. What is called experience becomes so dispersed and miscellaneous as hardly to deserve the name. Resistance is treated as an obstruction to be beaten down, not as an invitation to reflection. An individual comes to seek, unconsciously even more than by deliberate choice, situations in which he can do the most things in the shortest time.
>
> (Dewey, 1934: 45)

We are only too familiar with this lament. Perhaps what Dewey could have never appreciated back in 1934 is the way that experiences today may also contain a complete absence of 'doing' to the point where experience is one of sheer passivity, hours on end, evening after evening. Although maybe if we have spent much of the day lusting for action, this is only to be expected.

Hans-Georg Gadamer's thoughts on the nature of experience (*Erlebnis*) are uncannily similar to those of Dewey, to the point where almost the same expressions are being used to convey meaning. Gadamer (1989) commences his analysis with an historical overview of the meaning of *Erlebnis*, concluding that in Enlightenment Germany the word conveyed three senses at once: immediacy of experience, the idea that an experience makes a particular impression that gives lasting importance and that it does this through achieving a permanence that emerges out of the transiency of experience. Out of this romantic critique of rationalism emerged, according to Gadamer, a concept of experience that Dilthey employed in order to capture 'the special nature of the given in the human sciences' (65). But these units of experience are now philosophically transformed so that they become units of *meaning*, which are intentional:

> If something is called or considered an Erlebnis, that means it is rounded into the unity of a significant whole . . . an experience is no longer just something that flows past quickly in the stream of conscious life; it is meant as a unity and thus attains a new mode of being *one*.
>
> (66)

And a little later, Gadamer alludes to the idea of an experience as an adventure (in contrast with episodes that are a 'succession of details which have no inner coherence and for that reason have no permanent significance' (69), which must be 'undergone like a test or a trial from which one emerges more enriched, more mature'. Gadamer goes on to suggest that such an experience is taken out of the continuity of life and related to the 'whole of one's life'. For on the one hand there is the 'experiencing' in its immediacy and vitality but there is also the experience once it has been integrated into one's life so that its significance may go beyond the meaning it had while it was in the process of being undergone.

Thus Gadamer adds something to Dewey's account. First of all, he stresses that an experience is fused with the experience of life itself and so the meaning of a single experience is never completely exhausted through conceptual determination: the meaning of an experience may always be revised at some point. Gadamer suggests that some experiences are not only not easily forgotten, but also that they may take some time to assimilate, with the implication that this assimilation may never be complete even if one thinks it is. Second, having an experience – once we think of it as a kind of adventure – can be a risky business: it takes us out into the uncertain. But these observations are I think implicit in Dewey's account: the very fact that we *undergo* an experience suggests that it is something that is never completely under our control.

The nature of an educational experience

I now wish to further explore the nature of the kind of educational experience that Dewey's reflections on aesthetic experience allow us to identify. There are many different types of educational experience, but rather than enumerate some kind of discipline-based taxonomy I will look to see what the three philosophers – Wittgenstein, Grice and Oakeshott – suggest.

As Andrea English has recently pointed out, a central feature of learning is, or ought to be, its transformative quality (English, 2009). But how does this work? One way of approaching this problem is through Wittgenstein's discussion of 'seeing-as' in *Philosphical Investigations*. He supposes that: 'I may contemplate a face, and then suddenly notice its likeness to another. I *see* that it has not changed; and yet I see it differently. I call this experience "noticing an aspect"' (Wittgenstein, 1958: 212).

A little later he distinguishes 'continuous seeing' from the 'dawning' of an aspect (213). Wittgenstein's point is that we are not given raw material that we then somehow interpret and derive a meaning: rather that the perceptual grasp is also interpretative too – hence the aptness of the example of the duck-rabbit where what is seen does not change. It is also clear from his analysis that the duck-rabbit is for him a fairly primitive example for an aspect may dawn where states of affairs are more complex: 'what I perceive in the dawning of an aspect is not a property of the object, but an internal relation between it and other objects' (212).

I want to suggest that one of the ways in which learning transforms is just this: the dawning of an aspect. I have in mind times when pondering over an inchoate jumble of information starts to make sense as an 'aspect'; or perhaps the same information was seen in terms of a, b and c but is now seen in terms of x, y and z. It might be objected that aspect dawning is a part of learning, but only a small part; in particular what Wittgenstein describes are situations where a person is simply looking and pondering. Yet when a teacher does step out of a teacher-driven pedagogy and lets learning happen maybe aspect dawning is exactly what needs to take place. But for aspects to dawn there are three preconditions: first, there needs to be enough time, with breaks for chatting if needs be. Second, the pace mustn't be forced at the same tempo; intensive activity needs to be followed by slow reflection. And third, the subject under consideration must be self-contained – a poem, a problem, a short text – so that in the time available it becomes possible for the learning to make sense. Aspects don't dawn by trying too hard or by trying to do too much.

Interestingly, Wittgenstein is aware that aspect dawning may require 'someone capable of making certain applications . . . quite freely. The substratum of this experience is the mastery of a technique' (208) and goes on to surmise that here we have a 'different though related concept' to that of visual aspect dawning. And here, I want to suggest that skills are brought to fruition precisely at the point where they enable a new aspect to dawn. For example, students learning to think philosophically may start to see how concepts are linked: their tutor may *tell* them many times over how rationality and freedom are linked in Kant but it may take the explorations of personal or situated case studies for students to realise this.

For the second type of experience I turn to an argument by Paul Grice, sometimes called the 'communication-intention' theory of meaning. However, my interest is more in the concept of recognition:

> *A* must intend to induce by *x* a belief in an audience, and he must also intend his utterance to be recognised as so intended. But these intentions

are not independent; the recognition is intended by A to play its part in inducing the belief, and if it does not do so something will have gone wrong with the fulfilment of A's intentions.

(Grice, 1957: 383–384)

Something like Grice's theory of communication-intention is needed to underpin what can happen between tutor and student in terms of a dialectic of recognition. What is particularly important is that the recognition takes the form of an understanding: it is not the mere perlocutionary effect of a piece of discourse instrumentally designed and fashioned to achieve certain outcomes. Still less is it a piece of behaviour that works in the stimulus-response mode which would not be action at all.

In what might be called normal teaching, the teacher may give instructions or give explanations in which the meaning of terms used is not an issue: the teacher is not attempting to induce any new or different beliefs from what she may standardly expect in a given situation. But there may be times of 'trans-formative' teaching in which the teacher is trying to induce a belief precisely by intending this to be recognised by the child or student. An example is where the teacher is trying to elicit different modes of behaviour on the part of the child in terms of interaction with other children. Or a university lecturer has reached a decisive point in an argument in which an example is used to help induce new beliefs. What is happening in both cases is that an experience is being created through the dialectic of recognition, which depends not only on the teacher's intentions being recognised but also by the way in which the teacher *intends* this recognition to take place. And this discourse may be accompanied by a range of non-visual signs, all of which have an illocutionary effect. Grice's theory of meaning, then, helps us to identify a non-strategic method of teaching, which we could refer to as the 'communication-intention' style of teaching. And through style and context an experience is created, which has all the more power for being shared by teacher and child alike.

My third example of educational experience is taken from Michael Oakeshott when he discusses human agency in his book *On Human Conduct*. One mode of agency he terms 'self-disclosure' and it arises in the pursuit of aims, purposes and outcomes. Oakeshott describes it as follows:

Self-disclosure is in transactions with others and it is a hazardous adventure; it is immersed in contingency, it is interminable, and it is liable to frustration, disappointment and defeat . . . an agent's choice is a response to an understood contingent situation and is therefore infected with contingency, and becoming a performance it falls into the hands of other optative agents who may defeat it and will certainly compromise it. And even if what survives bears some relation to the meaning of the act, it may disappoint and it will certainly reveal itself as but another situation to be diagnosed and responded to.

(Oakeshott, 1975: 73)

My thought here is thinking of the classroom or seminar room as a scene of self-disclosure in terms of the personal journeys and the risks taken in coming to grips with complex learning. Everyone has what we might call a 'learning journey' and disclosing something of one's own journey as a teacher may help children and students understand better the process of learning and the simple, yet re-assuring fact that in all likelihood the teacher struggled to understand and master difficult concepts, methods and skills. For every straightforward learning journey (possibly Russell might be an example here) there will be another full of twists and difficulty (Wittgenstein, Churchill). The use of learning journals can be used to document and share journeys. They are not for everyone, of course: but a teacher needs a diverse set of tools in her knapsack in order to encourage learning and engagement. There will be many who respond very well to reading about and documenting their own and others' learning journeys.

As I have mentioned, there can be no taxonomy of educational experience and the examples of aspect dawning, recognition and self-disclosure are far from exhaustive. An educational experience often occurs in company with others but this is by no means necessary. Moreover, teachers may not even always be aware that any experience of educational significance has happened at all, at least at the time. It may have arisen through the normal interaction of the seminar or classroom without having been planned.

Conclusion

All three examples are ways of engaging in subject matter that is neither teacher-driven nor learner-driven. Rather, such engagement is *content-led* because both child and teacher – student and tutor – are following where the content of the subject matter, be it an interpretation of a poem or the details of a physics problem, is leading them. But what, it may be asked, has this to do with liberty? Perhaps it is easy to see that the teacher-driven approach – or, at any rate, too much of it – undermines the child's sense of their own liberty. Indeed, they become to feel that they are not liberty-bearing agents at all if nothing in their learning suggests that this could be the case, if everything that is learnt has been first of all vetted and supplied by the teacher. But the idea of the learner-driven approach may seem to many much more consistent with the ideals of liberty. Is not the learner in direct control of her learning? Is she not able to dictate the pace of learning? And if the learning is attuned to her needs, does not this place the learner (not the teacher) at the centre of education? Surely, it will be urged, the learner-centred approach is that which is most consistent with liberty.

The problem, I suggest, with the learner-centred approach is that it confuses self-mastery with liberty. It assumes that liberty requires full control over one's life. But the ideal of self-mastery, as emphasised in Chapter 2, is different from that of liberty. The belief that it is desirable to control as much of my life as is possible, including my learning and education, is understandable, especially if this is contrasted with a putative state in which my whole life is dictated by another. But if this then becomes the pursuit of self-management in which I attempt to plan, monitor and evaluate the course of my life then this aim, whether esteemed or not, has nothing to do with liberty. For if liberty is to be taken seriously then I should be free *not* to embrace self-management as a way of life. I may prefer to keep my planning to a minimum and to keep my life open to the unexpected and take the consequences. No doubt such a way of life to those wedded to the ideal of self-management is grossly irresponsible. But the attempt to cajole persons, through the organisation of the learning process, to adopt self-management as a form of learning – i.e. to embrace the ideology of auto-pedagogy – has nothing to commend it from the standpoint of liberty. It is precisely an updated example of what Mill complained of in *On Liberty* – a piece of interference based solely on the grounds that it redounds to the putative good of the individual.

I therefore suggest that the process of learning be best conceived as an engagement with content so that the experience of learning is primarily associated with the experience of such an engagement in the way that Dewey describes. But in order for this to happen, learners need to be regarded as the bearers of liberty because in this way they will be directed by the logic and structure of the content rather than the management of their learning. The chief way that this management takes place is through assessment and through self-assessment. Now, the view propounded here may seem nonsensical to all of those who assume that formal learning cannot really happen at all unless assessment is built into the process of learning.[4] Whereas what is being suggested is that assessment should be *separate* from the process of learning. Of course, as part of the learning experience we would expect essays, discussions and artefacts to be produced and we would also expect the teacher to comment on these and to discuss them with her children and students. We would expect those learners to be told how much they were successfully engaging with the content, as we would also expect them to comment on whether they are benefitting from their learning and what they themselves would like to explore. A teacher will employ a variety of informal methods of assessment, varying from the complex to the simple, and integrate these so that they become a seamless part of learning itself. But the need for formal summative assessment fulfills a role that is quite separate from the process of teaching and learning itself. That role is of a social character and serves the vital purpose of *validation*. The piece of paper that a person earns following successful assessment tells an employer or any other member of the public what the owner of it understands and what she is capable of doing. The role of formal assessment (which may take many forms including written examination, observation and demonstration) is therefore to be confined to validating knowledge and skills acquired. The confusion of formal assessment with learning not only undermines and poisons the experience of learning itself: it also systematically undermines the liberty of those engaged in learning.

Notes

1 For example, Paul Willis (1977) shows how 'having a laugh' at the teacher's expense, experienced by teenagers at a working-class urban school helps to promote a certain independence and solidarity, quite independent of any curriculum aims.
2 Winston Churchill's encounter with education is a case in point. Here he is in reflecting on his early life, in his 50s – 10 years before becoming Prime Minister:

> It was at the 'Little Lodge' I was first menaced with Education. The approach of a sinister figure described as 'the Governess' was announced. Her arrival was fixed for a certain day. In order to prepare for this day, Mrs Everest (his nanny) produced a book called *Reading Without Tears*. It certainly did not justify its title in my case. I was made aware that before the Governess arrived I must be able to read without tears. We toiled each day. My nurse pointed with a pen at the different letters. I thought it all very tiresome. Our preparations were by no means completed when the fateful hour struck and the Governess was due to arrive. I did what so many oppressed peoples have done in similar circumstances: I took to the woods.
>
> (Churchill, 1930: 11)

Later on, Churchill summarises his Harrow experience thus:

> But this interlude of school makes a sombre grey patch upon the chart of my journey. It was an unending spell of worries that did not then seem petty, and of toil uncheered by fruition; a time of discomfort, restriction and purposeless monotony.
>
> (46)

3 See Lyotard (1984: 51) for an account of the conception of knowledge as a transient phenomenon.
4 The following assumption, in a paper surveying assessment methods in Higher Education is typical: 'If you want to change student learning then change the methods of assessment' (Brown *et al.*, 1997: 9). By contrast, I wish to suggest the priority of the quality of the learning *experience*.

Chapter 7

Liberty and the curriculum

In this chapter we will look more closely at the relation between human powers and education in terms of implications for the curriculum. In particular, we will further develop the thesis that the curriculum – the school curriculum – must be knowledge-based. However, knowledge must not be interpreted propositionally solely along the lines of 'knowing-that'. The curriculum inhabits the space of reasons and is therefore orientated towards understanding and judgements. Furthermore, we must also recognise that the process of understanding within the space of reasons also involves what has come to be called, following the distinction made between the two forms of knowing by Gilbert Ryle, 'knowing-how' (Ryle, 1949: chapter 2). Knowing-how, as we shall see, is one of the key elements of those human powers that are needed to preserve liberty.

The metaphor of the Cave

The account of the Cave in Plato's *Republic* provides us with a powerful metaphor of the inadequacies and poverty of lives that are shaped by everyday experience and lacking systematic knowledge. To be more accurate, the metaphor provides a particular way in which that experience can be conceived, which takes the form of epistemic dependence. Not all everyday experience takes this form, however.

The broad features of Plato's account are well known, but one or two details are worth noticing as well. Plato supposes that the cave dwellers are so constrained that all they see are flickers on a wall opposite, caused by the light of a fire behind them throwing shadows through a curtain. Behind the curtain is a road on which there are comings and goings of people which cannot be directly seen. All the cave dwellers can do is observe the flickers and infer from them what are the point and purpose of the people, animals and other implements. To help them in this task the cave dwellers can hear noises from the road behind which they can associate with the shady figures in front of them. Plato speculates that they may get quite good at recognising these shadows and we can even suppose that they may award each other prizes for spotting the most interesting combinations of sound and image, not to mention prizes for being able to make correct predictions (Plato, 1987: 258). He further speculates that if someone had managed to escape from the cave and spent time above ground (so that they experienced sunlight and could see things correctly) on their return they would be somewhat less interested in the prizes that the cave dwellers so eagerly valued. What is more, the returnee may not be very good at discriminating the flickers for he may have let all his old skills go rusty. He may well make a complete fool of himself and the cave dwellers 'would say that his visit to the upper world had ruined his sight' (259). With his new knowledge the returnee could certainly explain the causes of what the cave dwellers took to be reality but he would no longer be able to play an interpretative part in their world.

The Cave is a powerful metaphor because it is utterly uncompromising. What the returnee knows is now entirely incommensurate with what he used to know, to the extent that what he used to know is now quite valueless. The incommensurability between the cave dwellers and those who have escaped has nothing to do with social position or social recognition. The incommensurability is not positional but epistemic. The uncompromising nature of the metaphor is driven home when one sees that the cave dwellers cannot even use the flickers on the wall as a basis for knowing because such knowing is based on error given that they can only see the flickers and not their source. The fact that they believe otherwise merely serves to emphasise the utterly hopeless position they are in. The only way to shift their perspective is to give them entirely different experiences on which to build an interpretative and explanatory structure.

The cave dwellers are in a position of what might be called *epistemic dependency*. We do not, of course, know why they are in the cave in the first place and the power of the metaphor could be lost once questions like that are pressed. All we need to note is that this dependency is structural and intended by no-one. This dependency arises in a twofold way. First, they do not know and have no way of knowing anything about the source of the sights and sounds they experience. All the inferences they might make could be wrong and if they are not that would only be by chance. Second, they are unaware of the sunlit world and are unable to conceive of such a world. (Perhaps they accuse those few who come back down to the cave of being 'elitists'.) Interestingly too, no-one benefits by this dependency. The only persons who might be said to 'benefit' are the cave dwellers themselves because, it may be supposed, their constraints are not particularly irksome, especially when they have the distractions of the flickers on the wall to look at. Their life could be considered as one which is comfortable and undemanding. After all, if one knows nothing else why would one ever complain? We might even speculate (although Plato does not go this far) that an escapee, while glad he has escaped and fully cognisant of the fact that there is no going back, might nevertheless occasionally feel pangs of regret at leaving behind a trouble-free existence even if he were to concede, if pressed, that he had no desire at all to go back to that kind of life.

The metaphor provides a frightening picture of what life could be like without the space of reasons and without a developed second nature. It would be a life in which second nature would be cramped, stunted and bent and in which the space of reasons would be bounded and inhibited by that dark cavern. If the McDowellian perspective can be seen as providing a setting in which there is what might be called epistemic freedom, the scene in The Cave, by contrast, is a disturbing dystopia.

We can see straightaway how the metaphor can work for education: the journey from the Cave to the sunlit world is a journey of enlightenment, from ignorance to knowledge. One of the key points is that in the process of that journey many things have to be *unlearnt*. The metaphor has relevance for education not because children and students are in the exact position of the cave dwellers but because some contemporary experiences may mirror the Cave in a way that might be found uncomfortable if dwelt upon for too long (for example, Plato's remarks about prizes they award each other and how the perceived prestige of such prizes no longer has any value for the returnee: the parallel with today would be celebrity culture). An important aim of education, then, is to liberate children from the perils of epistemic dependency or to ensure as far as possible that children can avoid this when they are adults. This requires some purposeful endeavour: mere socialisation is not enough, and neither is learning of an informal kind: after all, the dwellers in the Cave are thoroughly socialised and they learn (or think they learn) all sorts of interesting facts and tips from each other. It would therefore be misguided for an educator to suppose that she could take just any of the everyday experiences of the child as a starting point in the process of learning. Judgement has to be exercised as to which experiences are of value; not to do so would be to risk trying to build learning on the basis of the experience of the flickers in the Cave. Experiential learning may well provide a good starting point for building up understanding, but not every experience that a child brings with them into school may be of value. Some of the lessons learnt outside school may have to be unlearnt (for example, placing too much value on what celebrities have to say for themselves).

The kind of assumptions behind the Cave metaphor have been investigated by a range of educational theorists in recent times. For example, Elizabeth Rata has spoken of working-class children being incarcerated in a 'never ending present' as a result of the failure to equip them with the intellectual tools needed to transcend epistemic dependency. For Rata, this failure takes a particular form of a celebration of localised, social knowledge often undertaken as a way of protecting local cultures and ways of life (Rata, 2012: 106). She believes the danger is that children and students are not exposed to deeper structures of meaning associated with subject disciplinary understanding (113). It is not that local perspectives need to be given up (and here, the analogy with the Cave metaphor gives out) but rather they need to be supplemented by a cognitive perspective that is both explanatory (by drawing on causes the nature of which are unavailable to the local gaze) and interpretative (by drawing on perspectives that are outside the immediacy of the local). The point about introducing a knowledge perspective in this way is to acknowledge, as Suellen Shay has suggested, that 'knowledge matters' and that '. . . a knowledge claim cannot simply be reduced to who is making that claim' (Shay, 2012: 7). The notion that we are, each of us, locked into a subjective world, exemplifies epistemic dependency because we are unable to make a judgement that can be contested in such a way that I might reasonably be expected to modify my claim. For if there is no standard that I am prepared to acknowledge other than one set by myself then I do indeed end up 'spinning in a void', as McDowell terms it (see Chapter 4). My dependency ends up self-referring because there is nothing that I can recognise that will enable me to break out of that circle of dependency. It makes no difference if this circle is inhabited by one individual or a group.

From a standpoint of liberty, it is important that knowledge claims and assertions are detachable from the social status of the claimer. Hence, an evaluation of a claim is not dependent on the status of the claimer either. At the same time, an agent is ascribed the right to make such claims, without reference to peer groups (this ascription may well be normatively based rather than codified as such). The assumption by a claimer that claims may only be recognised if they are approved of is one of the most insidious ways in which dependency insinuates itself since the claimer may feel herself obliged to trim and fawn in order to secure approval; only then, she may feel, will her voice be listened to. But, by the same token, the claimer is responsible and account-able for the claim – and by 'responsible' I mean someone who accepts that making claims can have consequences and she is prepared to acknowledge that. The danger of relativism (for example, where knowledge is viewed as having constructivist foundations) is that knowledge claims are associated and judged in accordance with who is making them. This is a form of epistemic dependency – a first step towards political and social dependency. Thus one of the most effective ways of deploying power is to frame the perceptions of a claim in such a way that a claim is seen as partisan or self-serving – 'they would say that, wouldn't they'. It is difficult for individuals, in isolation, to counter these kinds of claims.

Ultimately, the only way of countering epistemic dependency is through establishing a curriculum in which claims to knowledge are grounded in criteria and procedures that derive from within subject disciplines and are immanent in respect of them, subject to scrutiny within the space of reasons. Through such a curriculum pupils and students acquire the expectation that their claims will be judged and evaluated in accordance with publicly defined criteria. This may seem a paradox: surely, it might be thought, constructivist epistemologies bestow the most freedom on agents since they are empowered through the construction of their own meanings. But the construction of meaning (supposing that this is epistemically possible in the first place)[1] only has value if that meaning can be evaluated and judged: and if only my evaluations are acceptable I will have no criteria of meaninglessness.[2]

In emphasising the role of knowledge within the space of reasons and its role *vis-à-vis* liberty it might be thought that I am advocating a sharp distinction between knowledge and experience, regarding the latter as untrustworthy and only the former as supplying the basis for education. This, for example, is the kind of view that seems to be suggested in his more recent works by Michael Young (2008, 2010). He gives a most interesting sociological account, drawing on Durkheim's distinction between the sacred and the profane, of the way in which all societies have had a symbolic order (the sacred) that is distinguished from the order of the practical (the profane) and suggests that modern societies are similarly characterised between knowledge and science on the one hand and the practical, every day experience on the other (Young, 2010: 14–15). There are two issues here. The first is whether the distinction applies to modern societies, which may be doubted if one takes the view that the domain of knowledge has long invaded the profane world, for good or ill (the example of information technologies is salient here). This, however, is a huge issue that cannot be pursued here. The second issue, however, is of concern. For the implication could be, from reading Young, that the realm of every day experience is a realm in which the criteria for the application of terms is hazy and that meanings are locked into the domain of the subjective. But this does not seem quite right, once we understand that the domain of the space of reasons reaches right down into the everyday. The giving and justification of reasons is as much a part of the home as it is of the classroom. To use McDowell's terminology, 'spinning in a void' is something that does not make sense whatever the circumstances.

Thus the metaphor of the Cave must be used with care because what it characterises is a certain way of viewing our everyday experiences and localised knowledge. It says that it is worthless, not to put too fine a point on it. But the way I am using the metaphor is as a warning against epistemic dependency, not as a warning against the worthlessness of ordinary experiences. There is no reason why the latter should necessarily be characterised by epistemic dependency. For, it may be urged, there is a practical knowledge (and a practical intelligence too), which is not only indispensible but a part of living. Thus, I do not need specialist knowledge to know how to be a friend, a lover, a parent or a sibling. When we enact ourselves as friends or parents, etc. we give reasons, offer justifications and do this well or badly. The domain of the everyday is no less part of the space of reasons than subject disciplines. The metaphor of the Cave is misapplied if it is thought to characterise the whole of the everyday. The concomitant conclusion has to be that there is no particular necessity to exclude ordinary experience from the domain of education, rather that one needs to be selective.

One should not underestimate the power of epistemic dependency. For in a world in which knowledge is rationed to a minority – or, what amounts to the same thing, where it is rationed for all – the process of practical knowledge and know-how will suffer as well. People need to learn how to give reasons and justify viewpoints in respect of the non-personal, that is in contexts where I must learn to bracket off, so to speak, my own particular concerns and interests. The adoption of the impersonal standpoint can be what, for many young people, is the most difficult feature of 'education' – it seems unedifying just because it does *not* engage a person at the level of the personal. The apparent remoteness of chemistry or much of history is precisely what seems most forbidding and while, as a pedagogic device, teachers may well attempt to engage interest by relating the subject matter to perceived personal concerns of young learners, as an overall strategy such devices are doomed to fail. What needs to be learnt is a vocabulary and symbols that have their own efficacy in the context of the grammar of a discipline, and to do this the realm of the personal must be discounted. Moreover, if the world of the practical itself is not to be consigned to motives driven by whim and caprice, the habits of assuming an impersonal stance must be adopted in any case. Thus, the requirement of knowledge is not just needed because it provides powerful explanatory tools unavailable at the level of the practical; the very mode of enacting practical intelligence can only be learnt through a sustained exposure to the logic of impersonal reasons. It is one of the illusions of those living in a state of epistemic dependency that self-effacement of the ego looks like weakness and that whim and caprice are superior to reason. That is *precisely* how the culture of masterhood operates, whether it be the slave-owner of old in southern USA, the modern gangster leader in urban neighbourhoods or indeed the boss of a large modern corporation used to getting his (and it is normally his) way.

As a matter of fact, there is no need to go as far back as Plato to find examples of epistemic dependency. We need only go as far back as what came to be known as the 'tripartite system' of education established by the 1944 Education Act in England. As is well known, the 11+ exam separated children into grammar schools, technical schools and secondary modern schools. The thinking behind this selection process was motivated by the belief that there were three different kinds of mentalities characterised in the Norwood Report (1943) as follows:

1   Pupils who are interested in learning for its own sake; who can grasp an argument and follow a line of reasoning.
2   Pupils whose interests lie in the applied arts and sciences.
3   Pupils whose interests are awakened by being touched by practical affairs.

(Goodson, 2005: 75)

In practice, the provision of those children in the second category (namely technical schools) was undeveloped and the majority of children (80–90 per cent) received a non-academic education in the secondary moderns. Many of these schools (by no means all) were characterised by a culture of low expectations and low achievement. An interesting interpretation of the 1944 policy was offered by G.H. Bantock as follows:

> Social Justice demands that every child shall, as a socio-cultural personality, have a right to that enlargement of his nature which a variety of educational provision can afford. The implication . . . is that there are numerous children who . . . have already been formed by historical socio-cultural forces which makes the segment of 'high' culture put before them pretty meaningless. And this implies seeing the secondary modern schools (and the lower forms of comprehensive schools) not as places for the failures, nor schools in which a certain number of children are 'wrongly placed', but as schools which offer cultural opportunities for satisfaction within what is rapidly emerging as the characteristic cultural forms of twentieth century man – the radio, cinema, TV and so on. Indeed, in so far as class divisions lead to cultural heterogeneity, some degree of class division may be said to enrich the State.
>
> (Bantock, 1965: 149–150)

Here, epistemic dependency is justified in pluralistic terms – it is the democratic right of the lower orders *not* to have high culture inflicted on them – rather it is their right to enjoy popular culture, and schooling provision should be arranged accordingly. In practice, the 1944 settlement led to a kind of social apartheid in which the lower orders were given an education fit for them. Only the 11+ intelligence test selected those who could leave the Cave: failure condemned one to a life of flickers on the wall.

Aims of the curriculum?

In Chapter 1 it was argued that republican liberty does not lend itself to eudaimonic interpretations. In a free state there is no need for those in authority to organise lives in such a way to promote what is termed the 'good life'. Exactly the same considerations apply to any school-based curriculum. The aim of the curriculum is to equip children and students with those human powers that they need to defend their liberty. In addition to this, it is important for children to learn that they are each of them responsible for their actions and while they are free to lead any life they choose they must also take the consequences (of, for example, a life of indolence). Of course, schools have a duty of care to children and this should extend beyond physical safety to include emotional care as well. But much of this kind of care arises from the nature of a school, as a community of persons living together and sharing their lives. Thus one would expect not only basic moral rules to be observed but also the development of appropriate dispositions to support those rules. For example, a school that neglected to develop in its pupils a spirit of sympathy and compassion would be an unhappy place with miserable and aggressive children.

However, the cultivation and encouragement of dispositions that are needed if children are to live together and share the same environment and take part in joint activities should not take the form of a programme of personal development driven and structured by a set of over-arching aims and purposes.

The notion that one should educate the 'whole person' and that one should proceed from an 'holistic' standpoint is one that in the educational environment has been very seductive. Judged from the standpoint of liberty, such approaches are well meaning but do not accord with the principles of liberty. The aims of education should be to provide the child with those human powers that they need; it should avoid trying to shape and structure the life of the child. The danger of such an approach is that it may end up fostering a culture of dependency – an environment in which needs are catered for but in which liberty may be neglected.

A recent example of this approach can be found in a monograph written by Michael Reiss and John White entitled *An Aims-Based Curriculum*. The authors declare that: 'A central aim of the school should be to prepare students for a life of autonomous, whole-hearted and successful engagement in worthwhile relationships, activities and experiences' (2013: 7). Reiss and White are concerned that a preoccupation with school subjects leads to a curriculum in which '*their* requirements get filled out' whereas they advocate a curriculum centred around the 'needs and wants of students' (2). The idea is that once these are correctly identified then school subjects will only play a part in the overall education of the child since the curriculum will also pay attention to broader social and emotional needs. They therefore envisage a curriculum that is designed to establish an environment that equips each child 'to lead a life that is personally flourishing' (1).

There are a number of features of this view that are troubling, from the standpoint of liberty. First of all, there is the emphasis on the need for 'wholehearted engagement' in 'valuable' activities, and the phrase 'wholehearted' is repeated throughout the book (e.g. pages 7, 17, 22 and 24). One wonders what the consequences for a child might be if she failed to display the requisite enthusiasm and commitment to activities that were deemed to fulfil her 'needs and wants'. One is immediately driven to a wholehearted desire to champion the right of the child to engage in a disinterested manner and the right to evince dispositions that do not always display enthusiastic engagement. This worry leads to a deeper one: it simply is not clear how 'needs and wants' are arrived at. The holistic approach is assumed without argument and it becomes clear early on that the option for interpreting 'needs' in terms of subject disciplines is never seriously considered. One of the great advantages of putting subject disciplines at the core of the curriculum is that curriculum aims arise out of those disciplines (their specific priorities, skills and content) without the need to decide on behalf of others what is supposed to constitute a flourishing life. The point behind the organisation of a curriculum along disciplinary lines is that it is liberty-friendly. What is asked of children and students is to fulfil those disciplinary requirements without their having to commit to any further agenda centred on the good life. A subject-based curriculum respects children's autonomy much more than a curriculum that is integrated through the promotion of holistic-based ends. The former leaves a child free to follow interests and pursuits with others *including* the option of doing nothing.[3]

One of the great advantages of taking subject disciplines as the core of the curriculum is that these disciplines are in fact a good way of framing 'needs and desires' of individual pupils. It enables them to find out what their preferences are, not merely at the level of choice but also in a way of testing commitments. These commitments attest to differing ways of engaging with the world – for example, a literary engagement at the level of the imaginary or a scientific engagement motivated by a deep interest in explanation of the detail of natural phenomena. The disciplines enable the expression of different levels and kinds of curiosity. They also – and this is decisive – enable the child to discover at an early age that he or she is not the centre of the world and that there is a world out there to be discovered. A curriculum that is built around personal flourishing is likely to lead to too great a pre-occupation with personal development and personal relationships. The purpose of education is not to re-enforce devotion to the personal – there are plenty of incentives for this outside of school. Rather, the purpose of education lies in the many pathways that lead away from a narcissistic preoccupation with the self and with personal relations. It helps pupils and students to attain a distance from the personal that enables them to cope with their lives with some degree of maturity. The subject disciplines are key to education because they open up pathways into the world.

It should, however, be noted that although the disciplines lie at the core of the curriculum it by no means follows that the *pedagogy* employed must be of an orthodox, standard transmissive mode. There are many ways of teaching physics or history that enable the learner to employ methods of enquiry and discovery: there are pedagogical approaches that permit and encourage children to express themselves and to work with others as comrades in arms. Nor should it be supposed that the curriculum should be divided into strict division of subject disciplines. For one thing, those experts and researchers engaged in the disciplines themselves are constantly exploring relations with other disciplines in order to seek out new perspectives. The disciplines are in a state of constant flux as new sub-disciplines emerge and others fall away. Interdisciplinarity in higher education assumes an increasing profile and yet sometimes critics of the academic curriculum assume as a matter of course that disciplines are framed in the form of self-contained silos. Thus it is not the case that disciplines are necessarily associated with 'specialist requirements' (Reiss and White, 2013: 14). Because they take a role as a window onto the world, if properly taught, disciplines open up perspectives rather than close them down.

A good example of someone who took disciplines as the basis for thinking about the curriculum was Lawrence Stenhouse. His principle ideas were ultimately based on an epistemological thesis that emphasised the provisionality of knowledge and research. He believed, however, that this thesis had implications for teaching in so far as a curriculum was itself an object of enquiry that is tested in the classroom and seminar by both teachers and students (or pupils). A curriculum was nothing more than a series of hypotheses that could be refined but never perfected. Consequently, Stenhouse stressed that education was a matter of process rather than achieving prescribed objectives: the aim of education was itself enshrined in the process of enquiry. Moreover – and this is crucial – he never believed that enquiry could only be confined to the most able. He held strongly to the view that adolescents of all abilities and backgrounds could be encouraged to think of their learning in terms of enquiry. Behind Stenhouse's educational theory was a firm and generous democratic conviction, which was thoroughly optimistic about what human beings could achieve. Moreover, this achievement was not the mere fulfilling of individual potential but the sharing and participating in a democratic culture.[4] One particular consequence with Stenhouse's approach (although by no means confined to him) was that knowledge was seen as plastic so that differing elements and content from subjects could be combined within a single topic of enquiry. The structure of knowledge is ordered through the disciplines. But it by no means follows that learning and using this knowledge should be through that same ordering: the skill of teaching lies precisely in being able to re-configure bundles of knowledge into differing modes of enquiry that appeal to the imagination and curiosity of the pupil.

I am arguing that an emphasis on a knowledge-based curriculum strengthens liberty for two reasons. First of all, the knowledge and understanding acquired develops the human powers needed to resist the depredations that are all too likely to occur without them. It is not enough to develop the confidence and social skills of the pupil: while these are not unimportant they need to be grounded in an engagement of the world that enables the pupil to play a part in the space of reasons in terms of making and defending judgements. Second, the *process* of acquiring learning is itself informed by a respect of liberty. This means, in particular, that there are boundaries around the child outside of which the school has less interest (developing friendships, enthusiasms outside the curriculum, social and romantic interests and so on). It is important that children realise and are made to realise that while the school has a duty of care which it takes seriously this duty still recognises boundaries outside of which the child must develop his and her own responsibilities. The problem with 'whole child' approaches to education is that such boundaries may not be recognised and, under the cover of a 'humane' approach, the child is patronised, nurtured and formed so that the child herself becomes ripe for a life not of liberty, but of dependency.

The relation between pedagogy and curriculum can have implications for liberty. Basil Bernstein distinguished between a collection code in which the classification boundaries between subjects was strong and integrated codes in which a more unified pedagogy weakened those boundaries. Interestingly,

Bernstein argued that strong classification increased the autonomy of the teacher but that an integrated code increased the power of the pupil. But one can see that this need not necessarily follow: a unified, integrated pedagogy that encompasses the whole school reduces autonomy for both teacher and pupil alike, independent of how strong the classification boundaries are. By contrast, strong classification may give the teacher more leeway in her own subject area: but whether this would have the effect of reducing pupil autonomy would be contingent on the teaching style. Indeed, strong classification may enlarge the scope of 'negotiation' between teacher and pupil while an integrated pedagogy may reduce the scope of that negotiation. The only integrated pedagogical approach that would not be seriously detrimental to pupil liberties would be in a school in which there was a strong pupil voice. On balance, I would say that if a school was interested in reducing the liberties of teacher and pupil then introducing a strong integrated code would be the best method. There may be independent good reasons for going down this path (for example, if there is a need to turn round a failing school) but once a culture of learning has been established and accepted then such a code can be relaxed and weakened.

Liberty and know-how

I have been arguing for the importance of knowledge acquisition as one of the key ingredients needed for the development of human powers in order to maintain resilience against possible threats of dependency. I have further argued that such knowledge should not be seen as lifeless and inert, as a series of propositions, but rather as a set of understandings that are not only deployed within the space of reasons but exemplify a reason-driven character. Knowledge acquisition is accompanied by argumentation and justification. But it is clear that one can extend such acquisition to that of know-how and ability – for example, the kinds of abilities linked to occupation. In the absence of land and estates to safeguard liberty the capacity for know-how becomes a supremely important human power if I am to mobilise personal resources in the face of possible threats. In a free state, everyone needs to be able to deploy know-how not only as a way of defending liberty but also as a way of extending the domains in which liberty can be exercised, in co-operation with similar liberty-bearing agents.

In this respect, Gilbert Ryle's *Concept of Mind* may be seen as striking a blow for liberty since in the second chapter he elaborated his well-known distinction between knowing-how and knowing-that. Ryle's targets, of course, were not the enemies of liberty. Rather the book set out to demolish the Cartesian 'myth' of the ghost in the machine – the mind conceived as a non-physical entity. In order to further this goal, Ryle showed that many forms of knowing could be described in terms of 'knowing-how' rather than the knowledge of propositional statements in terms of 'knowing-that'. For example, all those cognitive (as well as practical activities) that could be qualified adjectivally ('intelligently', 'cunningly', 'convincingly') could be seen as forms of knowing-how, since it was not possible for know-that to admit of degree. Furthermore, Ryle argued, knowing-how often preceded knowing-that – for example, I may learn how to solve quadratic equations long before I have any real understanding of the mathematics behind the procedure. As part of his attack on 'Cartesian' thinking Ryle sought also to demolish what he termed the 'intellectualist legend' which, he maintained, held that any form of knowing-how must be preceded by knowing-that. This demolition took the form of deploying the regress argument, which showed that for any piece of knowing-how I need to enact, if it is supposed that it must be preceded by a piece of contemplation then I will end up having to contemplate the contemplatory act of working out how to enact my know-how – and so on (Ryle, 1949: 31).

It could be argued, however, that the regress argument can be avoided by the simple expedient of enacting a declarative act of knowing, namely '*A* knows that *w* is the way to *V*'. The difficulty now is that though a regress is avoided a gap has emerged between the setting forth of *x*, *y*, *z* as elements of *w*, and the act of *V-ing* itself. Yet know-how does seem to imply, in normal circumstances, the ability to enact the know-how and not merely give an account of it (Winch, 2010: 28–29).[5]

In more recent years, Ryle's account has been both challenged and enhanced.[6] The chief challenge comes from the attempt to argue that if one takes any piece of know-how then it can be broken down into several individual pieces of know-that where each element of know-that answers to a specific proposition. In favour of this argument is the thought that if know-how is not to be thought of as some kind of magic box in which somehow knowledge is translated into performance then know-how must be capable of being analysed into a series of beliefs. The skills and dispositions required to turn these beliefs into a performance certainly need explanation, but that then takes on a psychological/behavioural character rather than an epistemological one. The difficulty with this approach is that it consigns know-how to something that seems to amount to a character trait, a habit or a disposition. On this reading, it would seem that know-how requires two stages: one, the acquisition of a set of propositions (and it may well be a very large number indeed) followed by appropriate behavioural and psychological training and motivation so that an agent is able to deliver. In other words, just at the point where we want the agent to be in full command of context, beliefs and skills the cognitive dimension is stripped away and replaced by 'training'. It is as if know-how is modelled on a clockwork toy, in which the beliefs form the mechanism and the training forms the winding up – once fully wound up, the primed agent springs into action and delivers. And on any credible account of know-how this does not ring true, if only because 'reflection-in-action' seems to be one of the central characteristics of the performance of know-how (Schön, 1983). Moreover, it is not clear that the complexity of know-how can be reducible in any credible way to a series of propositions that are objects of knowing-that. As Wiggins points out, in considering the 'know-how' involved by the head of a small family firm: 'There is no proposition, no conceivable form of words, that answers to and condenses his way of running the show' (2012: 120). Even supposing that his successor was given an instruction manual this would still have to be interpreted on each and every occasion it needed to be consulted.[7] The attempt to reduce knowing-how to a series of know-thats seems to risk over-simplification without shedding light on the processes that knowing how connotes.

Part of the problem lies in the characterisation of knowing-that. Typically this is spelt out in terms of propositions such as 'the city of Baku lies at 40 degree latitude north of the equator' or 'the England fast bowler Harold Larwood was born in Nottinghamshire' or 'the algorithm that performs the VAT calculation for this computerised billing system is called *VATCALC*'. It is often said, furthermore, that knowing-that (unlike knowing-how) does not admit of degree since I either know, or I do not know, the latitude of Baku and I cannot know that fact well or badly (see, e.g. Winch, 2010: 5). Yet one's *understanding* of a state of affairs may be said to be comprehensive, sketchy, accurate or impressive – whether this understanding be of the country of Azerbijan, the career of Harold Larwood or the computerised billing system that has just 'crashed'. The object of knowing-that is more realistically interpreted as a state of affairs that I can indeed know well or not so well, in outline or in detail, and my understanding may be said to be naive, workmanlike or superficial. The point is that it is not just know-how that can be construed in terms of a performance. A set of beliefs – including and especially beliefs of a propositional form – remain nothing more than inward beliefs unless they are explained, demonstrated, communicated, proclaimed or extolled. And all of these epithets involve some degree of know-how. Even the most academic, theoretical discipline requires explanation and the ability to explain complex propositions is one of the tests (both for others and myself) as to whether I have understood them in the first place. The division between know-that and know-how does not correspond to the division between the theoretical and the practical, and (to use a phrase of Stanley and Williamson) there is no set of beliefs that can escape the 'practical mode of presentation'.[8] Consequently one does not step out of the domain of knowing-that into a different domain of knowing-how. What one has, rather, is *one* domain of knowing, which is subject to a range of performances ranging from the (usually slightly easier) performance of explanation to the much more complex performance of creation, construction, evaluation and repair.

These considerations can be applied to a school curriculum, including one motivated by knowledge because children and students need to learn how to demonstrate understanding under a variety of 'practical modes of presentation' so that elements of 'knowing-how' can be an integral part of an academic curriculum. It is a fundamental mistake to suppose that knowing-how must be hived off to a strictly non-academic, vocational curriculum. Hence, it is that modes of assessment need to capture a wide range of performances, which include written and oral performance but also test and extend pupil powers of social interaction, creativity and speech.

Thus in learning trigonometry, I learn certain procedures that I can apply to problems (possibly drawn from surveying) so that I know how to use the sine and cosine. I can explain, at least in outline, how trigonometric functions are used in cartography or satellite navigation. The point here is that I do not learn these functions in isolation or separate from being able to demonstrate them and showing how they are applied. The ingestion of the propositions that are characterised by 'knowing-that' proceeds through exhibiting know how as part of that ingestion. The calculations that I know how to get right and that I am able to spot if they are incorrect are all part of the cognitive abilities that are required in *knowing*. A curricular approach that sees clearly that knowing-that and knowing-how operate in harness will be the stronger not only because it will facilitate the learning but also because the two modes of knowing operating together increase and enhance those human powers needed to enlarge and defend the realm of liberty.

Conclusion

Liberty-bearing agents need a considerable degree of know-how if they are to protect their liberties and, in particular, if they are to develop resilience against dependency. Their strength lies in developing varieties of knowledge and knowing – and the school curriculum must facilitate this. But the ends of liberty are not served if there is too great a stress on knowing-how because without a grasp of theoretical and methodological principles the range of know-how may become narrow and limited. There will be problems and issues that persons simply will not be able to address if they do not have a sufficient grounding in theoretical knowledge, which may include design principles as well as relevant maths and physics. The easiest way of coping with these demands is if children and young adults learn these topics as a natural part of growing up. Without a strong element of 'knowing-that' in their education children, when they become adults, may find themselves in a position of epistemic dependency, at the mercy not only of more knowledgeable individuals but also at the mercy of events, victims of *fortuna*.

Notes

1   It would be impossible if the logic of Wittgenstein's private language argument were applied to the construction of meaning since if the *criteria* of meaning are also constructed by me then I would never know if, in using meaning x at time t whether at time $t1$ I was using the same meaning or not. Yet constructivists persist in supposing that meaning can simply be 'created': 'meaning and understanding are created by individuals by means of their social interactions and their interaction with the environment' (Pritchard and Woollard, 2010: 7). The process of learning can,

of course, be encouraged through the creation of principles as *hypotheses* to be tested against or mediated through a body of knowledge, but that is quite different from creating meaning. The one domain in which meaning can indeed be created is that of the imaginary; but it is crucial that pupils are able to distinguish – and that their teachers can help them distinguish – between the domains of the imaginary and the domains of knowledge. That knowledge may inform the imaginary – and that techniques of the imaginary may be used in the domain of knowledge – does not alter the need to keep the two conceptually distinct and, in particular, to know when one is crossing from one domain to the other.

2   For a critique of constructivism see the discussion of the 'standpoint approach' in Moore (2004: 154–156).

3   It should be the right of any teenager to spend some of their time loafing about aimlessly, and schools should provide for this. For most young persons it will be the only chance they get to do this.

4   For a good recent account of Stenhouse, see Elliott and Norris (2012).

5   Winch also points out that in the English language the ambiguity in English regarding whether knowing-how entails ability is dispelled in French since a distinction is made between *savoir faire* and *savoir comment faire*; the former spells out ability while the latter implies only the ability to give an account that falls short of actual performance.

6   Most famously challenged by Stanley and Williamson (2001) and enhanced by Winch (2010) and Wiggins (2012). A good summary of the debate is given by Winch, chapter 2, who also further contextualises the debate in terms of occupational capacity. Wiggins adopts an Aristotelian approach, a singularly non-Rylean context with which to defend Ryle's basic arguments.

7   And in-house manuals are infamous for being comprehensible only to those who already know.

8   See Stanley and Williamson (2001: 428–429).

Part III

Liberty and authority

Chapter 8

Liberty and educational authority

Our theory of liberty as non-domination has sought to situate this concept in the notion of the free state. Crucially, for a state to be free there must be no dominion – neither externally through the oppression of other peoples nor internally through consigning its people, even a small number of them, to servitude. We have also seen that in a republican theory of liberty persons are viewed as free persons, that is, as liberty-bearing persons. The thought behind paying particular attention to education is twofold. First, the development and exercise of human powers owe much to the education of both young and older people. Education and learning are, for most people, complex activities that take up a great deal of time, whether as a child or student, a parent or a mature learner. From a republican standpoint it makes sense to evaluate the activity of educating from the standpoint of liberty because whatever advantages may accrue from education it should, whatever else it does, enhance the value of liberty itself. But in addition to this, the provision of education – the institutional structure – should also reflect the requirements of liberty; for example, its provision should be free from dominion and should reflect the importance attached to (from the standpoint of liberty) that of non-domination. This means that the provision of education needs to be *authoritative*, i.e. that there should be an authority to educate consistent with the requirements of liberty.

Relation between liberty and authority

The question of authority is significant for the question of liberty because of what might be called the internal relation between authority and liberty: liberty can only function within an authoritative normative order. Consequently education itself, given its immense significance in the lives of most people, is part of that normative order. Hence, whereas an account of human powers enables us to understand better what is involved in the exercise of liberty, an analysis of authority enables us to understand the place of liberty within a normative order. At the ontological level we have seen how a dialectic of recognition underpins what might be called the liberty relation. For freedom is nothing at all if it is not a relation *between* persons. Liberty calls for a relation that is neither one of servitude nor of mastery, that takes the form of recognition: my liberty is only as good as its recognition. But how can the dialectic of recognition be transformed from an ontological relationship into a normative relation that is socially grounded? The answer lies in laws and procedures whose authority is acknowledged by each as a necessity for realising the condition of liberty. A good example of this would be laws that regulate freedom of speech: the exercise of free expression is only possible providing each recognises that particular right as belonging to each. Accepting the authority of such law *ipso facto* enables each to recognise the other as free in that respect. There are, however, some modes of speech that are specifically premised on the denial of liberty-bearing status to some. Such would be speech that is racist or anti-Semitic. In so far as such speech acts are prohibited by a law governing free speech, then acknowledging its authority over me enables me to recognise the limits to free speech. In this way, we can see that Harrington and Locke have a better understanding of liberty than Hobbes. For the latter, laws merely impair liberty: for the former, law creates the possibility of liberty.[1]

We have seen, in Chapter 1, how Hobbes was able to articulate the basic conception of authorisation: 'A person is he, whose words or actions are considered, either as his own, or as representing the words or actions of another man . . . he that owneth his words and actions (*i.e. of the person authorised*), is the Author' (Hobbes, 1991: 111–112). But this account only serves to give us the bare bones of an authority relation. The reason is that where authority is conferred it is rarely unconditional and is done so for reasons. It is for this reason that the mere act of consent, in itself, is insufficient to ground authority except for actions that are limited in scope, where the purposes are clear and understood, the persons authorised are known and identifiable and the time-frame is limited. For actions that flow from institutional structures whose decisions are far-reaching both in terms of persons affected and an indefinite time-frame, then the bare act of consent is not enough. It does not perform what Dudley Knowles has referred to as the 'moral magic' that states sometimes make use of to legitimise their activities.[2] The mere act of consent does not confer a *carte blanche* on those thereby authorised. It makes no difference whether the consent is merely presumed (tacit consent) or whether it is openly given through words that have public utterance. No-one understood more than John Locke that the business of consent was hedged in by conditions and reasons. Therefore, it is worth examining briefly his *Two Treatises of Government*.

From a republican standpoint, it is striking how again and again Locke reiterates that the purpose of well-founded government is to free persons from arbitrary power and dominion. For example, early on, Locke says of Society that it permits:

a Liberty to follow my own Will in all things where the Rule prescribes not; and not to be subject to the inconstant, unknown, Arbitrary Will of another Man . . . This Freedom from Absolute, Arbitrary Power, is so necessary to, and closely joined with a Man's Preservation, that he cannot part with it.

(Locke, 1960: 324–325, paras 22–23)

For Locke, the 'natural liberty' of man entails a freedom from arbitrary power and this freedom carries straight through to Society, namely that state of affairs in which men have formed a body ('Society') prior to deciding on the form of legislature. This message is hammered home again and again. Speaking of the legislative power that is established through contract he says 'it can never have the right to destroy, enslave or designedly to impoverish the Subjects' (403, para 135). Moreover, where the Prince (or, by extension, government) 'has a distinct and separate Interest from the good of the Community', the people are to be looked upon 'as an Herd, of inferiour Creatures, under the Dominion of a Master, who keeps them, and works them for his own Pleasure or Profit' (423, para 163). Even towards the end of the *Treatise*, the same message is spelt out again – just in case anyone may have missed it – when Locke speaks of legislative authorities that overreach their powers:

either by Ambition, Fear, Folly or Corruption, endeavour to grasp themselves, or put into the hands of any other an Absolute Power over the Lives, Liberties and Estates of the People; by this breach of Trust they forfeit the Power, the People had put into their hands.

(461, para 222)

Locke, of course, did not subscribe to ideology of Republicanism. Moreover, it has been long established that when Locke wrote the Treatise he was responding specifically to the ideas of Robert Filmer, who argued for a natural dominion in personal and family relationships that then translated into political authority at the level of the state.[3] Nevertheless, it is Locke's words and tone that ring for us. It is not as if, having settled accounts with Locke, we are to treat these sonorous declarations as mere relics of a now forgotten dispute between two polemicists. Locke is pronouncing on the evils of domination and thereby setting limits to what authorisation through consent can bring about. Whatever people consent to, they can never consent to their own servitude.

Another consideration that limits authority is what is sometimes called the force of 'good reasons'. This can be interpreted in different ways. Sometimes it can be seen in a Kantian way such that the reasons apply not to a person in their capacity as someone with specific interests and wants but to a person in their moral capacity. In this case, a good reason would be a reason that could count for anyone no matter how they were personally situated.[4] For our purposes, the scope of this particular 'good reasons argument' is too wide. We need only consider reasons that apply to persons in their capacity as liberty-bearing. The real point of the good reasons argument is that it connects up with a point made by Peter Winch in an earlier discussion of authority:

'Authority is essentially bound up with systems of ideas and systems of *ideas* essentially involve the possibility of discussion and criticism' (Winch, 1967: 106). Winch is emphasising the point that what is recognised as authoritative is so in a context of beliefs such that authoritative pronouncements do not normally run counter to what we might standardly expect from that authority (Winch's example is of the Pope advocating free love). What this means, however, is that questions of authority cannot be treated separately from contextualised ideas and beliefs. For example, if persons are treated as *not* liberty-bearing and rarely, if ever, see themselves in that way, then what they are likely to accept as authoritative may turn out to be very different from someone who does. What, therefore, counts as good reasons or, better, 'adequate grounds'[5] depends on the historically-grounded human purposes and characteristics.

Thus it was that Locke (1960) was able, at one level at any rate, to give the process of consent a certain scope so that it was bounded by the requirement that consent was conditional on: 'the Preservation of their Property' (395, para 124) in which 'property' consists of 'Life, Liberty and Estate' (367, para 87). (It should be noted that Locke on a number of occasions makes this same point about the extended meaning of 'property' – see for example, paras 123 and 173.) Consent is therefore bounded by the purposes of human beings in society, and as Hanna Pitkin has observed this seems to imply that 'Your obligation to obey depends on the character of the government' (Pitkin, 1972: 57), since so long as government *does* pursue and succeed in preserving your property then you have no reason not to acknowledge its authority. And hence it is, too, that tacit consent can be easily presumed providing this condition is met through 'any possession or enjoyment of any part of the dominions of any government, whether this possession be of land to him and his heirs for ever, or a lodging for only a week' (Locke, 1960: 392, para 119). The difficulties with Locke's position at this point in his argument are well known because, as Pitkin says, 'your personal consent is irrelevant to your obligation to obey' (Pitkin, 1972: 57). As she goes on to observe, it is easy to conclude that 'express' consent must be grounded in deliberative, reflective conduct with the unfortunate conclusion that 'proper' consent is the preserve of a reflective minority with the majority of 'clods' (as she calls them) merely engaging in tacit consent, which scarcely amounts to consent at all since the 'clods' would presumably consent to virtually any kind of government which did not actively persecute them (61).

But from a modern republican standpoint, the difficulty with taking Locke's analysis as it stands, despite its attraction and its simplicity, has nothing to do with problems over tacit consent. It is that in the twenty-first century, property for the vast majority of persons extends no further than dwellings and personal possessions. Our 'estate', such as it is, is chiefly dependent on the exercise of our human powers. Our 'estate' therefore consists primarily of occupational knowledge, experience and skills and our only property that really counts is cognitive ability allied to practical know-how. If to this is added moral and

I have spoken of authoritative structures (by which I include both law and different kinds of institutional arrangements) as structures that both support free agents and enable agents to exercise their freedom. This implies that those structures are not going to be static. Although there will be basic constitutional arrangements and provisions of law (for example, much of criminal law) that will remain relatively stable, other institutional arrangements (and the concomitant patterns of authority) will shift and change as liberty-bearing agents respond to changing events through discussion, disagreement and eventual compromise. Whereas authoritarian regimes whose people are mere subjects in differing degrees of servitude much prefer silence, order and quiet, a free state will be characterised by 'tumult'. One of Machiavelli's innovatory doctrines was the acceptance of change and conflict and the belief that a well-ordered polity need not be perpetually stable. Thus, he recognised that 'all human affairs are ever in a state of flux and cannot stand still' (Machiavelli, 1960: 123) and attempted to establish principles of a polity based on that unalterable fact. By contrast, Hobbes and Locke (and most of their successors) assume that authoritative structures are based on a (illusory) permanency; and that without such structures we would be cursed with unavoidable instability, of the kind evidenced by the hypothetical state of nature.

For Machiavelli (1960), 'tumult' was occasioned by 'quarrels between the nobles and plebs' (113), but those who condemn them:

> seem to be cavilling at the very things that were the primary cause of Rome's retaining her freedom and they pay more attention to the noise and clamour resulting from such commotions than to what resulted from them, i.e. to the good effects which they produced.

For 'nobles and plebs' we can substitute, in our times, cultural clashes and even ethnic frictions. Machiavelli was not afraid of conflict, and nor should we be, today. Conflict and argument are the oil that helps turn round the wheels of a free state.

The problem of educational authority

What, then, is the basis of educational authority? There are two different kinds of answer to this question. The first asks 'how is educational authority justified?' and the second asks 'who or what is justified to be in authority?' The answer to the first question can be construed in terms of justifying reasons: the relevant authority instructs me to do what I would have reason to do in any case; it is through acknowledging the relevant authority that I am more likely to secure what I have reason to want. So, since I want to have my children educated (say), acknowledging the appropriate educational authority is the best way of achieving this.[6] One can see an immediate advantage in this line of thought, namely that, providing my wishes respecting my children are provided for, it

cultural experience then these elements, taken together, constit
liberty-bearing agency. Our estate is not made of soil and brick
is not mixed with the earth, as the Lockean fable would have
products and services that are often transitory and virtual
knowledge employed is itself unstable and provisional. The
government and normative structures are required not only t
tangible features of our lives but also our capacity as liberty
It is an agency that absolutely requires that appropriate norn
be maintained and preserved in such a way that they are done
continuing activity of liberty-bearing agents themselves.

Thus the question of political obligation, in these circun
so much 'under what conditions should individuals accept
authoritative', which puts the onus on individuals themselves t
otherwise comply. Rather, we ask: 'what do governments hav
are to be regarded as authoritative?', to which the answer is:
and institutional structures premised on the idea that agen
liberty-bearing. Furthermore – and this is decisive – these struct
the characteristic of permitting persons to recognise and be recog
bearing. This permits citizens to exercise their liberties both on
basis and through activities that encourage inter-recognition. The
no need to produce a hypothetical story or a 'just-so' story in orc
government and authoritative structures; it is enough that they
status of each and every person as liberty-bearing with all tl
that follow – namely those concerning recognition and the reli
activity to maintain that authority.

There are broadly three ways in which liberty can be exercis
that of pursuing activities and aims (or merely refraining from p
which are completely independent of the law that sanctions tl
that is, permits a whole range of activities which, from the
law, are entirely unpredictable. But the other ways in which
exercised are focussed on law and authority itself. One way is tl
of activities designed to criticise or, by contrast, enhance and str
The third way is the undertaking of activities that are permitted
have the effect of maintaining authoritative institutional structure
those governing education). What one might call adversarial ac
one hand and institutional activities on the other could be see
the *vita activa*, briefly discussed at the end of Chapter 1. Not
could claim, has an interest in pursuing adversarial or instituti
But we can see that those who choose to pursue, in the main, v
called independent activities are still contributing to the state ol
are, no less than others whose pursuits are more directed toward
laws and structures, contributing to the maintenance of a free st
the fact that they are indeed exercising their liberties.

cultural experience then these elements, taken together, constitute much of our liberty-bearing agency. Our estate is not made of soil and bricks and our labour is not mixed with the earth, as the Lockean fable would have it, but issues in products and services that are often transitory and virtual where even the knowledge employed is itself unstable and provisional. The upshot is that government and normative structures are required not only to preserve those tangible features of our lives but also our capacity as liberty-bearing agents. It is an agency that absolutely requires that appropriate normative structures be maintained and preserved in such a way that they are done so through the *continuing activity of liberty-bearing agents themselves.*

Thus the question of political obligation, in these circumstances, is not so much 'under what conditions should individuals accept government as authoritative', which puts the onus on individuals themselves to consent or to otherwise comply. Rather, we ask: 'what do governments have to do if they are to be regarded as authoritative?', to which the answer is: constitute laws and institutional structures premised on the idea that agents are free and liberty-bearing. Furthermore – and this is decisive – these structures must have the characteristic of permitting persons to recognise and be recognised as liberty-bearing. This permits citizens to exercise their liberties both on a self-regarding basis and through activities that encourage inter-recognition. There is, therefore, no need to produce a hypothetical story or a 'just-so' story in order to legitimise government and authoritative structures; it is enough that they recognise the status of each and every person as liberty-bearing with all the implications that follow – namely those concerning recognition and the reliance upon free activity to maintain that authority.

There are broadly three ways in which liberty can be exercised. One way is that of pursuing activities and aims (or merely refraining from pursuing aims), which are completely independent of the law that sanctions them. The law, that is, permits a whole range of activities which, from the standpoint of law, are entirely unpredictable. But the other ways in which liberty can be exercised are focussed on law and authority itself. One way is the undertaking of activities designed to criticise or, by contrast, enhance and strengthen a law. The third way is the undertaking of activities that are permitted by and which have the effect of maintaining authoritative institutional structures (for example, those governing education). What one might call adversarial activities on the one hand and institutional activities on the other could be seen as a part of the *vita activa*, briefly discussed at the end of Chapter 1. Not everyone, one could claim, has an interest in pursuing adversarial or institutional activities. But we can see that those who choose to pursue, in the main, what might be called independent activities are still contributing to the state of liberty. They are, no less than others whose pursuits are more directed towards authoritative laws and structures, contributing to the maintenance of a free state by dint of the fact that they are indeed exercising their liberties.

I have spoken of authoritative structures (by which I include both law and different kinds of institutional arrangements) as structures that both support free agents and enable agents to exercise their freedom. This implies that those structures are not going to be static. Although there will be basic constitutional arrangements and provisions of law (for example, much of criminal law) that will remain relatively stable, other institutional arrangements (and the concomitant patterns of authority) will shift and change as liberty-bearing agents respond to changing events through discussion, disagreement and eventual compromise. Whereas authoritarian regimes whose people are mere subjects in differing degrees of servitude much prefer silence, order and quiet, a free state will be characterised by 'tumult'. One of Machiavelli's innovatory doctrines was the acceptance of change and conflict and the belief that a well-ordered polity need not be perpetually stable. Thus, he recognised that 'all human affairs are ever in a state of flux and cannot stand still' (Machiavelli, 1960: 123) and attempted to establish principles of a polity based on that unalterable fact. By contrast, Hobbes and Locke (and most of their successors) assume that authoritative structures are based on a (illusory) permanency; and that without such structures we would be cursed with unavoidable instability, of the kind evidenced by the hypothetical state of nature.

For Machiavelli (1960), 'tumult' was occasioned by 'quarrels between the nobles and plebs' (113), but those who condemn them:

> seem to be cavilling at the very things that were the primary cause of Rome's retaining her freedom and they pay more attention to the noise and clamour resulting from such commotions than to what resulted from them, i.e. to the good effects which they produced.

For 'nobles and plebs' we can substitute, in our times, cultural clashes and even ethnic frictions. Machiavelli was not afraid of conflict, and nor should we be, today. Conflict and argument are the oil that helps turn round the wheels of a free state.

The problem of educational authority

What, then, is the basis of educational authority? There are two different kinds of answer to this question. The first asks 'how is educational authority justified?' and the second asks 'who or what is justified to be in authority?' The answer to the first question can be construed in terms of justifying reasons: the relevant authority instructs me to do what I would have reason to do in any case; it is through acknowledging the relevant authority that I am more likely to secure what I have reason to want. So, since I want to have my children educated (say), acknowledging the appropriate educational authority is the best way of achieving this.[6] One can see an immediate advantage in this line of thought, namely that, providing my wishes respecting my children are provided for, it does not matter too much *who* or *what* is in educational authority. It does not matter whether educational authority is claimed by the state, a local authority or merely the school itself. But one can also see an immediate disadvantage with this approach, which is that an educational authority may provide a type of education for my child that goes far beyond anything I might have reason to want for her. It may insist that the child is given an 'academic' education concerning which I can see no value; it might insist on standards of discipline that I consider to be outrageously brutal; or it might insist that my child be introduced to religions and cultures that from my point of view have very little merit.

The difficulty with the normal justification thesis is that authorities – any authorities – have the habit of inventing new reasons for acting which didn't exist before that authority came into being. It is not simply that authority creates obligations where none existed before; it creates new reasons for acting as well. It does this because the scope of authority extends well beyond an individual or subset of individuals – and the reasons for action tend to track this broader scope. Thus it is that citizens find themselves supporting causes, through taxation, that they didn't know even existed before it was pointed out to them. And thus it is that citizens and parents may find themselves having to accept actions of educational authorities that they (the parents) find not so much innovative as downright bizarre. The upshot is that the justification of authority, through reasons that I would act on myself if I were able to, needs to be extended by means of an acknowledgement of the *public* role of authority. And this means that I also must see myself as a member of the public for whom reasons apply, reasons that may be different – possibly very different – from reasons that would apply if I were just an individual. Authority creates individuals who have public identities, and those in authority therefore have a public role as well. This extends to the teacher herself who is obliged to enact a form of educational practice that may go far beyond what parents might wish for their children. Nevertheless, they (the parents), generally speaking, take on trust that what is taught is for the good of their children. And although it is natural for parents (in their role as parents) to want the best for their children to whom they have a natural duty of personal care, what is also happening is that children are being educated not merely as children of a particular parent but as children who will soon be fully fledged members of the public.

Thus education has an inescapable public role and it is not for nothing that in England the private schools of Eton, Harrow and so on have historically always been known as public schools, even though access is restricted to the very wealthy. Consequently, the answer to the second question concerning the justification of authority – namely 'who or what is justified to be in authority' becomes rather important. Given the public scope of education it matters that the source of educational authority is one in keeping with its public character: this I term a *well-founded* educational authority, namely an authority recognised by children, parents, employers and members of the public. There have been relatively few examinations of the basis of educational authority in recent years, but much of the debate surrounding school choice makes better sense when seen from this perspective.[7] For the issues surrounding the parental right to choose an education raises the question as to the source of educational authority: does this reside in the state, in parents, in teachers or the community?

Three sources of educational authority

A book that does consider educational authority in a comprehensive way, however, is Amy Gutmann's *Democratic Education*. Gutmann proposes four models of education, three of them drawn from explicit philosophical sources. The first is termed 'the family state' and the idea behind it is Platonic in that the state, as a unitary authority, teaches the good life to all. In this form it is clearly paternalistic:

> The defining feature of the family state is that it claims exclusive educational authority as a means of establishing harmony – one might say, a constitutive relation – between individual and social good based on knowledge. The purpose of education in the family state is to cultivate that unity by teaching all educable children what the (sole) good life is for them and by inculcating in them a desire to pursue the good life above all inferior ones.
>
> (Gutmann, 1999: 23)

Gutmann suggests that this theory of educational authority fails to recognise the parental involvement in education (indeed, in *The Republic* parents are deliberately excluded) and that the direct link between political power (in the form of the state) and moral probity is suspect. It might well be thought that the 'family state' form of education is a relic that philosophers dutifully dust down in order to pay scholarly respects, but has clearly no relevance or application today. This would be a mistake. Take, for example, the following statement on education from the UK Labour Party 1997 election manifesto:[8]

> It is not just good for the individual. It is an economic necessity for the nation. We will compete successfully on the basis of quality or not at all. And quality comes from developing the potential of all our people. It is the people who are our greatest natural asset. We will ensure they can fulfil their potential.
>
> (Labour Party, 1997)

At first sight it is not a moral imperative that links the individual to a wider fate but one of 'economic necessity'. Nevertheless, the Labour Party is here proclaiming its desire to harness the 'potential' of the people who are the nation's 'greatest natural asset' to the development of 'quality'. The only difference between the Labour Party and Plato is that the ends for which individuals are to be mobilised and harnessed are different, because in Plato's case the end is justice, informed by a philosophical conception of what justice consists. But what Gutmann identifies as the constitutive relation between individual and state is at the very heart of the Labour Party declaration. We are to be considered as a family in the quest for economic prosperity and thereby fulfil our human destiny.

Indeed, leaving aside authoritarian regimes and dictatorships, one could say that state direction of education in democratic states reached its zenith with the UK 1944 Education Act in which 80 per cent of children were consigned to state-provided inferior education (in the form of secondary modern schools) and which, through selection based on intelligence tests, created an educational apartheid with the top 20 per cent of children selected for an academic education in grammar schools. The state, using local authorities as proxies, assigned children to their designated school, with no room for discussion. The views of parents were systematically ignored and it is no wonder that this was resented, so that there was a gathering movement to confer greater educational authority on parents.[9]

This is explored in the second theory of educational authority that Gutmann (1999) refers to as the 'state of families', which: 'places educational authority exclusively in the hands of parents, thereby permitting parents to predispose their children, through education, to choose a way of life consistent with their familial heritage' (28). Sometimes Locke is used as philosophical support since, as Gutmann notes, Locke assumed that parents were the natural persons to look after their own children's education: 'The Nourishment and Education of their Children, is a Charge so incumbent on Parents for their Children's good, that nothing can absolve them from taking care of it' (Locke, 1960: 355, sec. 67). Locke goes on to add: 'There is little fear that Parents should use their power with too much rigour; the excess is seldom on the severe side, the strong byass of Nature drawing the other way' (ibid.).

Locke was unaware of what lay in store for children of the future at the hands of zealous parents. Here, for example, is Mr Gradgrind in Charles Dickens' *Hard Times*:

> 'You are to be in all things regulated and governed', said the gentleman, by fact. We hope to have, before long, a board of fact, composed of commissioners of fact, who will force the people to be a people of fact, and of nothing of fact . . .'
>
> (Dickens, 2003: 14)

Dickens goes on to tell the reader that 'No little Gradgrind had ever associated a cow in the field with that famous cow with the crumpled horn' (24). Mr Gradgrind, of course, does all this for the good of his children, as indeed does a more recent, updated version of Gradgrind, Amy Chua, the 'tiger mother' from North America:

> When Lulu turns in a poor practice session on the piano, Chua hauls her
> doll's house to the car and tells her she'll donate it to the Salvation Army
> piece by piece if she doesn't have The Little White Donkey mastered by
> the next day. When Sophia does the same, she screams: 'If the next time's
> not *perfect*, I'm going to *take all your stuffed animals and burn them*'.
>
> (*Guardian*, 15 January 2011)

Nevertheless, faced with a modernised version of the 'family state' as the
basis for educational authority, from the standpoint of natural liberty no state
or normative order generally should ever have the authority to take a child out
of its home and put it through it system of enforced schooling – the very idea
seems preposterous.[10] Advocates of parental basis for educational authority have
the huge advantage of support from an apparently impeccable quarter: article
26 of the Universal Declaration of Human Rights document (United Nations,
1948), which states 'Parents have a prior right to choose the kind of education
that shall be given to their children'. But this 'prior right' is a right only
conceivable in terms of a natural liberty, that is a liberty which stands outside
a normative order.[11] It is a liberty that is not so much grounded in a normative
order but proclaims its sovereign right to lie *outside* such an order. Thus no
parent (and nobody else for that matter) has a 'prior right' with respect to
educational choice or any other choice. Rather, a right flows from liberties that
are grounded in authoritative structures through which recognition of liberties
are constituted. Thus, even if parents did have an absolute, unfettered right to
choose their children's education it could never be a *prior* right. Such a right
appears to be 'prior' only because it is assumed that parents have a natural
authority over their children who are dependent on them. But the dependency
of children on parents in respect of warmth and sustenance cannot be extended,
without further argument, to embrace a general dependency that is intellectual,
moral and cultural. Parents have no such rights to have mastery over their
children in any of these respects. Parents certainly have a legitimate interest in
their children's education, which stems from the caring relationship that both
parties (parents and children) help to establish; but this relationship does not
warrant or sanction the absolute right of parents to determine their children's
education. For if education is formative in developing agents of a liberty-bearing
nature then if such education is determined by a specific group in order to
maximise control both over those educated and over those doing the educating
then the liberties of both sets of persons are threatened. If it be countered that,
as a matter of fact, no parent wishes to interfere in their child's education it
can then be asked: in that case, why insist on a prior right?

However, in England the locus of educational authority has gradually
changed in the 70 years or so since World War II. The state now provides
education but often in the name of parental authority. Thus there is offered a
combination of Gutmann's first and second approaches to educational authority:
the aims of the family state are proclaimed (in the form of economic well-being)

but parents are enlisted as willing supporters; parental aspiration for their children happily coincides with government aims for the economy and economic growth. The Lockean 'state of families' is put in service of the overarching requirements of the 'family state'. The UK Conservative Party election manifesto of 1987 put these two together perfectly when it proclaimed:

> Parents want schools to provide their children with the knowledge, training and character that will fit them for today's world. They want them to be taught basic educational skills. They want schools that will encourage moral values: honesty, hard work and responsibility. And they should have the right to choose those schools which do these things for their children.
>
> (Conservative Party, 1987)[12]

The Manifesto is significant for education since it contained outline proposals for a national curriculum, which was introduced in 1988.

Nevertheless, as Gutmann (1999) suggests, the argument in favour of parents as the basis for educational authority is flawed. In part, misgivings flow from the dangers of placing too much authority with parents who may simply use their influence to inculcate their children with views that are disrespectful to persons of different religions or cultures, using schools as a means to further partisan aims. But as Gutmann also suggests, it is not that this is decisive since this risk is run with any kind of educational authority (31). It is, rather, that the concomitant consequence of investing parents with sole educational authority is that the dependency of children on their parents becomes absolute. Not only are children dependent on parents for food, warmth and emotional care; their only chance of developing as independent persons is denied to them because the principal route for that – education – is put into the hands of their parents. Of course, Locke is quite right: most parents are not Gradgrinds or Amy Chuas and any move in the direction of authoritarianism with respect to their own children is corrected with kindness, usually with interest. But as we have seen, dependency, no matter how benign, is still dependency.[13] Parental-based educational authority risks directly undermining the liberties of children because it may frame both the content and methods of education in accordance with the vision of the parents. It condemns children to benign servitude. It is an attempt, not to prevent children from growing up but to prevent them from growing different.

The third theory of educational authority arises out of dissatisfaction with the Lockean approach. Amy Gutmann draws on J.S. Mill's argument in *On Liberty* that neither the state nor parents should have exclusive control over education. She terms this the 'state of individuals', observing that it 'responds to the weakness of both family state and the state of families by championing the dual goals of opportunity of choice and neutrality among conceptions of the good life' (1999: 34). She reads this as an attempt to create an 'impartial' education authority, staffed by experts and practitioners, and goes on to show that not only could a 'neutral' education be impossible to attain but also that children and students would actually be deprived of the opportunity to share in a received culture (34–35). Gutmann also suggests that the effect of the 'state of individual' conception is to place de facto authority in the hands of professional educators. And it is here that its weakness lies – that is, not so much misplaced notion that such an educational system could be neutral but that it puts inordinate authority (and power) into the hands of professional educators, without there being effective means of holding them accountable.

England: a case study of contested authority

Interestingly, there are some signs of this happening in the UK (briefly) for a period of 15–20 years from the 1960s through to the early 1980s. While professional educators never wielded total influence because of the strength, in those times, of local education authorities, at the same time the direct influence of central government on both educational provision and curriculum was weak. In the early 1960s the 1944 settlement became increasingly questioned as doubts were raised about the justice and accuracy of selection tests for children. As local authorities were encouraged by central government to abandon selective schools and introduce a single common school (the 'comprehensive' school), the influence of teachers and professional educators, for a time, increased.[14] At the same time, in 1964, the School Council was formed, which was specifically designed to enable teachers and professional educators to have a direct influence on educational policy and curriculum design. Although doubts (even at the time) were expressed as to how much impact the Council had, it was a body that was staffed and funded by government and signified a recognition that professional educators had a key role to play in the development of education, not merely at the level of delivery but also at the level of policy and strategy.[15]

There are a number of examples of teacher influence. For example, in 1967, the Plowden Report advocated a greater emphasis on placing the child at the centre of the process of learning, stressing the role of experiential learning and the importance of learning through discovery (Plowden, 1967: 185–186). What the report does not emphasise quite as much as it possibly should have is the immense responsibility this places on schools and teachers to devise an improvisatory pedagogy that allows this kind of learning to take place. Moreover, such an approach to learning must involve a curriculum that is characterised by a loose framework rather than fixed outcomes. Both the pedagogy and the view of the curriculum implied by that pedagogy, if taken seriously, inevitably places the *teacher* at the heart of the educational process and all the concomitant responsibilities that follow. Child-centred teaching means that the teacher lies at the very heart of educational authority.

Another example is the bold aim of Lawrence Stenhouse and his associates to introduce a form of education designed to raise standards for average-ability and lower-achieving adolescents – the Humanities Curriculum Project that ran from 1967 to 1972. The HCP placed the teacher at the heart of curriculum research through the idea that the curriculum was to be conceived of as a series of hypotheses that needed to be tested by teachers in the classroom. The idea was to enable both teachers and students to explore the curriculum as a process, in contradistinction to merely achieving a series of already-prescribed outcomes. The aim was to help learners become more mature and responsible through acculturation; but the method was to place the teacher at the very heart of the learning process. Again, this placed immense responsibility – and authority – on the teacher.[16]

Looking back, we can now see that no institutional mechanisms existed at the time whereby the immense authority of teachers could be recognised and made accountable. The projects inspired by Plowden and the HCP eventually foundered because teachers and schools simply lacked the authority to make them work. It therefore made it appear that educational ideas, untested and unproven, were merely being foisted on an unwilling constituency. And just as the state previously, through the 1944 provisions, ignored parents, so now did teachers and schools. I say nothing here of the merits of either Plowden or of the HCP (which I believe to be considerable): I merely observe that teachers simply did not have the authority to carry them through on the scale that was needed if they were to work.

However, by the mid-1980s, central government began to take more and more control of education, increasingly marginalising the position of professional educators to one of delivery only. In the UK, the 1988 Education Act (and its successors) conferred tremendous authority on the Minister of Education who is now responsible both for the content and the delivery of the curriculum in schools.[17] Moreover, the Minister has the power to close schools and to change the governance of a school in defiance of the wishes of both parents and teachers. With nearly half of all secondary schools opting out of local authority control in favour of Academy status, the Minister now has direct authority for over 1000 schools in the UK, even if day-to-day school governance is devolved. If current trends are maintained, the state, in the form of the Department of Education, is set to become the main source of educational authority in the UK, having direct authority for school governance as well – the Minister can appoint a new head, for example.

Thus the fate of the (very short-lived and somewhat tenuous) 'state of individuals' basis for educational authority was overtaken by the pressure of events emanating from *both* the 'family state' and the 'state of families'. This took the form of both the desire of parents to wield greater influence and the desire of successive governments to harness parental power in favour of greater state direction so that education could be utilised, in the words of the Labour 1997 manifesto, as 'an economic necessity for the nation'. Yet given the *public* scope of education, to base the source of its authority on a single government minister seems odd and is scarcely well-founded. To vest so much authority in a single person – even if an elected member of parliament – gives that person an overwhelming influence over an activity that is a collective endeavour.

The democratic conception of educational authority

From the standpoint of republican liberty, educational authority can be neither vested in parents nor in the state. Rather, educational authority is by its nature distributed and needs an elected body to reflect the variety of legitimate interests there are in educational provision, of which the parental interest is but one. This suggests that schools – all schools – need to be sanctioned and legitimised through a single point of authority, the legitimacy of which is recognised by all stakeholders and citizens. Moreover, this point of authority needs to be demonstrably educational in character so that authority extends only to education and not to other sundry, doubtless important, services. Indeed, it is vital that education is *not* seen as another form of service on equal footing with public utilities and social welfare. Education is not a service and neither are teachers mere service-providers (to be so would merely make teachers dependent on service users and so undermine *their* liberties).

A democratic conception of educational authority is the fourth approach that Amy Gutmann sets out, and she favours this approach on the grounds that 'educational authority must be shared among parents, citizen and professional educators'. Moreover, she advocates local democratic control, within an overall national framework, with members of school boards being elected. But if one were to ask why Gutmann favours democratic authority we are given three principle reasons. First, it gives voice to parental influence in perpetuating conceptions of the good life; second, it gives effective expression to the value accorded to professional practitioners; and third, such an educational authority enables a democratic civic culture to flourish (Gutmann, 1999: 42). One is struck by the fact that the first two reasons do not necessarily require a *democratic* authority for their realisation and therefore much hinges on the third reason, the building of a democratic civic culture, as the best way of reflecting, managing and realising the diverse concerns of a citizen body (11).

But from a republican standpoint, a democratic conception of educational authority is justified in terms of liberty. First of all, it enables liberty-bearing persons to effectively exercise their liberty in respect of maintaining authority structures that govern an activity – namely, education – that has a direct and immediate impact on the development of human powers and the opportunity to exercise them. In addition, in a domain of human activity that is central to the pursuit of liberty, it is essential that relations of dependency and servitude are not permitted to gain a foothold – whether it is an excess of parental influence that undermines teacher authority; or an excess of influence of professional educators in setting the educational agenda; or the excess of centralised state power – all these influences have both in the past and in the present prevailed. It is an affront to the liberties of parents and their children to have them assigned to an inferior education, without redress.[18] It is an affront to the liberties of teachers to have teaching methods prescribed for them and to be subject to inspection procedures in which their concerns are simply disregarded as having no weight whatsoever.[19] It is for these reasons that educational authority needs to be democratic: the protection and maintenance of liberty.

In her book, Amy Gutmann uses the USA as the main context for her discussions and so accepts as part of that context the school board system of educational authority. In England (I exclude Wales, Scotland and Northern Ireland) the control and funding exercised by local authorities is rapidly being diminished in favour of the Academy programme in which schools exercise self-governance and are accountable directly to the Minister of State for Education from whom they receive their funding. Local democratic control over secondary education is therefore almost non-existent in many areas of England. Contrast this position with that in California where there are over 1000 School Districts, each with an elected Board of Education. These district boards themselves report to County Boards which are also elected. The only divergence from this eminently democratic-based system of governance is at the State level where the State Board of Education is appointed by the State Governor, although the State Senate must ratify appointments. Yet despite this well-founded system of educational authority, schooling in California is in more or less permanent crisis. The reason is not far to seek. In terms of funding for public education, California would need to spend around 16 billion dollars extra per year to reach the national average of state spending in the USA. The surprise is not that there is a growing Charter Schools movement[20] but that it is not greater than it is – currently around 5 per cent of children in California are in Charter schools (see CSBA, 2010). In California, the system of education can truly be said to have a public reach yet confidence in it has been weak. However, in November 2012, voters in California approved, by 54 per cent to 46 per cent, a plan introduced by the Governor, Jerry Brown, designed to rescue the state's crumbling schools. The measure raises 6 billion dollars annually through raised taxes, thus overcoming decades of anti-tax sentiment in that state.[21]

In England, the structure of educational authority is as far removed from California as could be imagined, falling short (but not that far short) of a system that is entirely directed, managed and funded by the central government. Yet, curiously, there was a system of School Boards in England that existed from 1870 to 1902, the experience of which is perhaps worth revisiting.[22] These were formed in order to supervise the implementation of elementary education and the members of the Boards were elected through a wider franchise than existed at the time for parliamentary elections. The Board system was closed down by the Conservative government of Lord Salisbury and the responsibilities of the Boards were transferred to local authorities. But for a time the School Board movement flourished and a variety of persons succeeded in being elected –

including women, professionals, employers and representatives of religious organisations together with a fair sprinkling of radicals. Of course, the School Boards of old, operating in the circumstances of the late nineteenth century, had concerns we would now scarcely recognise. A major one was the resentment of many working-class parents against compulsory school education. The London School Board issued over 1.5 million truancy warnings over a 16-year period (Auerbach, 2009: 758). This elicited the following response from an anonymous author:

> The state, as represented by the tyrannical majority in parliament, has usurped the natural authority of the father, who is no longer treated as a person with independent and special privileges as a free citizen of a free state, but simply as one of millions of units whose sole use is to support the vast fabric of the state.
>
> (Auerbach, 2009: 775)

Unfortunately, the complainant was only concerned with the liberties of the father (as opposed to his children), but the content of the last clause can only evoke sympathy. There was, of course, very strong working class support for the School Boards, particularly from the trade union movement (Rubinstein, 1979: 234). In addition, in many cases, Boards acted as conduits for middle-class concerns; thus the Boards in the northern cities of Bradford, Manchester and Sheffield helped to set up a higher-grade school movement principally aimed at children of better-off parents, at least initially (Roach, 1991: 95–97). The attempts by School Boards to set up higher-grade schools met some opposition from the supporters of the well-established grammar schools as well. Boards also met opposition from traditional Church of England supporters, who suspected the Boards of undermining Anglican schools, though often they were supported by non-conformists (Simon, 1965: 158).

Despite these difficulties, School Boards acted as a forum for local debate and discussion in a way rarely seen these days (in England, at any rate). Indeed, it was the fact that educational debate raged in many parts of the country (above all with the London School Board) that prompted increasing calls for the already existing, all-purpose machinery of local government to be used instead of the Boards. In this way, national policy could be implemented at local level in a regulated and uniform manner. And although, from the standpoint of liberty, some debate, discussion, anomaly and even a degree of disorder is to be welcomed this only provokes the anger of those whose interest in liberty is only slight. The abolition of School Boards was strongly opposed, throughout the country, leading to many demonstrations and petitions. The largest demonstration seems to have been at Woodhouse Moor in Leeds, where a crowd of over 70,000 persons attended in the autumn of 1902 (Simon, 1965: 222). Many people in England at the time knew what exactly was at stake: the

School Board movement, though imperfect and flawed, was the first and only gesture at popular control over education in England.

The local control of education in England by local authorities (city and county) is now, 100 years later, gradually (though with increasing acceleration) being reduced as educational authority is dispersed directly to parents (who can set up their own 'free schools') or to business and religious sponsors, with the state directly financing a growing number of secondary schools through the Academy programme. One outcome of this state of affairs is that educational authority is fragmented: local authorities have been severely weakened while the Secretary of State for Education carries immense power but is remote. The formation of independent schools (Academies) entails that the schools themselves are, in effect, the sole local source of educational authority. But this is not, I suggest, the well-founded basis that is needed since such schools are no longer accountable to the public, save the Secretary of State through the system of schools inspection. It is not, therefore, surprising that the authority – the legitimacy – of the Inspection Agency itself is challenged by schools and colleges when the inspection results do not go their way.[23]

It is suggested that revitalised School Boards, with elected representatives, could act as a conduit for the expression and establishment of equality of self-expression on educational matters. Moreover, these discussions could take place at the appropriate local level. The idea would be that a Board could sanction a variety of schools in its area of jurisdiction. Even 'free schools' could be set up with this big difference: unlike the free schools in the UK today such free schools would carry the stamp of educational authority. Each Board could have reserved places for parents and for professional educators, and each would have a degree of autonomy so as to be able to respond to local conditions and reflect local concerns. A democratic mandate would, over time, strengthen the authority of the Board and also the authority of teachers and schools. The national schools inspection scheme could remain in place, but it would need to justify its findings to School Boards. The Boards could become creative influences within localities and providing the terms of Office for School Board representatives were limited to two or three, the democratic process would prevent vested interests from manipulating the system. Parental choice of schools could be spread across the geographical area of Board jurisdiction. Unlike local authorities, Boards would have a single purpose: education. They would, of course have flaws and imperfections – that is the price of democracy.

Conclusion

The relation between liberty, education and authority can be summarised as follows: education is critical for liberty since only through education are those human powers developed that are needed to protect liberty and to be resilient against attempts to diminish it. At the same time, an empire of liberty can only be established through authoritative mechanisms at the level of civic order, through which citizens are recognised as liberty-bearing. These two strands come together in the provision of education, which itself needs to be both authoritative and consistent with the claims of liberty. It is pointless having a curriculum that may be wonderful in many different ways if it is provided through *authoritarian* (not authoritative) means. But this is precisely the situation in England at the moment; the provision of the school curriculum lies in the personal fiefdom of the Secretary of State for Education, whoever he or she is. One does not need to be wedded to ultra-progressive ideas to find this troubling and there needs to be a way that lifts education out of the debilitating adversarial party political debate so that it serves the interests of a free society.

Notes

1 See Chapter 1.
2 See Knowles (2010: 96–97).
3 See the introductory essay by Peter Laslett in Locke (1960: 80–84).
4 Something along these lines is argued for by Knowles (2010: 53–54).
5 See Tuck (1972: 198).
6 See Raz (1990: 129) for a more formal exposition of what he terms the 'normal justification thesis'.
7 See Haydon (2010) and Pring (2008) for a summary of some of the issues.
8 Labour won the election by a landslide, making education one of their key platforms.
9 The role of parents was acknowledged by Prime Minister James Callaghan in his famous 1976 Ruskin speech on education – see http://education.guardian.co.uk/thegreatdebate/story/0,9860,574645,00.html (accessed 22 March 2014).
10 For a typical argument in favour of the 'state of families' approach see Tooley (2007).
11 See Chapter 1.
12 The Conservatives went on to win the election convincingly.
13 Dependency and its modes feature much in Dickens' novels. For example, it is a *motif* that runs right through *Little Dorrit* (Dickens, 2008): take, for instance, the wholly kind yet utterly condescending attitude of Mr and Mrs Meagles to the young woman in their care, Tattycoram. She is torn between a desire for independence (which leads her to the uncertain and somewhat menacing influence of Miss Wade) and a genuine fondness of the Meagles: eventually she goes back to them, as the pull of kindness triumphs. Independence is personified by the male professional engineer, Daniel Doyce, who finally succeeds in his projects, but only after escaping the bureaucratic ensnarements of the Circumlocution Office. He is knowledgeable, resourceful and entirely trustworthy. Whether Dickens sees women as capable of similar independence is another matter. Yet not all women are in a position of dependency: Little Dorrit herself cares for her father without being in a relation of servitude.
14 For a survey of these developments see Sally Tomlinson (2005).
15 See Plaskow (1985) for a fuller account of the workings of the School Council.
16 For an excellent and recent account see Elliott and Norris (2012), especially pages 19–33.
17 For a more detailed account of the implications of the 1988 Act, see Maclure (1988).
18 I refer, of course, to the notorious 11+ selection scheme in England, once nationwide but which still exists, notably in the county of Kent.
19 I discuss this further in the next chapter.

20 This refers to schools which are permitted to opt out of the school board form of governance and are directly controlled by bodies of parents, business groups, charities and other sponsors. Charter Schools are akin to the 'free schools' in England.

21 www.mercurynews.com/ci_21943732/california-proposition-30-voters-split-tax-that-would (accessed 22 March).

22 See Simon (1965) for a basic account.

23 www.dailymail.co.uk/news/article-2174753/Ofsted-inspectors-offered-counselling-clash-teachers-brings-college-visit-untimely-end.html (accessed 22 March).

Chapter 9

Liberty and teacher authority

The role of teachers

Given the importance of education in a free state it would be unsurprising if the role of teachers was not to come under scrutiny. Their significance is not only found in the role that they play in education and learning but also because they are in daily, personal contact with children and young adults with whom they often form close bonds. Teachers have a particular responsibility in contributing to the development of young persons in their care who will become free individuals, that is to say, liberty-bearing. At the same time, teachers operate within a structure of educational authority from which their own authority as teachers is derived. Finally, teachers are themselves liberty-bearing persons which means that, in a free state, they are not the mere instruments of the state, of parents, of employers, of the Church or of anyone else. Of all the professions, their position is unique because of the enormous trust placed in them by parents in particular but also by the whole body of citizens. Other professions have their clients, of course; but not even nurses, with the exception of chronic illness, are in daily contact with their patients over a sustained period of time. Moreover, this 'contact' takes the form of a personalised relation typically characterised by dispositions (on both sides) of trust, encouragement, disappointment, endeavour, striving and success. Because of the personal relation they have with children and young adults, teachers become one of the main bearers of the culture of a free state as it is transmitted to another generation. Hannah Arendt once proclaimed that teachers must have a 'love of the world' if they are to do this successfully and there is some truth in this.[1] For teachers are introducing the world to children in order that they can make it their home. This is just what servitude does not do; rather it denies the world to people who thereby have no other place to go, except a private imaginary. If teachers are treated as mere instruments of others then the world is denied to them, the teachers: it remains a mystery, in such circumstances, how they are supposed to introduce to their young charges a world that is the object of curiosity, wonder and enjoyment. The idea of 'love of the world' is an excellent metaphor for the relation of liberty-bearing beings to their world because their liberty is as nothing if they are unable to enjoy their brief time in it. This is often the true curse of servitude and dependency: it robs people of all enjoyment or, at best, makes enjoyable moments fleeting instances in a life otherwise given over to task-driven drudgery in which the agenda of one's life is set by others.

In this chapter I examine the role of teachers and the peculiar nature of their servitude and subaltern role. I offer a possible way of re-thinking the occupation of teacher which, I hope, is sufficiently grounded to make sense to any teacher who happens to be reading this book. I then move to a discussion of teacher authority and in the process of that say a little more about the importance of the public role of education and how that affects the role of the teacher.

However, it would be a mistake to suppose that a defence of the professionalism of teachers amounts to a call for teacher *autonomy*. For one thing, as we have already seen in Chapter 2, liberty is not the same as autonomy. What this chapter argues for, rather, is the recognition of teacher *authority*. This means identifying the source of that authority and identifying its scope. Moreover, actions taken under authority are accountable by dint of their authoritative nature so there is no question of supposing that if the liberty of teachers is better recognised they will become less accountable. If the authority of teachers is not publicly recognised and well founded, if the teacher is obliged to found her authority in the classroom and with parents on her own personal qualities and charisma, then her job is made impossible. Teacher authority has to be derived from a broad-based educational authority.

Teacher dependency

In Chapter 3 we discussed some of the more general features of domination and the dependency that results from this. In this chapter, I wish to focus on the specific example of teachers in England. But before doing so, it is worth making clear at this stage that an authority relation, whereby one person is authorised to give another person or persons instructions, need not in itself be liberty-threatening. Indeed, it is perfectly possible to retain one's status as liberty-bearing in such situations. The reason is because the relation is one of authority, not one of domination. The person in authority does not have arbitrary power over those in her jurisdiction. The scope of the authority will be set: there will be limits, known to all concerned, regarding what kind of instructions can and cannot be given. Moreover, the authority attaches to the role occupied not to the person him or herself. Finally, those who receive instructions from a relevant authority have consented to this situation (for example, by taking up employment). However, as we saw in the previous chapter, the mere act of consent does not give employers or those in authority a blank cheque to do whatever they wish on pain of dismissal. In consenting, I have by no means given up my liberty-bearing status: indeed, any consent given is conditional on this being recognised throughout the period of the agreement. Specifically, this translates into the recognition of what I term *occupational powers*, and I will say a little more about this in the next section.

In the field of education it is what might be termed *instrumental dependency* that is pervasive, in which teachers, pupils, students and whole schools are made into the effective instruments of educational policies and directives concerning assessment, the tracking of pupil progress and behaviour and the monitoring of standards. The motives, of course, are apparently impeccable: the raising of educational standards. But in England, these are achieved not through the co-operation of teachers but through compliance with an inspection regime managed through Ofsted (the Office for Standards in Education). The Ofsted Framework for Inspection signals its intent early on: 'Ofsted is required to carry out its work in ways that encourage the services it inspects and regulates to improve, to be user-focussed and to be efficient and effective in the use of resources'[2] (Ofsted, 2012a).

It goes on to say: 'School inspection acts in the interests of children, young people, their parents and employers. It encourages high-quality provision that meets diverse needs and fosters equal opportunities'.[3] At no point in the document does it say that the views and concerns of teachers are taken into account as part of the informational base on which judgements are made. In fact, the role of the teacher is not mentioned in its three primary objectives, which are to provide *parents* with an assessment of how a school is performing, to provide information to the Minister of Education and to help improve schools. While there are ample opportunities for parents to give views online about schools and teachers, no such opportunity is given to teachers. The judgement of teachers is made entirely and only through observation of pupil learning. In the *School Inspection Handbook*, some mention is made of discussions of teaching and learning with teachers but these only revolve around, and are determined by, observations already made.[4] Head teachers are consulted during the inspection process but they are only permitted to 'comment on the inspector's recommendations to ensure that these are understood'.[5] Feedback is given to teachers based on observations but at no time are inspectors required to enter into an extended discussion with teachers. The *Handbook* emphasises again the need to investigate parent's views of the school – a statutory obligation – and also instructs inspectors to talk to a range of pupils to ascertain their views on the work of the school; talking to teachers, however, is not needed.

This inspection regime treats teachers as the mere instruments of children's learning who are not recognised, I suggest, as being capable of bearing liberty: the basic powers of self-determination and of co-operating with others are not so much explicitly denied as simply ignored and overlooked. Teachers are expected to perform duties that are laid down for them. It may be objected that this paints too black a picture and schools may win for teachers a much greater degree of freedom, including freedom from inspections. But the point about dependency is that there are always exceptions, lapses, lacunae and spaces within which agents may have the opportunity to act independently: *but only at the discretion of their masters or as a result of oversight.*

A second form of dependency is what I term *service dependency,* in which it is the supreme purpose of agents (e.g. teachers) to be at the service of a range of service users (e.g. parents, children, employers, local authorities, central government). Service provision may be seen as having the following characteristics:

1   The standards of the service are not set by the providers but by the users or customers, or at least by the presumed perception of the customer or user. Individual service providers are judged by standards of service, which they rarely set themselves.
2   Any professional development – training – must be entirely task- and service-related. There is no question of development that in any way enhances personal goals beyond the strict requirements of the service.
3   There is no question of any kind of extended dialogue between service provider and user. Essentially, the user (or his agent) requests and the provider responds.
4   Service providers may be given some scope for individual initiative, since most services require some degree of flexibility. But this initiative is heavily circumscribed since too much flexibility would undermine the unity of the service provided (in service-speak this is called 'clarity').
5   Unity of service is delivered through a top-down management structure. Managers ensure that staff are well-motivated and understand processes and tasks. Individual idiosyncrasies and eccentricities are erased through the employment of a common vocabulary, the use of which is policed by management.
6   Service providers are controlled, in particular, by their work being 'full-on' throughout the whole day and the whole week.

All of these six functions and characteristics of service provision now characterise the teaching profession in schools and colleges to a greater or lesser extent, not only in England and North America but increasingly elsewhere.

1   Parents (not children) themselves become service users and it is the presumed wishes of parents that set the standards and character of the service.
2   The development of teacher training in such a way that all references to educational theory must be erased in favour of 'on the job training' is entirely consistent with the development of education provision as a task-focussed service.
3   The ability of teachers to enter into constructive dialogue with parents and members of the community is severely constrained by schools management and governors. Moreover, the introduction of the national curriculum

has not become a framework in which dialogue could take place but a prescriptive mechanism through which service users hold service providers (teachers) to account.

4   A practice of pedagogy is gradually being introduced which documents both process and outcomes and progressively reduces teacher initiative and judgement.[6]

5   On the side of government and policy makers there is now common consent that 'good' schools are almost entirely the product of effective leadership. Teachers are the willing, enthusiastic followers of managers endowed with a golden touch.[7]

6   The astonishing lack of free time that teachers actually have is perhaps the single most visible sign of the emergence of teachers as service providers.[8] Teachers have very little time to develop their own research and networks: but then, why would a mere service provider want to do any of these things in the first place?

The transformation of the teacher into a service provider is, of course, not yet complete and it would not be too difficult to find many counter-examples to each of the points just made.[9] Moreover, even when policies, procedures and institutions take on increasingly the character of service provision, teachers themselves continue, stubbornly, to think in terms of a profession. But the imperatives created by service dependency make the discourse of educational theory, research and professional development increasingly at variance with the discourse of service dependency: the questions raised by the former are simply an irrelevance to the latter.

Occupational powers

The historic theorists of republican liberty assumed that servility and dependency were always ever-potent threats to liberty. Moreover, it was never enough to rely on institutional mechanisms for the safeguarding of liberty. One needed to cultivate a set of virtues including courage, prudence and resourcefulness. The humanist movement of the Quattrocento, originally motivated by a textual quest for the recovery of ancient Roman and Greek writings, in the process reignited interest in the civic virtues and the role these could play in protecting the liberty of citizens in the Italian city states. Great play was made of the *vir virtutis* who was able to subdue the onslaughts of *fortuna* and at the same time explorations were made of man's free and creative powers.[10] How might this need for virtue associated with liberty be interpreted in the twenty-first century?

I suggest the answer lies in the development of capacities and social powers as ways of realising the basic human power of self-determination. And I wish to suggest further that one of the prime ways in which a person's powers can be developed is through a work-based occupation. Christopher Winch has recently done much to help us see how, when properly understood, the possession of an occupation allows the development of human powers, providing the basis of social freedom and liberty. Having an occupation makes us less likely to be servile and dependent. Winch draws our attention to the German term *Beruf* and notes that it is a broader term than the English term 'occupation' with closer similarities to 'vocation'.[11]

He goes on to explain that a *Beruf* signifies a multi-layered activity including the exercise of task-related skills and also abilities (such as initial assessment, planning and evaluating) that enables the practitioner to cope with a variety of situations within which particular skills need to be exercised. In addition, *Beruf* also involves the exercise of systematic and theoretical knowledge relevant to the occupation and finally it also includes those complex moral and civic dispositions (for example, meeting ethical standards or setting reasonable expectations), which are indispensable for the practical and effective exercise of *Beruf*. Winch suggests that this gives the worker a certain degree of independence and control over his work. When these elements are taken together in an integrated way (i.e. skills, abilities, practical and theoretical knowledge together with normative dispositions) we have what Winch terms 'occupational action capacity'.[12]

In the case of a teacher, this would include relevant theoretical knowledge underpinning pedagogical method, including psychological and philosophical perspectives. This is *in addition* to the abilities relating to classroom management, monitoring of pupil learning, communicating with parents and co-ordinating work with colleagues. It also implies having an understanding of the principles of curriculum development and having a fair degree of influence over its implementation within a school. If the occupation of teaching reflected better the implications of *Beruf*, then a UK-based teacher would have all this as well as the basic assessment and pedagogical skills currently required.

We can see how occupational capacity might work if we take the example of assessment. Currently, much of classroom-based assessment is performative in that (especially in England) the teacher implements procedures already laid down. There is a great emphasis on the recording of procedures and especially the recording of results, including the retaining of any documentary evidence pertaining to pupil performance that has been formally assessed. Whereas the deployment of an occupational capacity would involve a critical perspective on assessment, drawing on relevant historic practice as well as educational theory plus an ability (and authority) to adapt recommended procedures in the light of specific pedagogic situations. The teacher would be in command of a range of assessment methods and be able to justify a particular approach *both* in pragmatic, situational terms and in theoretical terms. Moreover – and this is crucial – these abilities would be *recognised* so that the teacher would be entrusted with pupil learning such that the performative requirements currently in place would no longer feature so prominently. In particular, teachers would be entrusted with devising formative assessments throughout the school year while summative assessments would cover a range of learning in an integrated way.

The development and exercise of occupational capacity is a specific example, within the education sector, of the way in which human powers have to be nurtured if liberty is to be preserved and dependency avoided. The teaching profession at the moment suffers from both instrumental and service dependency, to the detriment not only of teachers' occupational status but also to the detriment of their liberties. The basic human power of self-determination is denied to the teaching profession, but the development of occupational capacity is one way of reclaiming it.

The concept of occupational capacity consists of that range of cognitive, technical and practical abilities that enables a professional – in this case a teacher – to function within a professional setting. When we view a professional in this way and link occupational capacity to the normative recognition of the professional as liberty-bearing then we can speak of occupational *powers*. We have spoken all the way through this book of the fundamental importance of the element of recognition in any theory of liberty and I have suggested that one way this recognition is given practical effect is through the authority of the law. Another way in which this recognition can be given is through the recognition of the powers of an occupation holder. Occupational powers are what the Ofsted inspection process denies to teachers at its very heart, because it is primarily interested in measurable learning outcomes and its inspection process therefore systematically reduces the significance of those who bring about those outcomes. Occupational powers are not, it needs to be added, confined to the traditional professions. The builder, the communications engineer, the car mechanic, the nurse – in a free state, all of them will share and recognise each other's powers.

Teacher authority and the sphere of the public

R.S. Peters (1966) in his chapter on Authority in *Ethics and Education* suggested that a teacher was in possession of two types of authority. First of all, a teacher is 'in' authority in so far as she has the right to 'decide, promulgate, judge, order and pronounce' in accordance with procedural rules backed up by a normative order. For Peters, this order is rule-governed and therefore it determines the sphere and scope of teacher authority, that is, her right to decide and promulgate on matters educational. In particular, this designates the right of a teacher to instruct and request in the classroom with the expectation that this authority is acknowledged by parents, children and the public. Second, Peters suggested that the teacher was also 'an' authority in so far as she was in possession of certain knowledge and expertise concerning subject matter.

For the purposes of this discussion I do not wish to challenge Peters' basic distinction (1966: 238–240). For reasons to be explained, I do wish to modify slightly the way in which a teacher can be 'an' authority so that a teacher is better thought of as an authority on educational practice as well as certain types of subject matter.

In so far as a teacher is in authority in the sense described, we assume that this stems from the broader normative order of educational authority, broader than the school or institution in which the teacher is a practitioner. Thus, for teachers to be 'in' authority in the way that Peters suggests, they need to be able to exercise authority on the basis of, and in the context of, a well-founded (and well-funded) educational authority. Teachers are the visible, tangible face of that authority. Therefore, just as educational authority has a public scope so the authority of the teacher is public in character.

However, although I have insisted on the *public* character of education, this may be disputed on the grounds that there is no unique public sphere as such. The classical account of the public sphere can be found in Habermas' *Structural Transformation of the Public Sphere* (1962) in which the rise and fall of the bourgeois – liberal public – is traced. But the central contention of Habermas – that there is an 'ideal-typical' public sphere in which competing views can find a voice – has itself been subject to criticism. Nancy Fraser (1977) in her essay *Rethinking the Public Sphere* has summarised a range of research, concluding that there are many publics (including counter-publics) and she doubts if there ever was (or could be) a 'single' public. Moreover, these different publics may come into being and then gradually fade away; some publics may compete with each other (e.g. faith and secular publics); and sometimes one public may supplant another. To be wedded to the idea of a single over-arching public is misguided because it assumes the presence of a single normative discourse that can in some way include a range of diverse perspectives whereas the strong likelihood is that a single public discourse will end up failing to recognise and failing to accommodate all the various publics that happen to exist in most of today's societies.

These matters have been taken up in a recent series of articles in the journal *Educational Theory*. For example, Kathleen Knight Abowitz (2011) has described the activities of the IAF (Industrial Areas Foundation) in Austin, Texas, and its attempts to influence public schooling through parent assemblies and questioning of school officials with a view to promoting greater self-governance at a local level (486). It has to be said, in reading Knight Abowitz's descriptions of local politics one gets the distinct impression that as far as teachers are concerned matters have changed little since Peters' remarks on the American teacher 50 years ago. Writing in the 1960s, Peters comments that in the USA:

> teachers are hired to promote ends which the parents consider they know almost as much about as the teachers . . . they are at the mercy of school boards who decide matters of salary, curriculum and courses . . . and

teachers are expected to conform closely to the norms of the local community both in and out of school.

(Peters, 1966: 253)

They still, today, appear to be regarded as little more than hired hands, to do the bidding either of school board officials or of the dynamic leaders of new-found pressure groups or 'publics'. ('Achieving publics for public schools requires leadership habits and skills spread across school organisation and across multiple civic sectors … parent leaders participate in trainings and public actions … they learn how the school system works including curriculum and budget …' (Knight Abowitz, 2011: 482).) It would appear that much has to be done before some teachers are recognised as both in authority and an authority.

But the main point I wish to make is that far from this being an example of a counter-public, it strikes me as exactly what one would expect in a public arena where educational priorities and goals are in dispute. The idea of there being a single public does not imply that somehow there is a single public discourse. It is rather that there is a single arena – a public space – in which inequalities and lack of empowerment get recognised. In a different article in *Educational Theory*, Terri Wilson explains how Habermas' concept of the public sphere needs to be supplemented by the theory of communicative competence so that the order of rational discourse is precisely aimed at recognition. It is not that there is a normative order to which emergent publics must conform: it is rather that this normative order is itself created precisely through rational argumentation at the level of practical discourse (Wilson, 2010: 657–659). The model of counter-publics may allow for a public gaining some of its objectives but this is quite different from a recognition that those objectives are legitimate. Thus the idea of a public sphere does not rest on a consensus so that differences are eliminated but rather on the idea that differences can be recognised and then following up the implications of what this recognition might mean. This is precisely implied by the idea of the 'space of reasons' that we examined in Chapter 4; a public sphere constitutes the domain in which the asking for and giving of reasons becomes possible.

Epistemically, Donald Davidson makes a parallel point when he argues against the possibility of different conceptual schemes that entail that we are, each of us, the prisoner of our own scheme. Davidson (1984) argues that there is no 'fixed stock of meanings, a theory neutral reality' (195), which can provide a ground for comparison between schemes. But he does think that translation from a sentence uttered by A into sentences used by B is possible through the attribution of beliefs resultant on sentence interpretation. We can form a picture of what a speaker holds to be true and what she holds to be false and in this way even the most divergent beliefs can be understood. The only stipulation in this process is that of epistemological charity: as he puts it, 'if we want to understand others, we must count them right (*'correct'*, GH) in most matters' (197). Davidson's ideas on interpretation therefore provide an epistemic basis for rational discourse: it holds the promise that attempts to work towards rational discourse are not doomed before we start.

I take it, therefore, that Habermas and Davidson offer us different ways of thinking about the coherence of the concept of a public. If the idea of the public were incoherent, in the way that Nancy Fraser suggests that it might be, then the future for establishing educational authority and, following on from that, teacher authority, would be difficult if not impossible. Teachers would end up as hired hands with no more authority than that permitted by those who employ them.

There is, however, the other dimension of authority that Peters identified, namely that the teacher is 'an' authority as well. Peters suggests that this kind of authority is disciplinary-based and is challengeable in the way that being 'in' authority is not. For while I may make a poor decision as a teacher with respect to some matter of school discipline and order, the authority I have to make that decision does not rest on its particular merits. By contrast, my authority to pronounce on some matter of knowledge can always be challenged through evidence and argumentation: as Peters (1966) points out, 'nothing is made right on (my) say so' in this respect (240). But I think that it is important to recognise that the scope of this kind of authority is broader than discipline-based knowledge. Educational practice can be seen as having three elements – process, content and development. By 'process' is meant those different kinds of learning activities and the pedagogies that support them. By content is termed that knowledge and those skills that our teacher is supposedly master of, at least provisionally. Content may be construed as composed of combinations of knowing-that and knowing-how: it may be organised along the lines of Hirst's forms of knowledge; it may be topic- or interdisciplinary-based. But however construed, process engages with content to produce pupil and student development, which can be identified and evaluated across a range of cognitive, practical and creative set of skills and understandings. I suggest that the teacher is an authority on all three elements of educational practice – process, content and development, and not only content. Teacher authority – that is, the authority 'on' – is diminished if she is no longer seen as having any particular expertise on any or all of these three strands. For the scope of teacher authority needs to extend across the whole of educational practice.

This is a matter of some importance because even if educational authority is well-founded, teachers may lack authority simply because social and historical factors have contributed to an unwillingness to recognise that teachers may ever be an authority on educational practice. Merely because educational authority is founded on a democratic basis is no reason to suppose that, as a result, teachers will be regarded as having authority 'on'. But recognition of teacher authority in respect of educational practice is not the same as teacher autonomy, which is a quite different idea. Teachers can never be autonomous as long as they derive their authority 'in' from an educational authority. The only time one might want to regard a teacher as being fully autonomous with respect to authority is if educational authority itself no longer deserves acknowledgement; then one may indeed transfer one's allegiance to a particular teacher and regard her as both the agent and source of educational authority. But such a move would be *in extremis* and could only be justified if an educational authority had been taken over by racists, fascists or suchlike.

The shifting nature of teacher authority

Suppose we characterise the two basic types of teacher authority ('in' and 'on') as pedagogic authority and epistemic authority respectively. The shifts and movements of this authority – both possibilities and limitations – may be seen as determined by organisational conditions, for which a framework of understanding was worked out by the British sociologist, Basil Bernstein in his seminal 1971 paper, *Classification and Framing*.[13] With one modification, which I will come to shortly, Bernstein's framework has proved to be remarkably robust, not to say prescient. 'Classification' refers to the relation between curriculum contents – for example, subject areas. Strong classification indicates contents that are insulated from each other with clearly defined boundaries, whereas weak classification indicates loosely defined boundaries between contents. Thus a curriculum with clearly defined subject areas and specialist teachers is said to be a 'collection code'; where the boundaries are much looser Bernstein suggests the term 'integrated code'. By 'framing' Bernstein designates the strength of pedagogical relations – or as he puts it, 'frame is used to determine the strength of the message system, pedagogy' (50). In particular, 'frame' conceptualises the 'degree of control over the selection, organisation and pacing of the knowledge transmitted and received in the pedagogical relationship' (51). In Bernstein's hands, this somewhat abstract terminology starts to get interesting when he proceeds to combine and apply the concepts of classification and frame. For example, an integrated code may vary as to framing: strong framing implies a unified pedagogic approach in which teachers are expected to participate in the delivery of a knowledge code that may be interdisciplinary in character and institutional in scope (for example topic-based, enquiry-led learning). By contrast, a collection code with strong classification and weak framing may give teachers considerable independence within their subject discipline; but arguably, pupils and students have much less control over their learning. Bernstein suggests that strong classification permits staff to hold a range of personal ideologies in contrast to an integrated code in which staff are expected to adhere to (depending on the strength of the framing) a shared pedagogic vision. It will be seen that the terms 'strong' and 'weak' do not signify normative approval or disapproval. It will also be seen that one of the major justifications of the terminology is that it creates a distancing from entrenched educational debate and conflict between 'progressive' and 'traditional' positions.

I mentioned one modification that is needed and this arises from the fact that Bernstein, certainly in 1971 when his ideas were first broadcast, would not have been familiar with subsequent increased government and intervention in the deployment of educational codes. This has particularly affected the concept 'frame' since Bernstein assumed, for the most part, that framing was internal to an educational code. While there may be social influences on framing, the pedagogic relation was largely determined at school level. However, framing can also be 'external': for example, as we have already observed, in England the government-sponsored inspection regime which has been in place since 1990 has had considerable impact on the framing of educational codes. External intervention can also impact on classification; however, not all external classification necessarily undermines the position of teachers. The introduction of the national curriculum in England in 1988 while curtailing the *autonomy* of teachers did not necessarily undermine their authority. This was partly because both the method and organisation of teaching was left to individual schools and partly because it introduced stronger classification and so helped re-enforce subject identities among teachers (though not all).[14]

It is worth noting that epistemic authority does not necessarily require strong classification to support it. There is no reason *per se* why the introduction of an integrative educational code should undermine such authority since epistemic authority can be deployed across subject areas, whether individually or collaboratively. Indeed, in higher education, arguably strong classification is breaking down anyway and maybe eventually this greater interdisciplinarity will be translated into the school curriculum. Nor should pedagogic authority be reduced by strong framing. Bernstein himself notes that the introduction of an integrative code need not undermine the position of teachers providing certain conditions are met. These include a clear consensus on the integrating idea, an explicit link between knowledge and pedagogy and clear criteria of evaluation and assessment. It is true, however, that *external* framing through inspection regimes may well undermine pedagogic authority of teachers. On the other hand, since the final arbiter is pupil learning achievements then providing these are met it is assumed that the internal framing of a school supports these and so teachers may be left unscathed.

These considerations strongly suggest that as far as the occupational powers of teachers are concerned attention needs to be directed towards the development and maintenance of both epistemic and pedagogical authority. Armed with this authority, teachers can withstand and even flourish in the changing scene of educational codes. It does no service to teachers to associate teacher professionalism with any particular combination of framing and classification. By the same token, the best way in which teachers can withstand external pressures is by building up and developing their authority. By contrast, the conversion of teacher into service provider is likely to result in a severe diminution of both epistemic and pedagogical authority and an accompanying loss of liberty.

However, despite the pressures of external framing, it may be that teachers can succeed in maintaining a degree of pedagogic authority concerning the methods and organisation of learning. This, however, needs to be buttressed by epistemic authority, which not only includes subject knowledge but extends to the theory and practice of pedagogy itself. The components of epistemic authority are largely under the direct control of teachers themselves and can be used to underpin pedagogic authority. Given the external pressures that are being brought to bear on the profession, teachers who undervalue epistemic authority are akin to turkeys voting for Christmas.

Conclusion

Suppose – and this seems highly unlikely for the foreseeable future – a well-founded educational authority could be established and the public role of education were recognised by all the various 'publics' that now exist. Would this then solve the problem for teacher authority? I argue that it would not, at least not completely. The reason is that the authority of the teacher is continually tested in the classroom, even in cultures in which there is a tradition of receptive learning. The testing I have in mind is not merely that of a disciplinary nature in the behavioural sense. Even when behavioural problems are minimal, the epistemic authority of teachers may still weaken. For the teacher, in the eyes of the learner, takes on the ownership of the curriculum, the subject matter. The learner has to be convinced that the subjects and skills are actually significant and this often involves a transformation of learner preferences. The curriculum itself must carry authority and it is the teacher who bears its weight. Sometimes this weight is difficult to bear, no matter how experienced or accomplished the teacher and no matter how sophisticated the learner might be. For the learner is always sceptical and what is surprising is how many people outside the profession assume that the default position of the learner is one of 'willingness'. The best one can hope for is that the learner is willing to be convinced that what they are being asked to do is worthwhile. The learner has to take this on trust.

Now if the aim is to convince the learner that the mental struggle of learning is necessary for instrumental reasons no exercise of authority is required by the teacher: all that is needed is a demonstration of means-end reasoning, although even this can sometimes be tough. It is far more difficult to require from initiates the hard work needed just because the teacher says it is important. As we know, the paradox of learning is that its importance can't always be recognised until one has accomplished all the hard work. Often it happens that the learner does it 'for the teacher' – but it isn't always a good idea to rely on one's own personal magnetism as a teacher to motivate. One can also, of course, resort to tricks, gimmicks, prizes and rewards – all in a day's work. But there are also times, I suggest, when both teacher and student may recognise the epistemic authority of the subject matter itself. The authority is presented not so much as a series of facts, theories and interpretations but as an experience to be negotiated and tried out and investigated. The subject matter holds authority because it always holds out the promise of better things to come. It is able to do this on account of the new vistas that it opens up for those engaged in it.

Notes

1 See *The Crisis in Education* in Arendt (1977: 174–196).
2 Ofsted *Framework for School Inspection* (2012a: 4) www.ofsted.gov.uk/resources/framework-for-school-inspection-january-2012 (accessed 22 March 2014).
3 Ofsted *Framework for School Inspection* (2012a: 13).
4 Ofsted *School Inspection Handbook* (2012b: 35) www.ofsted.gov.uk/resources/school-inspection-handbook-september-2012 (accessed 22 March 2014).
5 Ofsted *Framework for School Inspection* (2012a: 23).
6 This does not mean that teachers do not try to develop new initiatives – see Pollard and James for many examples, e.g. the varying questioning techniques (2004: 7). But arguably, overall, the effect on pedagogy has been marginal: orthodox transmission pedagogy is still the preferred teaching method, according to Sue Cox who summarises research into the effects of organisational change on actual practice in the classroom (2011: 90–97).
7 See, for example, Sachs who analyses the rise of individualism and the charismatic in the context of a developing entrepreneurship model in education (2003: 129–130).
8 See the analysis of the effects of workload on teacher retention by Day and Smethem (2009: 146–147).
9 Day and Smethem (2009) try to argue that teachers are managing to retain professional autonomy but they are not wholly convincing:

> Yet they [teachers] were able, it seems, to exercise substantial autonomy. It was not that the government had created . . . the conditions . . . for a transformation that would be led and created by the schools themselves . . . but more that these teachers' work was founded upon hope, a sense of agency.
>
> (152)

They go on to concede:

> Surveillance has increased and those who fail to perform against standards established by the government are punished, directly or indirectly.
>
> (154).

10 For an account, see Quentin Skinner (1978: 94–101).
11 See Christopher Winch (2010).
12 See Winch (2010: 73–74).
13 See Bernstein (1971).
14 This mixed response by teachers is explored in McCulloch, Helsby and Knight (2000: 64, 67–71).

Part IV

Liberty and hegemony

Antonio Gramsci

Dependency, resilience and resistance

The significance of Gramsci

Up to this point we have been concerned with elaborating a certain concept of republican liberty and then exploring how that concept can be used to inform an understanding of knowledge, pedagogy and educational authority. But at this point, critics may indicate a difficulty that so far has been ignored. For neither pedagogy nor curriculum exist as processes independent from the dimensions of culture and power. Indeed, pedagogy and curriculum could be seen as one of the critical sites in which culture and power are contested. Nowhere is this more evident than in the sphere of education in the United Kingdom (particularly England) since 1944 (to take a significant but none-theless arbitrary date since contestability predates 1944 by the best part of a century). We therefore need to adopt a theoretical approach that convincingly situates education and schooling within a broader framework. Such a framework, however, needs to recognise the durability of educational traditions: if education is the site in which power and cultural contestabilities are played out, it is not, on that account, merely reducible to them. Indeed, the very durability of educational traditions may help to modify and influence those contests. A good example of such a tradition is the humanist curriculum itself, borne out of a dissatisfaction with medieval schooling and training. Even today the academic curriculum still has a recognisable affinity with the *studia humanitatis* of the fifteenth century. Just as enduring is the tradition of 'learner centred' pedagogy, which most certainly has roots that can be traced back to the seventeenth century, John Locke himself cast doubt on the efficacy of imposing humanist studies on youthful, unwilling material.[1]

Moreover, the contextualisation of educational process through reference to culture and power needs, if possible, to accommodate considerations pertaining to republican liberty, especially those relating to dependency/non-dependency and the development of human powers. We need a theory of liberty that recognises the domain of culture and education as a dimension of power, which at the same time integrates within its perspective an appropriate account of the conditions of liberty. Such a theory would provide a certain economy of thought which spares us, having elucidated the place of education within a contextualised setting, the task of then further grafting on to such an account the claims of republican liberty. Far better then, to have these claims situated and integrated within an overall account of educational process appropriately contextualised. This also helps to avoid the temptations of a methodological individualism which serves to inhibit the thought that liberty itself may be socially founded: we need, then, to resist the supposition that we must construct a timeless notion of the self with appropriate attributes of freedom and then judge to see if social and political conditions measure up to it. If this were merely one of a number of theoretical strategies deployed then it could be instructive; but if it is the only strategy taken up then it is simply naive. We need to avoid, if at all possible, an account of liberty that entails the condemnation of most, if not all, social and political arrangements for failing to measure up to our most treasured concepts.

An integrated account, however, is made even more complex. The reason is that some role must be assigned to knowledge. If education is concerned with the production and transmission of knowledge then at the very least a view needs to be taken up as to the status of knowledge. If knowledge is viewed as essentially determined by a particular social and political configuration of power and culture then, admittedly, the 'problem of knowledge' solves itself: a system of education merely relates knowledge production to the pragmatic needs of that particular configuration. Thus (it could be argued) the character of knowledge differs: a society characterised by significant social stratification and elite governance will adopt a proprietorial perspective wherein 'knowledge' is the precious preserve of the few (Young, 1971: 19–47); whereas knowledge in a society characterised by democratic governance and a high regard for the status of popular culture will take on a pragmatic, social needs-driven character. However, if the domain of knowledge is viewed as largely or even partly self-determining (in the sense that knowledge is built through specific disciplinary requirements and imperatives, which though not immune to social and political determinants are never entirely reducible to these) then there is a sense in which education may be seen as serving the requirements of knowledge production and transmission, among other aims it may have.

The natural starting point of the kind of complex account I have outlined could be taken to be John Dewey. And it is true that Dewey does indeed try to integrate an account of curriculum and pedagogy within the framework of the conceptualising of a democratic society, in which the role of education is that of developing individuals with a democratic cast of mind. However, there are certain shortcomings with Dewey's account.[2] The first is that while Dewey eschews a simple-minded reductionism concerning the role of knowledge *vis-à-vis* its putative social basis, the workings of a pragmatist epistemology tend to make the drivers of knowledge consist of the emergence of problems that arise through experience. The idea that knowledge has its own drivers, contained within disciplinary prerogatives, is not one that Dewey entertains with any sustained purpose, and certainly not in a way that could inform an account of educational change. The second difficulty with Dewey is that he is loath to take seriously the idea of educative traditions. Indeed, he is in earnest when he wishes to dissolve those traditions so that education (in the form of pedagogy and curriculum) is essentially a response to current societal conditions. But the most significant weakness in Dewey's approach is a failure to situate a vision of a democratic concept of education within a configuration of culture and power which, as it happens, tends to undermine that vision. The problem is not so much that the democratic vision is hard to realise but that in Dewey's account we are at a loss to understand why this might be the case. It is for this reason – and this is to cast no doubt on Dewey's radical credentials – that a deeper, more nuanced account is needed. It needs to shed light on this initial question: 'How does one conceptualise the *dual* role of education which both *maintains* a power-cultural complex and also *holds out the promise of change*?' And one person had some answers to this question. His name: Antonio Gramsci.

In the domain of educational theory Gramsci's claims rest, in the eyes of many, on a short passage of fifteen pages or so in the *Selections from Prison Notebooks*[3] (1971) where Gramsci seems to be extolling the virtues of what in England, at any rate, would pass for a traditional grammar school education.[4] That is, Gramsci appears to be advocating the merits of a knowledge-driven curriculum over those of a more vocational curriculum, and moreover appears to be strongly in favour of an instructional component lying at the heart of pedagogy, evincing a certain scepticism of activity-based learning.[5] Making use of Gramsci in order to make a polemical intervention can be traced back to the 1970s (at least, in the UK) with the publication of Harold Entwistle's *Antonio Gramsci: Conservative Schooling for Radical Politics* in 1979. Entwistle (unlike some of Gramsci's later advocates) broadly endorsed the Marxist politics of Gramsci, but argued that 'conservative schooling' was in the interests of a radicalised working class. Entwistle's book was soon sharply attacked in a review symposium that included the advocate of radical pedagogy, Henry A. Giroux.[6] But before evaluating some of the claims and counter-claims regarding Gramsci's ideas on curriculum and pedagogy it is necessary to consider the role that the concept of hegemony plays in Gramsci's broader theory of politics.

Hegemony and education

The concept of hegemony emerged through a study of Italian political history in which Gramsci noted that for a social group to emerge supreme, two factors are involved: domination – the exercise of coercive power which could include subjugation through armed force; and the exercise of 'intellectual and moral leadership' so that such a group 'becomes dominant when it exercises power, but even if it holds it firmly in its grasp, it must continue to 'lead' as well' (Gramsci, 1971: 57–58). According to one commentator, hegemony is exercised primarily through the consent given by subaltern groups[7] to the leadership – moral, intellectual, cultural – exercised by dominant groups (Femia, 1981: 31). Hegemony consists in the supremacy of a set of ideas that privilege some social groups over others, that privilege certain activities over others. A good example would be the near-universal hegemonic position of business activity and the associated role of business leadership in most developed countries. Femia's point is that hegemony is exercised through *voluntary* agreement by subordinate groups and initially suggests that hegemony consists solely in dominance of ideas (24). A further implication is that dominance can be achieved through the configurement of institutions and agencies of civil society, with the state playing a subordinate role in establishing supremacy. But within a few pages, Femia goes on to suggest that there is an 'interpenetration of the two spheres', i.e. state and civil society (27), leaving the reader perplexed as to just what hegemony actually consists of.

The most convincing analysis is that of Perry Anderson (1976). Anderson suggests that there are three versions of hegemony elaborated by Gramsci in his *SPN*. In the first, it is suggested that there is a preponderance of civil society over the state, which is equivalent to a preponderance of 'hegemony' over coercion. This echoes Femia's initial analysis (noted above) in so far as hegemony is seen as being exercised through cultural dominance so that the acceptance of hegemony is largely consensual. Anderson's complaint about this version is that it neglects the 'juridical-political component of the state' (29): notwithstanding the role played by what might be termed 'cultural hegemony', it needs to be supplemented by state activity and back-up. This leads us to the second version in which hegemony is distributed between state and civil society.[8] Anderson suggests that this is an advance on the first version and only needs to be supplemented by a recognition that the state plays an explicit coercive role *in addition* to its juridical-political activities (31–32). The third version is only hinted at by Gramsci but Anderson detects, in Gramsci, the thought that state and civil society are merged into a larger unity. But since this abolishes the distinction between state and civil society by making all ideological/cultural activities a putative domain of the state, Anderson rejects this as being unrealistic.

We are left, then, with the second version, which gives the state a role in maintaining hegemony through a variety of activities – some of which include legalised coercion. If we confine ourselves to examining the role of education in maintaining hegemonic domination the role of the state can, of course, vary widely. In some European countries (e.g. Prussia in the nineteenth century) the state set up schools and universities partly to produce a trained cadre of civil servants (in Prussia, these were seen as providing a counter-balance to the influence of the aristocratic Junker class – see Moore, 2004: 67–71). In the United Kingdom, the state has progressively increased both the scope and intensity of its educational activities. These include non-coercive measures (e.g. the introduction of a national curriculum in 1988) and coercive measures that are explicitly designed to modify teacher behaviour, such as the formation of the current schools inspection regime in 1992. Moreover, the hegemonic influence of business interests in the UK is also reflected in the growth of performance management systems in schools, systems which originated in the private sector (Mahony and Hextall, 2001: 175). All of these initiatives show the way in which the state acts to correct and neutralise possible counter-hegemonic tendencies (e.g. ones that emanate from the teaching profession itself). All of these measures command the broad support from those involved in school governance: they are not merely 'imposed' on unwilling local interests by an arrogant and overweening state; rather the justifications are couched in terms of a discourse of efficiency and standards which is widely accepted. The discourse of efficiency therefore provides a supportive background in terms of which the state is able to make its interventions through guidelines and codes of practice. At the same time, the sanction of the schools inspection regime is always on hand, just in case the message has not got through.

It is important to note that from Gramsci's standpoint the analysis of hegemony and the role of education was not merely a question of theoretical speculation. Despite being held in prison while elaborating these thoughts, Gramsci had a particular purpose that was orientated to a question of 'praxis', as he would have put it: given a particular historical configuration, what is the precise role of the 'New Machiavelli', as he imaginatively termed the modern political party, drawing explicitly on the 'activist' stance that he detected in Machiavelli's *The Prince*. His writings have an urgency that Anderson succeeds in capturing as he orientates his discussion of Gramsci in the context of political conflict in the 1970s. In particular, Anderson notes that oppositional forces need to establish a leadership through hegemonic activity (Anderson, 1976: 45; Gramsci, 1971: 57–58).[9] This opens up one role for education in the 'political activist' sense: for Gramsci, education was a key means whereby cadres of the working class and oppositional groups could challenge the prevailing hegemony and establish a supremacy in the domain of ideas prior to taking state power. This would make education, from a Gramscian standpoint, another potent political weapon but still a means to an end (political power). However, Gramsci's analysis of the role that education plays goes much deeper than that of the activist perspective.

In considering the role of education, Gramsci observes that 'the relationship between teacher and pupil is active and reciprocal' and then goes on to observe, however, that this educational relationship 'should not be restricted to the field of strictly scholastic relationships'. He then suggests that:

> this form of relationship exists throughout society as a whole and for every individual relative to other individuals. It exists between intellectual and non-intellectual sections of the population, between rulers and the ruled, elites and their original followers, leaders and the led, the vanguard and the body of the army. Every relationship of 'hegemony' is necessarily an educational relationship.
>
> (Gramsci, 1971: 350)

What is interesting here is that Gramsci is not merely saying that hegemonic relations are *cultural* but that they are educational – that is, hegemony is maintained and developed through a directed endeavour that while not always scholastic or school-based nonetheless is purposive in a number of respects: to re-enforce the moral authority of those in power, to develop perspectives that include some ideas and exclude others and to assist in the development of a self-identity for persons appropriate to their station in life. The contrast with cultural relations between persons is evident, since relations of hegemony are not ones that are merely participative, sharing and optional: these educative relationships have a certain necessity inscribed within them.

Gramsci is here alluding to more than government concern over curriculum, pedagogy and teacher education although the activities of central government in this respect certainly amount to the promotion of hegemonic relationships. Less visible in terms of policy but still potent are the differing educative tropes that serve as powerful signifiers that modify both perceptions of self-identity and behaviour. One of the most significant of these is that of 'the lifelong learner' in which pedagogy is transferred from the teacher to the individual whose identity is structured through what we have already termed an auto-pedagogy (see p. 78) that has a number of features. Essentially, auto-pedagogy can be seen as constituting a set of disciplinary procedures and methods through which individual identities are constructed *by the individual him or herself*. Thus, the individual becomes their own teacher who has to 'learn how to learn' and 'manage' their own learning. There is virtually no experience that cannot count as learning and there is virtually no activity that cannot be learnt. In this way the individual must acquire the identity of a learner from cradle to grave.[10] Finally, learning needs to be translated into assets that can be marketed. It should be noticed that the trope of 'learner' excludes or minimises the trope of 'researcher', 'reflector' or 'creator', not because learning is passive (after all, lifelong learning consists of 'active' learning if nothing else) but because of the implication that learning is a form of consumption.[11] The learning that goes on is primarily orientated to the consumption of knowledge and skills.

It was Jean-Francois Lyotard, in *The Postmodern Condition* (Lyotard, 1984: 47–54) who declared that it would no longer be enough to acknowledge the possession of understanding and knowledge in themselves as indicating effectiveness. What would count, rather, would be the extent to which knowledge and understanding could be operationalised. Moreover, understanding over and above what was needed for operationalisation was redundant. Correspondingly, the idea that value could be attached to learning for its own sake was also redundant. Post-modernity, therefore, heralded a ruthless pragmatism in the production of knowledge. Moreover, operationalised knowledge itself could – indeed would – become swiftly redundant. There was simply no *point* in attaching value to something so transitory: our knowledge worker needs to discard outmoded knowledge – and move on. Lyotard thought that criteria which legitimated knowledge would cease to be discursive and instead become performative, where performance is defined in terms of measurable outputs and impacts that can be quickly used, transferred and disseminated. The 'learner' therefore has this dual role of both the consumer of learning 'services' and the consumer of operationalised knowledge that is packeted up into bundles.

By contrast, it is instructive to consider the educative trope that Gramsci entertained since it permeates much of his thinking about education and the relation between education and hegemony. In the section of the *Notebooks* entitled *The Study of Philosophy*, Gramsci proposes the idea that 'it is essential to destroy the widespread prejudice that philosophy is a strange and difficult thing' and goes on to suggest that 'it must first be shown that all men are philosophers' (Gramsci, 1971: 323). He does not mean, as a matter of fact, that all persons think in a critical manner and are familiar at handling arguments and abstract concepts. But he does think that all 'men' have the potential to be philosophers and gives a number of reasons as to why this is the case. One reason is that engagement with language carries with it a specific conception of the world, even if this is disjointed. Moreover, 'there is no human activity from which every form of intellectual participation can be excluded: *homo faber* cannot be separated from *homo sapiens*' and Gramsci amplifies this thought as follows:

> Each man . . . carries on some form of intellectual activity, that is, he is a 'philosopher', an artist, a man of taste, he participates in a particular conception of the world, has a conscious line of moral conduct, and therefore contributes to sustain a conception of the world or to modify it, that is, to bring into being new modes of thought.
>
> (1971: 9)

The idea of the modern intellectual was further seen as someone who is no longer engaged primarily in rhetoric but someone who has an 'active participation in practical life, as constructor, organiser' (1971: 10). This is not someone who exists as a mere learner: for Gramsci, each person has a philosophical-intellectual dimension that enables them to play a part in constructing society both in terms of its physical, material character and at the level of meaning. The trope of philosopher lies at the very heart of the counter-hegemonic education that Gramsci favoured. The hallmark of the philosopher, then, is a certain critical stance within an historical juncture. It is not so much the discovery of an essential self that lies within but the creation or construction of an historical/political self whose dynamic is sustained through critical activity. The philosopher-intellectual is not merely 'bookish'; rather his or her critical stance arises directly out of a sustained engagement with the world, an engagement that could take on a technical or professional character (Coben, 2002: 271).

Brief reflection on the trope of 'lifelong learner' makes it clear why this is entirely unsuitable for use in counter-hegemonic activity. For this trope is utterly immersed in a world of employability in which *criticality* is not a feature that requires any more than a passing recognition. By contrast, counter-hegemonic activity needs a different trope that is built on critical engagement and which therefore is to some degree dependent on a familiarity with theory and philosophy. For the lifelong learner no alternative imaginary is required and so the intellectual and creative resources needed to construct such an imaginary are simply redundant.[12] In particular, whereas the trope of the philosopher-intellectual requires a deep engagement with historically grounded possibilities, the lifelong learner must be locked into the present; history is for the merely curious.

For Gramsci, the emergence of a philosopher does not happen by chance and cannot be left to a person's own efforts. There needs to be a sustained educative process, which has to be directed towards the development of a critical stance. Gramsci does not adopt the approach associated with Rousseau for whom intellectual growth could occur of its own accord providing the child/student is placed in an appropriate environment (Entwistle, 1979: 55–57, Adamson, 1980: 156). For Gramsci, the non-Rousseauian approach arises out of the philosophy of praxis, particularly redolent of Marx's third and sixth theses on Feuerbach (Easton and Guddat, 1967: 401–402). It is there that Marx critiques the concept of an essence of man as a 'dumb generality' and calls attention to the need of 'educating the educators'; Entwistle suggests this implies that in educating we must select *from* the environment so that learning becomes a purposive, organised endeavour (Entwistle, 1979: 61).[13]

For Gramsci, just as the philosopher-intellectual is historically formed so is the non-critical raw material on which education is to work. The teacher educates children/students who *already* have perspectives and outlooks which amount to the non-critical baggage of what Gramsci terms 'common sense'. Common sense too has a history (Gramsci, 1971: 325–326) and counter-hegemonic education may have to directly challenge and confront it.

By 'common sense', Gramsci is referring to what he terms a 'chaotic aggregate of disparate conceptions' though he goes on to say that this 'does not mean that there are no truths in common sense'. Yet he immediately qualifies his qualification by saying that 'common sense is an ambiguous, contradictory and multiform concept and that to refer to common sense as a confirmation of truth is a nonsense' (422–423). There is no definitive conception of common sense termed 'the philosophy of non-philosophers', of which 'its most fundamental characteristic is that it is a conception which, even in the brain of one individual, is fragmentary, incoherent and inconsequential, in conformity with the social and cultural position of the masses whose philosophy it is' (419).

Earlier in *SPN* he gives common sense an almost post-modernist character by terming it 'an infinity of traces, without leaving an inventory' (324). At the same time, Gramsci qualifies this view by insisting that 'we are all conformists of some conformism or other, always man-in-the-mass or collective man' and that these views and beliefs associated with common sense are an amalgam of 'stone age elements and principles of more advanced science, prejudices from all past phases of history at a local level and intuitions of a future philosophy' (324). The business of raising oneself above common sense is a task that confronts all individuals and the implication is that this is a continuous process. Aspects of common sense do indeed contain what Gramsci terms 'good sense' and in *SPN* (328) he gives an example of the belief in the need to 'overcome bestial and elemental passions through a conception of necessity which gives a conscious direction to one's activity'. The educator must start by accepting and acknowledging the beliefs associated with common sense in order to develop more critical and coherent perspectives on the part of her students. Above all, we can say that common sense reflects and helps to maintain a particular hegemonic order. One example of such a belief was the view held by most Englishmen and women prior to 1642 that the King not only had a right to rule but that Parliament was subordinate to this right. There are many examples of 'common sense' in contemporary times. For example, in the twenty-first century in most western countries there exists the widespread belief that aesthetic opinions are 'subjective' and that no criteria exist by which one piece of art could be judged 'superior' to another. Or again, many subscribe to what may be termed the 'condescension of posterity' in that persons (for example) who engaged in religious controversy and conflict at the time of the Reformation were essentially misguided; fortunately (so it is commonly held), we now know better. Mixed with these questionable views are others of a more solid, reassuring kind – those, for example, that involve the treatment of children and the importance of kindness.[14] For Gramsci, an educative order simply fails if it merely consolidates common sense. Pedagogies that fail to move learners on from common sense, no matter how benign and comfortable, also fail to recognise that 'all men are philosophers'.[15]

There is, however, another aspect to common sense too: namely those beliefs held by subaltern groups, beliefs that confirm their members in their state of dependency. Thus the common sense of subaltern groups takes on a specific character of fatalism, submissiveness and a certain helplessness and resignation. Gramsci suggests that a 'mechanistic conception of reality has been a religion of the subalterns' (337) and goes on to link such a conception with a particular form of Christianity, which focuses on the interiority of the soul. But he also explores another aspect of 'mechanism', which is the separation of theory and practice, observing that this separation is merely conventional (335) and that 'people speak about theory as a 'complement' or an 'accessory' of practice, or as a handmaid of practice'. As Diana Coben (2002) observes, the notion that theory should be subordinate to practice is another facet of the religion of the subaltern (270). And it is with some degree of clarity that Gramsci firmly distinguishes the outlook of dependency from one that is self-determined:

> Is it better to take part in a conception of the world mechanically imposed by the external environment, i.e. by one of the many social groups in which everyone is automatically involved from the moment of his entry into the

conscious world (and this can be one's own village or province; it can have its origins in the parish and the 'intellectual activity' of the local priest or ageing patriarch whose wisdom is law, or in the little old woman who has inherited the lore of witches or the minor intellectual soured by his own stupidity and inability to act)? Or, on the other hand, is it better to work out, consciously and critically one's own conception of the world and thus, in connection with the labours of one's own brain, choose one's sphere of activity, take an active part in the creation of the history of the world, be one's own guide, refusing to accept passively and supinely from outside the moulding of one's personality?

(Gramsci, 1971: 323–324)

Gramsci worked within the Marxist tradition and does not evince any explicit commitment to republican liberty. Moreover, his reading of Machiavelli appears to be mainly structured by *The Prince*, with little or no awareness of *The Discourses*; his interest in that figure is mainly in drawing links between the political activism expressed in Renaissance Italy and the activism needed in the early twentieth century in the struggle against fascism. Nevertheless, Gramsci does not merely evince a sympathy for some of the main tenets of republican liberty but he also, through the concept of hegemony, provides a theory of dependency/supremacy which lifts this relation out of person-to-person and into the domain of the social and political. Through the concept of hegemony, republicans are armed with a concept of *power*.

The concept of hegemony provides a framework in which the absence of liberty can be identified through an elaboration of the subaltern role. It also provides a way of understanding how education can play a part in producing and sustaining this role – both through the organisation of education and through the tropes and signifiers that create a web of meaning, which apparently confirms subalternship. However, education is also the site on which counter-hegemonic activities can be developed. Understood in terms of liberty, these activities signify attempts to escape dependency and to found a different kind of hegemony – one which heralds relations between liberty-bearing persons, relations free of ties of dependency. In the next section we shall examine some of the ways in which Gramsci thought this could be achieved.

Gramsci's concept of education

It is in the light of this theoretical orientation that Gramsci's views on education are best understood. Too often he is used, when he is used at all, by advocates of one pedagogy or another as a respected intellectual with which to beat their opponents. In so far as such terms have any meaning at all, he can be seen in turn as 'conservative' or 'radical' in his educational views. But before discussing these in more detail there are two points worth remembering. The first is that his ideas on education were part of a broader political theory and in so far as he appears to be advocating a specific pedagogical or curricular approach then these particular views should not be interpreted as being his *permanent* views. Those views were mediated by a specific historical conjuncture so that it is somewhat fatuous to suppose that what Gramsci advocated in the Italy of the 1920s and 1930s would be identical to what he would say, were he alive, in Britain or the United States in the twenty-first century. The second point to remember is that Gramsci clearly thought long and hard about education. The pages in *SPN* where he puts forward his views are bristling with ideas, all the more potent because of the compressed way in which he was prone to write – those pages require two or three reads to understand fully and they comprise, without doubt, one of the best essays on education that has been written in the twentieth century. However, one still needs to remember that Gramsci had never taught in a formal school and that although he had certainly engaged in worker education as part of his political activities, his views had never been tested through a continuing professional engagement either with the practice of education or with some of its theoretical foundations. Moreover, Gramsci himself, certainly in the *SPN*, never had the opportunity while in prison to debate and discuss his views and through discussion come to modify them. It would be mistaken, therefore, to assume that specific pedagogical recommendations represent Gramsci's definitive and final word.

Although the discussion in *SPN* is wide ranging and discursive a number of themes emerge which help us to structure Gramsci's ideas. In fact about halfway through his account he introduces one of the main themes, namely the search for what is termed an 'educational principle'. Perhaps rather surprisingly he says this comprises 'work', which some have interpreted in terms of a pedagogy that is task-driven and intensive.[16] But it is precisely here that some awareness of the Marxist/humanist provenance of Gramsci's thinking is needed. The discussion of work is first of all premised on the twin observation that schooling has had two purposes: first to educate children into the principles of scientific ideas (in contrast to superstition and folklore) and second into the principles governing civil society (in contrast to the arbitrary nature of local customs). But then the discussion moves up a further gear when Gramsci observes that 'work is the specific mode by which man actively participates in natural life in order to transform and socialise it more and more deeply' (34). He goes on to say that work involves 'theoretical and practical activity' through which a human world is created that is free of magic and superstition and which is populated by people who 'appreciate the sum of effort and sacrifice which the present has cost the past and which the future is costing the present and which conceives the contemporary world as a synthesis of the past ... which projects itself into the future'. Thus 'work' takes on the character of that practico-theoretical activity that Marx started to identify in his 1844 manuscripts as forming the basis of his 'materialist' conception of human activity: a conception that fuses technical, practical and theoretical activity into *praxis*. Gramsci, of course, had not had any sight of the 1844 manuscripts which were not to be published until 1932 in German – which makes his achievement all the more remarkable. For Gramsci, this *praxis* has an historical dimension and this conception determines the way he thinks about education, which becomes the purposeful direction of human activity that transforms its agents. This is why work is not confined to the workplace and why any attempts to conceive learning along the conventional ideas of 'work' are seriously misconstrued.[17]

Once we have grasped the significance of work and the way in which it is conceived as historical praxis, other themes mentioned by Gramsci start to fall into place. First, we can see education as a purposeful endeavour in which pupils and students learn to become bearers of praxis through learning activities. This forms the basis around which relations of care and well-being are conceived: thus well-being (for example) is not an inert mental state: rather our well-being is to be determined through human relations, which always already have an historical character and determination. But even more importantly than this, we can see why Gramsci thinks that there is no automatic unity between school and 'life'. For if, within an historical conjuncture, there is a rupture between life as characterised by folklore, localism, fatalism and subaltern values of dependency then the role of pedagogy becomes even more difficult for the teacher since there will be 'a contrast between the type of culture and society which he represents and the type of culture and society represented by his pupils' and a corresponding need 'to accelerate and regulate the child's formation in conformity with the former and in conflict with the latter' (35–36). It is for this reason that Gramsci believes that an instructional component to pedagogy is inescapable since without it there will be no escape from the values of the subaltern. The aim of pedagogy, therefore, is not to regiment the child along predetermined paths which confirm that child as to her place in the world: the aim of pedagogy (and instruction) is precisely to do the exact opposite. Pedagogy therefore has a counter-hegemonic urgency.[18]

That the educational principle of praxis also has an historical dimension goes a long way to explain Gramsci's attitude to the curriculum. For if praxis – practical and theoretical activity – is seen as the 'synthesis of the past which projects itself into the future' then the curriculum itself would be a reflection of this synthesis. Indeed, we would expect the curriculum to be the active working out of this synthesis, if we construe learning itself as a form of praxis. This means, of course, that the curriculum has an historical provenance and so it should come as no surprise that for Gramsci it should not only be 'formative' but that it should impart a 'general, humanistic culture' (27). That, historically speaking, this form of curriculum had only been available to an elite does not detract from its being the product of praxis, the engagement with which is a precondition for a formative education for persons who are not merely self-determining but are able, of themselves, to carry on 'projecting into the future'. And although Gramsci fully recognises that Latin and Greek need to be replaced by modern languages as curricular subjects, he nonetheless insists that a broadly humanistic curriculum is needed as a precursor to future specialisation, including vocational education. Specialisation (of a vocational nature) that took place too early would mean that children and students would be disengaged from their past and disconnected from possible futures; as mere prisoners of the present, children would already be set up for a life of dependency in which the creeds of the subaltern classes would be taken as great truths.

Linked, however, with the common curriculum is another educative principle: the common school. It was Gramsci's great historic achievement – despite his incarceration – to have successfully identified one of the key features of the Gentile Reform Act of 1923.[19] This was the multiplication, not only of types of curriculum (with a vocational, activity-based curriculum held to be more 'suitable' for most children and young adults) but the multiplication of types of school. Gramsci's words are worth quoting in full here:

> Schools of the vocational type, i.e. those designed to satisfy immediate, practical interests are beginning to predominate over the formative school, which is not immediately 'interested'. The most paradoxical aspect of it all is that this new type of school appears and is advocated as being democratic, while in fact it is destined not merely to perpetuate social differences but to crystallise them in Chinese complexities.
>
> (40)[20]

Gramsci was concerned that, in the Italy of his day, the move away from a common school to a variety of provision with a more vocational orientation would lead back 'to a division into juridicially fixed and crystallised estates rather than moving towards the transcendence of class divisions' (41). Thus, for Gramsci, the common school was counter-hegemonic not in the sense that it was a revolutionary weapon in the manner of a 'new Machiavelli' but because it formed the basis of a counterweight to social division, in which some classes and groups were destined for a dependent or subaltern role. At the same time, the temptation to diminish curricular strength in favour of social relevance also ran the risk of merely confirming members of lower social groups in their subaltern role. For if, under the call of 'relevancy', the appeal was to that of 'interests' then this could only mean the interests of those already characterised by dependency. The purpose of schooling, for these children, would be merely that of training them up for a future subalternship.

It is for the same kind of reasons that Gramsci was concerned that the instructional component of learning be preserved. The danger of what he termed the 'new pedagogy' was that if the 'nexus between instruction and education is dissolved, while the problem of teaching is conjured away by cardboard schemata exalting educativity, the teacher's work will as a result become yet more inadequate' (36). However, it is worth noting that Gramsci does not endorse the teaching of more information: while he is concerned that the customary 'baggage of concrete facts' may be imperilled he recognises that even the acquisition of this, by itself, does not amount to an *education*, for the accumulation of information only amounts to the mechanical part of teaching (36). Thus, for Gramsci, there are two features of what characterises an inferior pedagogy: the first is where there is no instructional component at all and where schools are merely 'rhetorical'; the second is where instruction is mechanical and produces the mere accumulation of facts and information. While criticism of the latter feature was entirely legitimate, the replacement of this with a pedagogy of 'cardboard schemata' was no answer either. It is at this point that

Gramsci does not, unfortunately, deepen what he means by instruction. But it is not too far-fetched (given his strictures against mechanical teaching of facts) to suppose that a theory of instruction along the lines of his contemporary, Vygotsky, would not have been uncongenial; the domain of instruction being precisely defined as the difference between what the learner knows and what she is able to achieve with assistance. This indicates the well-known 'zone of proximal development' (Vygotsky, 1962: 103) and identifies the kind of instruction which 'marches ahead of development and leads it' (104). Vygotsky's methodology assumes that the learner is, or can be, 'active' and this is precisely the point Gramsci (1971) makes when he criticises the view that holds that education is *separate* from instruction since 'for instruction to be wholly distinct from education, a pupil would have to be pure passivity, a 'mechanical receiver' of abstract notions – which is absurd' (35).

However, there is one other important aspect to Gramsci's thinking about pedagogy which others have not overlooked (Giroux *et al.*, 1980: 317). This concerns the passage from an instructional mode of learning to one that is more creative, in which the pupil passes to a phase of 'independent, autonomous work'. Indeed, Gramsci makes a distinction between an 'active' school – that is one in which learners are not merely passive – and a creative school which does not indicate a school of 'inventors and discoverers' as much as a 'method of research and of knowledge', in which the teacher exercises a function of 'friendly guide'. For, according to Gramsci, there can come a stage in a pupil's maturity – particularly regarding the emergence of investigative powers – when 'to discover a truth oneself is to create – even if the truth is an old one' (1971: 31–33). Gramsci clearly has in mind the idea that the creative phase is preceded by a phase of education that is instructional and even 'dogmatic (31) and here, one feels, one would like to demur. Why, one wonders – accepting the point that instruction is a part of education – cannot the creative phase be one that is entertained for younger children, even very young children? Given, as Gramsci emphasises himself, that creativity does not imply 'originality of research' why is it not possible to envisage learning as taking a creative character that complements learning in its instructional mode?

As an example of what I mean, one can do no better than to turn to an illustration of a comparative analysis of children's essays as set out by Lawrence Stenhouse in his 1967 *Culture and Education*. There, Stenhouse discusses contrasting work by 11-year-old children with a view to assessing contrasting teaching methods. The first piece of work that he presents was written under relatively formal pedagogic conditions with the given title, 'A Happy Day'. A brief extract will suffice:

As the children walked along the country lane, in the beautiful island of Tiree. They felt very happy. The sun was shining, the sky was cloudless and a lovely blue.

'Oh! I'm so hot!' said John

'So am I!' said his sister Mary. They walked on in silence until John stopped and said,

'Listen!' They listened, and then decided to go and see.

'Oh!' exclaimed Mary, 'It's a little stream!'

They pulled off their socks and shoes and ran in, exclaiming at the coolness. They paddled around for a while in the bubbling sparkling water and then decided to carry on, walking beside the stream.

The two of them walked on until they came to a small wooden hut, which had a boy of about the same age in it.

(Stenhouse, 1967: 79–81)

Stenhouse comments that this composition shows considerable accomplishment in that the grammar and spelling is virtually perfect. The teaching has been effective: it has extended the children's vocabulary, for example. He also remarks that the composition does rather conform to expectations, that the emotions expressed are somewhat trite and the writing is not to be taken too seriously; he goes on to wonder if the children themselves were writing (albeit effectively and successfully) for an approving audience (1967: 79–81).

He then provides an extract of a quite different piece of writing from children of a similar age:

My name is Maria. My home is in the Pyrenees, the Pyrenees being high mountains in Spain. I live in the poorer part of the country where people find it hard to survive. The only pleasure we have in life is drinking our wine which we take from the vine but this too is getting poorer. The reason for this is that the soil is barren. It has been farmed for countless centuries and is old and tired. To make matters worse the strong winds that blow every autumn carry it away. Life gets harder and harder every year. Soon after I married a man called Fernando Bertally. You see I was promised to him and I was only a child and he also. My father and his were friends when boys. So it is in Spain. For after his marriage he gew to love me in his fasion. The fasion of all men in Spain who think it is the lot of women to work like a beast of burden. But he is kind and does not whip me as is also the fasion in my country. For me it is all bad . . . One day I will look in the mirrow and find myself an old woman, no longer beautiful.

(Stenhouse, 1967: 82)

Stenhouse then explains that the second piece of work had developed out of a reading of a poem by Hilaire Belloc, *Tarantella*, which depicts a deserted, ruined place that had once been a place of human enjoyment. This had evolved into a play in which most of the children had a part: the composition above emerged out of a child's reflections on the particular role she had chosen to play. As Stenhouse himself says, the teaching involved here is one of particular skill. But for him, it represents a creative approach to learning which involves a different standard of what is regarded as excellence in writing. For the second piece is marred by spelling and grammatical imperfections: these, however, do not detract from its merits. For it is more ambitious and the writer is right at the limits of her accomplishment in the attempt to capture a felt experience, from the inside. Above all she is trying to be creative: as Stenhouse puts it, 'They are artists, and the standard they set themselves will accordingly always be a little beyond their grasp' (83).

It is not necessary to wait until post-puberty years for creativity to flourish, as Gramsci thought. And while every pupil requires a platform of capability, which may well need to be established through instructional forms of learning, it is not only those platforms themselves which are the object of good teaching: from an early age, each new platform can be the site of creativity. The danger (and this will not have escaped many perceptive readers) of waiting until the child is a young adult before creative forms of learning are unleashed is that already the habits of the subaltern may be formed: the writing and arithmetic may be accurate but the mentality – the *habitus* – of dependency may already have started to crystallise. On the other hand, the child who, from an early age, has set themselves tasks 'a little beyond their grasp' is unlikely to be successfully groomed for a life of dependency.[21]

Conclusion

Gramsci's reflections on education have a fourfold significance.

First, Gramsci situates the role of education within a wider theory of hegemony, which enables us to grasp the links between education, culture and power. Yet at the same time, this is not a reductionist approach: education is still seen as having a history and a dynamic. It is because Gramsci takes a non-reductionist stance that education can also be a counter-hegemonic force. Theorists who see educational process as the mere epiphenomenon of a structural interplay of power no longer have the option of employing education as an oppositional force. This leads to an excessive reliance on political activism and a crude anti-intellectualism.

Second, Gramsci, through grounding education on the philosophy of praxis, is able to take a wider view of what counts as education. Since the organic intellectual is both a thinker and an organiser, educational development can take place in the workplace and in different stages in life – a point emphasised with good effect by Entwistle (1979), particularly in the second half of that book in which he discusses adult education.

Third, because the philosophy of praxis has itself an historical dimension – so that praxis is the outcome of historic accruals and is never complete – education itself also has an historic dimension. Learning is no longer the prisoner of the present but has a critical dimension precisely because the historical perspective is the only way of achieving praxis as a reflective activity. For Gramsci, reflection without history is meaningless.

Fourth, Gramsci provides proponents of republican liberty with a theory of power – i.e. hegemony – in which liberty as non-dependency is at its very heart. For the exercisers of hegemony over subaltern groups keep those groups in a state of dependency, which is reflected both in actions and beliefs. These beliefs enter into their very awareness of their own identities and configure for them what is possible and what is not possible. At the same time, Gramsci gives those who occupy a subordinate role a way of overcoming their dependency and of attaining emancipation – namely, a state of liberty. The principal method is that of education because it is this that drives political activism. The path to liberty lies through education.

Notes

1 'Children may be cozen'd into a Knowledge of Letters; to be taught to read, without perceiving it to be anything but a Sport, and play themselves into that which others are whipp'd for' (Locke, 1989: 209).
2 See Dewey (1916: 87–106).
3 Henceforth referred to as *SPN*. The passage comprises pages 24–43. A few other, apparently scattered, remarks are also frequently alluded to.
4 This, for example, appears to be the view of the UK Secretary of State for Education, Michael Gove. For a speech given in February 2013 warmly praising Gramsci, see www.smf.co.uk/media/news/michael-gove-speaks-smf/ (accessed 22 March).
5 An advocate of a knowledge-based curriculum in the USA, E.D. Hirsch (1996: 6–7) reads Gramsci as saying just this.
6 See Giroux *et al.* (1980) for an unremittingly hostile review of Entwistle on the grounds that he had systematically distorted Gramsci's thinking. But in the same symposium, the translator of Gramsci, Quinton Hoare, though not uncritical, is much more sympathetic to Entwistle's position. Giroux returned to the fray again in 1999, attacking Entwistle once more, as well as Hirsch – see Giroux (1999).
7 The term 'subaltern' is used by Gramsci to refer to subordinate groups or persons. Subalterns are in a position of dependence.
8 'Every state tends to create and maintain a certain type of civilisation and of citizen . . . then the Law will be its instrument for this purpose together with the school system and other institutions and activities' (Gramsci, 1971: 246).
9 Oppositional forces may be said to engage in 'counter-hegemonic' activity; but it should not be thought that this amounts to actions against all forms of hegemony. Rather, oppositional forces are merely countering a specific kind of hegemony with the aim of establishing a different kind of hegemony. Hegemony as such cannot be abolished.
10 See also Chapter 6. One must 'acquire the self-image of a lifelong learner' (Knapper and Cropley, 2000: 49). See also Michael Barber's *The Learning Game* for an account of the 'learning society' (e.g. 1996: 239–241 and *passim*). Barber was an education advisor to the New Labour government of Tony Blair, 1997–2001.
11 These ideas are further discussed in Hinchliffe (2006). For an entertaining account of the evangelism that can surround the trope of learning, see Frank Coffield (2000: 1–8).
12 Throughout the UK government investment in humanist-based adult education has collapsed since 2000.

13   Interestingly, this approach also tells against the methodology of learning outlined in Plato's *Meno* in which the teacher elicits cognitive skills and even knowledge that lay buried in the mind of the learner who merely needs the teacher to stimulate and bring forth what is *already there*.

14   One of the signs that a hegemonic order may be undergoing modification is when groups of persons in authority who have hitherto enjoyed extensive social respect, as a matter of routine common sense, now find that authority questioned: priests, elected representatives, bankers. The disruption of trust amounts to a direct assault on one of the elements of an historically determined common sense.

15   For a reliable account of common sense, see Coben (2002) to which my account is, in part, indebted.

16   e.g. Hirsch (1996: 6–7); Entwistle (1979: 53–54).

17   See Easton and Guddat (1967: especially 308–314). Marx crystallised his views in the *Theses on Feuerbach* – see the reference to 'practical-critical activity' (1967: 400–401).

18   See Giroux (1999: 7). Giroux, I think, is perfectly correct to criticise Entwistle's claim that 'a proper inference to be drawn from the work of Gramsci is that it is unrealistic to look to schools for a radical, counter-hegemonic education' (Entwistle, 1979: 176). However, Giroux himself does appear reluctant to fully acknowledge Gramsci's disdain of pedagogies that have no or little instructional component, a point that Entwistle fully grasps (see Entwistle, 1979: 64–68), pointing out that Gramsci himself does not suppose that instruction is premised on the passivity of pupils: different types of instruction may, on the contrary, call for a range of activity-based learning. But it is learning that is carefully set by the teacher in terms of the pre-preparation of stages and achievements of understanding and skills.

19   See Entwistle (1979: 92–104).

20   E.D. Hirsch deliberately assumes, in a misconstrued extract from *SPN* that 'Chinese complexity' refers to new pedagogical methods (see the epithet in Hirsch, 1996), whereas in fact it is absolutely clear that this refers to the multiplication of types of school and not (as Hirsch makes his readers believe), new types of pedagogy. Hirsch's misleading quote is taken over directly by Gove (2013), in which the whole point of what Gramsci is in favour of (namely, the common school) is passed over. As the subsequent discussion will make clear, for Gramsci, the common school and a common curriculum were fused.

21   There are many examples of innovative pedagogies that strive to develop creativity in the child. One such is the 'mantle of the expert', inspired by the teacher of drama, Dorothy Heathcote: 'Mantle of the Expert is based on the premise that treating children as responsible experts increases their engagement and confidence' – see http://dramaresource.com/strategies/mantle-of-the-expert (accessed 22 March). For a school that uses this methodology as part of its pedagogy, see the website of Recreation Road Infant School, Norwich: www.recreationroad.com/pages/ (accessed 22 March). The school's professed aim is to treat children as critical thinkers and enquirers – see the school mission statement.

Conclusion

This book has covered much ground. The chapters that traced the genealogy of liberty are necessary because we, today, must understand that the quest for liberty by no means belongs to the recent past and that many of the essential arguments involved in the idea have been with us for centuries. This does not mean to say, of course, that what was meant by liberty in seventeenth-century England or fifteenth-century Florence is exactly the same for us today. I have tried to capture this thought in the historical approach that has been taken. For example, one thing that a historical perspective makes clear is that the discourse of liberty has receded in favour of what is essentially a discourse on individuality and the two are not the same. I have also been at pains to emphasise that the idea and the enactment of liberty is constructed and crafted through normative relations within a polity. Thus the idea that 'all men are born free' no doubt has metaphorical significance but both historically and philosophically it makes no sense at all. Our liberty can only be justified and preserved through decisions and judgements made within a state.

Perhaps one of the most widespread characteristics of developed states in the twenty-first century are the ties of dependency that have insinuated themselves in so many aspects of life. Indeed, so prevalent and sophisticated are these ties that individuals typically conceive their self-identity in terms of the roles they enact rather than thinking of themselves as liberty-bearing as such. These roles confer on individuals' differing degrees of mastery and subaltern status. Much of the language of managerialism produces precisely this effect: namely the designation of degrees of dependency and service status. By the same token, the endless vaunting of the importance of 'leadership' confers on individuals in senior positions absurd expectations that cannot possibly be fulfilled. Yet it is amazing how many persons, once elevated to higher stations in life, suddenly themselves realise and understand just how important leadership is.

But all is not lost. Those discourses on leadership, for example, can be turned round to a greater emphasis on shared leadership and shared responsibilities within organisations. This would mean that the culture of 'ownership' be shifted: rather than owning the responsibilities and ethical outlook characteristic of a subaltern, ownership could be an inclusive concept in which individuals take on responsibility for the wider concerns of an organisation. But the corollary of this is that those same individuals would also have the right to criticise and debate the ends of that organisation and the methods employed. So whereas our modern manager might well welcome the idea of shared responsibility he or she must also welcome critique – not a word that usually belongs in the manager's vocabulary.

I have tried to show, in particular, how the practice of education can be thought of in a way that would buttress and inform our thinking about liberty. For example, the idea of the space of reasons not only powerfully contributes to our understanding of knowledge; it also provides us with some idea of how liberty-bearing persons can conduct themselves with each other. The idea is that in an empire of liberty, within a genuinely free state, something like the space of reasons pervades all aspects of social life. This would include the corporate organisation so that the judgements that are made have to be defended and argued for. The business of living within a space of reasons is what life is for those who are endowed with liberty: education is best seen as a preparation for this.

I have also tried to show the connection between liberty and authority. It is appropriate authoritative structures that both enable the exercise of liberty and limit its scope. This is important because too often claims for more freedom, stripped of the authority context, merely end up as claims for control and mastery over others. Mastership, in all its many forms, often likes to claim liberty for itself and constructs sophisticated discourses that dress up control in the guise of freedom. By the same token, if authority is lacking – as is the case in England with respect to educational authority – then so are the liberties of those affected diminished accordingly.

I am acutely aware that certain ideas that could be very helpful for my argument still need to be explored further. For example, I have not availed myself of the writings of Foucault, and especially his views on the disciplinary self that is inserted within a nexus of complex power relations. It should be possible to explore the effects of micro-power relations on the possibility of constructing ourselves as liberty-bearing. Perhaps I (or indeed others) may be able to take this forward at some future date. But there is one idea in particular, however, about which a few more words could be said. I am thinking of the role of interference in free actions and how this can be justified and in particular, the role that interference may play in order to inhibit actions that may lead, whether intentionally or not, to greater dependency. For example, vast accumulations of wealth inevitably foster greater dependency through ties of patronage, something that the classical republicans were acutely aware of. But it should be noticed, from the standpoint of liberty, that it is not wealth as such that is objectionable. In a free state, some individuals may end up more prosperous than others, whether through luck or their own efforts (although it is noticeable that those who have become prosperous rarely attribute their good fortune to luck alone). Nevertheless, some restrictions on individual wealth accumulation are inevitable, on the grounds that it may come to threaten the liberty of others. Particularly pernicious are the vast accumulations of wealth for those who hold positions of authority. Thus something like the operation of Rawls' difference principle would become necessary to ensure that the distribution of wealth does not become such that a skewed distribution starts to seriously threaten the liberties of all. But the exact nature of distribution would vary.

However, the need for this kind of interference may be tempered by the presence of a culture of liberty. In particular, such a culture may generate feelings of horror that one might be assuming a position of mastery of others. This would be a culture in which the abhorrence of servitude is only matched by an equal abhorrence of mastery. What might be called the practice of mastership may, in time, come to be seen as something shameful and thoroughly degrading. One can but hope.

For many who have got this far, it may seem odd that I have failed to mention dependency in its most recognisable context: the supposed dependency on the state of those in receipt of welfare benefits. It is clear to me that this indeed is one possible form of dependency that may be accompanied by an unwillingness to take responsibility for one's actions. But it also seems to me that a free state simply cannot leave it at that. First, one needs to recognise the requirement for creating opportunities for breaking out of this dependency, and here the state has a clear role to play on the grounds that persons in this particular dependency relationship are, for whatever reason, not fully liberty-bearing. Second, it is imperative that the link between insurance and welfare is fully restored so that those taking, for example, unemployment benefit, do so as a matter of right. Finally, it goes without saying that a free state has a duty of care to those who are ill and frail.

One final point. There may be those who find it surprising that a book on republican liberty does not advocate full-hearted participation in civic affairs as one of the key elements of what is sometimes termed 'the good life'. Perhaps my reluctance fully to embrace civic rectitude arises from someone who belongs to a generation whose parents fought against the enforced participation in political life threatened by fascist elements and other totalitarians. On a theoretical level, my approach to republican liberty attempts to steer a path between communitarianism on the one hand and the baleful consequences of negative liberty on the other. I leave it to readers to judge how successful I have been.

Bibliography

Ackrill, J.L. (1980) 'Aristotle on Eudaimonia', in A.O. Rorty *Essays on Aristotle's Ethics*. Berkeley: University of California Press, pp. 15–33.

Adamson, W. (1980) *Hegemony and Revolution*. Berkeley: University of California Press.

Anderson, P. (1976) 'The Antinomies of Antonio Gramsci'. *New Left Review*. 100 (November 1976–January 1977).

Arendt, H. (1958) *The Human Condition*. Chicago: University of Chicago Press.

Arendt, H. (1977) *Between Past and Future*. London: Penguin Press.

Aristotle (1946) *Politics*. Translated by D. Ross. Oxford: Oxford University Press.

Aristotle (1980) *Nicomachean Ethic*. Translated by D. Ross. Oxford: Oxford University Press.

Auerbach, S. (2009) 'Some punishment should be devised: parents, children and the state in Victorian London'. *Historian*. 71 (4), pp. 757–779.

Aviram, A. and Assor, A. (2010) 'In defence of personal autonomy as a fundamental educational aim in Liberal Democracies: a response to Hand'. *Oxford Review of Education*. 36 (1), pp. 111–126.

Backhurst, D. (2011) *The Formation of Reason*. Oxford: Wiley-Blackwell.

Bailey, R. (ed.) (2010) *The Philosophy of Education*. London: Continuum.

Bantock, G.H. (1965) 'Education, Social Justice and the Sociologists', in G.H. Bantock *Education and Values*. London: Faber & Faber.

Barber, M. (1996) *The Learning Game*. London: Victor Gollancz.

Baron, H. (1966) *The Crisis of the Early Italian Renaissance*. Princeton, NJ: Princeton University Press.

Berlin, I. (1969) *Four Essays on Liberty*. Oxford: Oxford University Press.

Bernstein, B. (1971) 'Classification and Framing', in M. Young (ed.) *Knowledge and Control: New Direction for the Sociology of Education*. London: Collier-Macmillan.

Braddick, M. (2009) *God's Fury, England's Fire*. London: Penguin Books.

Brandom, R.B. (1994) *Making it Explicit*. Cambridge, MA: Harvard University Press.

Brown, G., Bull, J. and Pendlebury, M. (1997) *Assessing Student Learning in Higher Education*. London: Routledge.

Callan, E. (1997) *Creating Citizens: Political Education and Liberal Democracy*. Oxford: Oxford University Press.

Carter, I. (1999) *A Measure of Freedom*. Oxford: Oxford University Press.

Carter, I. (2008) 'How are Power and Freedom Related', in C. Laborde and J. Maynor (eds) *Republicanism and Political Theory*. Oxford: Blackwell Publishing, pp. 58–82.

Charvet, J. (1974) *The Social Problem in the Philosophy of Rousseau*. Cambridge: Cambridge University Press.

Charvet, J. (1993) 'Quentin Skinner on the idea of freedom'. *Studies in Political Thought*. 2 (1), pp. 5–16.

Churchill, W.S. (1930) *My Early Life*. London: Fontana Books.

Coben, D.C. (2002) 'Metaphors for an Educative Politics: "Common Sense", "Good Sense" and Educating Adults', in C. Borg, J. Buttleig and P. Mayo (eds) *Gramsci and Education*. Lanham, MD: Rowman and Littlefield, pp. 263–290.

Coffield, F. (2000) *Differing Visions of a Learning Society, Vol. 2*. Bristol: Policy Press.

Cohen, G.A. (1993) 'Equality of What? On Welfare, Goods and Capabilities', in M. Nussbaum and A. Sen *The Quality of Life*. Oxford: Oxford University Press, pp. 9–29.

Conservative Party (1987) *Election Manifesto*. [Online] available at: www.conservative-party.net/manifestos/1987/1987-conservative-manifesto.shtml (accessed 22 March).

Copeland, T. (1998) 'Constructing History: All Our Yesterdays', in M. Littledyke and L. Huxford (eds) *Teaching the Primary Curriculum for Constructive Learning*. London: David Fulton Publishers, pp. 119–130.

Cox, S. (2011) *New Perspectives in Primary Education*. Maidenhead: Open University Press.

CSBA (2010) *Education Issues Brief*. Californian School Boards Association. [Online] available at: www.csba.org/~/media/AC5BF2C5672340BB9482C3221C645FC9.ashx (accessed 22 March).

Day, C. and Smethem, L. (2009) 'The effects of reform: have teachers really lost their sense of professionalism?'. *Journal of Educational Change*. 10, pp. 141–157.

Davidson, D. (1984) 'The Very Idea of a Conceptual Scheme', in D. Davidson *Inquiry into Truth and Interpretation*. Oxford: Clarendon Press, pp. 183–198.

Davidson, D. (2001) 'A Coherence Theory of Truth and Knowledge', in D. Davidson *Subjective, Intersubjective, Objective*. Oxford: Clarendon Press, pp. 137–158.

Dearden, R.F. (1972) 'Autonomy and Education', in R.F. Dearden, P.H. Hirst and R.S. Peters (eds.) *Education and the Development of Reason*. London: Routledge, Kegan & Paul.

Derry, J. (2008) 'Abstract rationality in education'. *Studies in Philosophy and Education*. 27 (1), pp. 40–62.

Derry, J. (2013) 'Can inferentialism contribute to social epistemology?'. *Journal of Philosophy of Education*. 47 (2), pp. 222–235.

Dewey, J. (1916: 2007) *Democracy and Education*. Sioux Falls, SD: NuVision Publications.

Dewey, J. (1934) *Art as Experience*. New York: Minton, Balch and Company.

DfES (2004) *Key Stage 3 National Strategy: Pedagogy and Practice*, Unit 2: Teaching models. London: DfES.

Dickens, C. (2003) *Hard Times*. London: Penguin Books.

Dickens, C. (2008) *Little Dorrit*. London: Penguin Books.

Easton, L.D. and Guddat, K.H. (1967) *Writings of the Young Marx on Philosophy and Society*. New York: Doubleday.

Elgin, C.Z. (2007) 'Education and the Advancement of Understanding', in R. Curren (ed.) *Philosophy of Education*. Oxford: Blackwell.

Elliott, J. and Norris, N. (2012) *Curriculum, Pedagogy and Educational Research: The Work of Lawrence Stenhouse*. London: Routledge.

English, A. (2009) 'Transformation and education: the voice of the learner in Peters' concept of education'. *Journal of Philosophy of Education*. 43 (1), pp. 75–95.

Entwistle, H. (1979) *Antonio Gramsci: Conservative Schooling for Radical Politics*. London: Routledge.

Femia, J. (1981) *Gramsci's Political Thought*. Oxford: Clarendon Press.

Fraser, N. (1997) 'Rethinking the Public Sphere', in N. Fraser *Justice Interruptus: Critical Reflections on the 'Postsocialist' Condition*. New York: Routledge, pp. 67–150.

Gadamer, H.G. (1989) *Truth and Method*. Translated by J. Weinsheimer and D. Marshall. New York: Crossroad.

Garin, E. (1965) *Italian Humanism: Philosophy and Civic Life in the Renaissance*. Translated by P. Hunz. New York: Harper Row.

Ghosh, E. (2008) 'From republican to liberal liberty'. *History of Political Thought*. 29 (1), pp. 132–167.

Giroux, H. (1999) 'Rethinking cultural politics and radical pedagogy in the work of Antonio Gramsci'. *Educational Theory*. 49 (1), pp. 1–19.

Giroux, H., Holly, D. and Hoare, Q. (1980) 'Review Symposium: Antonio Gramsci: Conservative Schooling for Radical Politics'. *British Journal of Sociology of Education*. 1 (3), pp. 307–325.

Goodin, R. (2003) 'Folie républicaine'. *Annual Review of Political Science*. 6, pp. 55–76.

Goodson, I. (2005) *Learning, Curriculum and Life Politics: The Selected Works of Ivor Goodson*. London: Routledge.

Gove, M. (2013), *The Progressive Betrayal*, speech given to the Social Market Foundation, 5 February 2013. [Online] available at: www.smf.co.uk/media/news/michael-gove-speaks-smf/ (accessed 22 March 2014).

Gramsci, A. (1971) *Selections from Prison Notebooks*. Translated by Q. Hoare and G. Nowell Smith. London: Lawrence and Wishart.

Gray, J. (1991) 'Mill's Conception of Happiness', in J. Gray and G.W. Smith (eds) *J. S. Mill On Liberty in Focus*. London: Routledge, pp. 190–211.

Green, T.H. (1927) *Lectures on the Principles of Political Obligation*. London: Longmans.

Grice, H.P. (1957) 'Meaning'. *Philosophical Review*. 66 (3), pp. 377–388.

Guardian (2011, 15 January). 'Amy Chua: "I'm going to take all your stuffed animals and burn them!"' [Online] available at: www.guardian.co.uk/lifeandstyle/2011/jan/15/amy-chua-tiger-mother-interview (accessed 22 March 2014).

Gutmann, A. (1999) *Democratic Education*. Princeton, NJ: Princeton University Press.

Habermas, J. (1962) *Structural Transformation of the Public Sphere*. Cambridge: Polity Press.

Hale, J.R. (1977) *Florence and the Medici*. London: Thames and Hudson.

Haller, W. (1934) *Tracts on the Puritan Revolution*. New York: Columbia University Press.

Hand, M. (2006) 'Against autonomy as an educational aim'. *Oxford Review of Education*. 32 (4).

Harrington, J. (1992) *The Commonwealth of Oceana* and *A System of Politics*, ed. J.G.A. Pocock. Cambridge: Cambridge University Press.

Haydon, G. (ed.) (2010) *Educational Equality*. London: Continuum.

Hegel, G.W.F. (1977) *Phenomenology of Spirit*. Translated by A.V. Miller. Oxford: Oxford University Press.

Higgins, C. (2011) *The Good Life of Teaching: An Ethics of Professional Practice*. Malden, MA: Wiley-Blackwell.

Hinchliffe, G. (2006) 'Rethinking lifelong learning'. *Studies in Philosophy and Education*. 25, pp. 93–109.

Hinchliffe, G. (2011) 'What is an educational experience'. *Journal of Philosophy of Education*. 45 (3), pp. 417–431.

Hinchliffe, G. (2013) 'On the need for well-founded educational authority in England'. *Oxford Review of Education*. 39 (6), pp. 811–827.

Hirsch, E.D. (1996) *The Schools We Need*. New York: Anchor Books.

Hirst, P. (1972) 'Liberal Education and the Nature of Knowledge', in R. Peters (ed.) *The Philosophy of Education*. Oxford: Oxford University Press, pp. 87–111.

Hirst, P. (1998) 'Philosophy of Education: Evolution of a Discipline', in G. Hayden (ed.) *50 Years of Philosophy of Education: Progress and Prospects*. London: Institute of Education.

Hobbes, T. (1991) *Leviathan*, ed. R. Tuck. Cambridge: Cambridge University Press.

Kant, I. (1929) *Critique of Pure Reason*. Translated by N. Kemp Smith. London: Macmillan.

Kenny, A. (1977) 'Aristotle on Happiness', in J. Barnes, M. Schofield and R. Sorabji (eds) *Articles on Aristotle*. London: Duckworth.

Knapper, C. and Cropley, A. (2000) *Lifelong Learning in Higher Education*. London: Kegan Paul.

Knight Abowitz, K. (2011) 'Achieving Public Schools'. *Educational Theory*. 61 (4), pp. 467–489.

Knowles, D. (2010) *Political Obligation*. London: Routledge.

Kramer, M.H. (2003) *The Quality of Freedom*. Oxford: Oxford University Press.

Kramer, M.H. (2008) 'Liberty and Domination', in C. Laborde and J. Maynor (eds) *Republicanism and Political Theory*. Oxford: Blackwell Publishing, pp. 31–57.

Laborde, C. and Maynor, J. (eds) (2008) *Republicanism and Political Theory*. Oxford: Blackwell Publishing.

Labour Party (1997) *Election Manifesto*. [Online] available at: www.labour-party.org.uk/manifestos/1997/1997-labour-manifesto.shtml (accessed 22 March 2014).

Larmore, C. (2001) 'A critique of Philip Pettit's republicanism'. *Philosophical Issues*. 11, pp. 229–243.

Livy (1960) *The Early History of Rome*. Translated by A. de Selincourt. London: Penguin Books.

Locke, J. (1960) *Two Treatises of Government*, ed. P. Laslett. Cambridge: Cambridge University Press.

Locke, J. (1989) *Some Thoughts Concerning Education*, ed. J. Yolton. Oxford: Oxford University Press.

Lyotard, J-F. (1984) *The Postmodern Condition: A Report on Knowledge*. Manchester: Manchester University Press.

MacCallum, G. (1967) 'Negative and positive freedom'. *Philosophical Review*. 76, pp. 312–334.

McCulloch, G., Helsby, G. and Knight, P. (2000) *The Politics of Professionalism: Teachers and the Curriculum*. London: Continuum.

McDowell, J. (1994) *Mind and World*. Cambridge, MA: Harvard University Press.

McDowell, J. (2009a) *Having the World in View: Essays on Kant, Hegel and Sellars*. Cambridge, MA: Harvard University Press.

McDowell, J. (2009b) *The Engaged Intellect.* Cambridge, MA: Harvard University Press.

Machiavelli, N. (1960) *The Discourses.* London: Penguin Books.

MacIntyre, A. (1981) *After Virtue.* London: Duckworth.

Maclure, S. (ed.) (1988) *Education Reformed: Guide to the Education Reform Act.* London: Headway.

Macpherson, C.B. (1971) *Democratic Theory.* Oxford: Oxford University Press.

Mahony, P. and Hextall, I. (2001) 'Performing and Conforming', in D. Gleeson and C. Husbands (eds.) *The Performing School.* London: Routledge.

Mallett, M. and Shaw, C. (2012) *The Italian Wars, 1494–1559.* Harlow: Pearson Education.

Mill, J.S. (1859: 1991) 'On Liberty', in J. Gray and G.W. Smith (eds.) *J. S. Mill On Liberty in Focus.* London: Routledge.

Moore, R. (2004) *Education and Society.* Cambridge: Polity Press.

Norwood Report (1943) [Online] available at: www.educationengland.org.uk/documents/norwood/norwood1943.html (accessed 22 March 2014).

Nussbaum, M. (2000) *Women and Human Development: The Capabilities Approach.* Cambridge: Cambridge University Press.

Nussbaum, M. and Sen, A. (1993) *The Quality of Life.* Oxford: Oxford University Press.

Oakeshott, M. (1975) *On Human Conduct.* Oxford: Clarendon Press.

Ofsted (2012a) *Framework for School Inspection.* [Online] available at: www.ofsted.gov.uk/resources/framework-for-school-inspection-january-2012 (accessed 22 March 2014).

Ofsted (2012b) *School Inspection Handbook.* [Online] available at: www.ofsted.gov.uk/resources/school-inspection-handbook-september-2012 (accessed 22 March 2014).

O'Hagan, T. (1998) *Rousseau.* London: Routledge.

Patterson, O. (1982) *Slavery and Social Death.* Cambridge, MA: Harvard University Press.

Peters, R.S. (1966) *Ethics and Education.* London: George Allen and Unwin.

Peterson, A. (2011) *Civic Republicanism and Civic Education.* Basingstoke: Palgrave Macmillan.

Pettit, P. (1997) *Republicanism: A Theory of Freedom and Government.* Oxford: Oxford University Press.

Pettit, P. (2001) *A Theory of Freedom.* Cambridge: Polity Press.

Pettit, P. (2008) 'Republican Freedom: Three Axioms, Four Theorems', in C. Laborde and J. Maynor (eds) *Republicanism and Political Theory.* Oxford: Blackwell Publishing, pp. 102–130.

Pitkin, H. (1972) 'Obligation and Consent', in P. Laslett, W.G. Runciman and Q. Skinner (eds) *Philosophy, Politics and Society, Fourth Series.* Oxford: Basil Blackwell, pp. 45–85.

Plaskow, M. (1985) *The Life and Death of the Schools Council.* London: Taylor and Francis.

Plato (1987) *The Republic.* Translated by D. Lee. London: Penguin Books.

Plowden Report (1967) *Children and their Primary Schools.* London: HMSO.

Pocock, J.G.A. (1975) *The Machiavellian Moment.* Princeton, NJ: Princeton University Press.

Pollard, A. and James, M. (2004) *Personalised Learning.* ESRC Report.

Price, R. (1991) *Political Writings*, ed. D.O. Thomas. Cambridge: Cambridge University Press.

Pring, R. (ed.) (2008) 'The common school and the comprehensive ideal'. *Journal of Philosophy of Education*. 4 (1).

Pritchard, A. and Woollard, J. (2010) *Constructivism and Social Learning*. London: Routledge.

Quintilian (1920) Institutio Oratoria, Vol. III (Loeb Classical Library edition).

Rata, E. (2012) 'Politics of knowledge in education'. *British Educational Research Journal*. 38 (1), pp. 103–124.

Rawls, J. (1972) *A Theory of Justice*. Oxford: Oxford University Press.

Raz, J. (1986) *The Morality of Freedom*. Oxford: Oxford University Press.

Raz, J. (1990) *Authority*. Oxford: Blackwell.

Reiss, M. and White, J. (2013) *An Aims-Based Curriculum: The Significance of Human Flourishing for Schools*. London: Barnes and Noble, Bedford Way Papers.

Roach, J. (1991) *Secondary Education in England, 1870–1902*. London: Routledge.

Rorty R., Schneewind J.B. and Skinner, Q. (1984) *Philosophy in History*. Cambridge: Cambridge University Press.

Rousseau, J-J. (1762: 1979) *Emile*. Translated by A. Bloom. New York: Basic Books.

Rubinsten, D. (1979) 'Socialisation and the London School Board 1870–1904', in P. McCann *Popular Education and Socialisation in the Nineteenth Century*. London: Methuen, pp. 231–264.

Rubenstein, N. (ed.) (1968) *Florentine Studies: Politics and Society in Renaissance Florence*. London: Faber and Faber.

Ryle, G. (1949) *The Concept of Mind*. London: Harmondsworth.

Sachs, J. (2003) *The Activist Teaching Profession*. Buckingham: Open University Press.

Sandel, M. (1996) *Democracy's Discontent*. Cambridge: Harvard University Press.

Schön, D. (1983) *The Reflective Practitioner*. New York: Basic Books.

Sellars, W. (1953) 'Inference and Meaning'. *Mind*. 62, pp. 313–338.

Sellars, W. (1956) 'Empiricism and the Philosophy of Mind', in H. Freigl and M. Scriven (eds) *Minnesota Studies in the Philosophy of Science. Vol. 1*. Minneapolis: University of Minnesota.

Selley, N. (1999) *The Art of Constructivist Teaching in the Primary School*. London: David Fulton Publishers.

Sen, A. (1982) *Choice, Welfare and Measurement*. Oxford: Oxford University Press.

Sen, A. (1993) 'Capability and Well Being', in M. Nussbaum and A. Sen *The Quality of Life*. Oxford: Oxford University Press, pp. 30–53.

Sen, A. (1999) *Development as Freedom*. Oxford: Oxford University Press.

Sen, A. (2009) *The Idea of Justice*. London: Allen Lane, Penguin Books.

Shay, S. (2012) *Contesting Purposes for Higher Education: A Curriculum Point of View*, paper delivered to the Annual Conference for the Society for Research into Higher Education (SRHE), Newport, South Wales, December 2012.

Simon, B. (1965) *Education and the Labour Movement 1870–1920*. London: Lawrence and Wishart.

Skinner, Q. (1978) *Foundations of Modern Political Thought, Vol. 1*. Cambridge: Cambridge University Press.

Skinner, Q. (1984) 'The Idea of Negative Liberty: Philosophical and Historical Perspectives', in R. Rorty, J.B. Schneewind and Q. Skinner *Philosophy in History*. Cambridge: Cambridge University Press, pp. 193–221.

Skinner, Q. (1998) *Liberty before Liberalism*. Cambridge: Cambridge University Press.

Skinner, Q. (2002a) 'A third concept of liberty'. *Proceedings of the British Academy*. 117, pp. 237–268.

Skinner, Q. (2002b) *Visions of Politics, Vol. II*. Cambridge: Cambridge University Press.

Skinner, Q. (2003) 'States and the Freedom of Citizens', in Skinner, Q. and Strath, B. *States and Citizens*. Cambridge: Cambridge University Press, pp. 11–27.

Skinner, Q. (2008a) 'Freedom as the Absence of Arbitrary Power', in C. Laborde and J. Maynor (eds.) *Republicanism and Political Theory*. Oxford: Blackwell Publishing, pp. 83–101.

Skinner, Q. (2008b) *Hobbes and Republican Liberty*. Cambridge: Cambridge University Press.

Skinner, Q. (2008c) 'Genealogy of the state'. *Proceedings of the British Academy*. 162, pp. 325–370.

Smith, N.H. (2002) *Reading McDowell*. London: Routledge.

Spinoza (2000) *Political Treatise*, eds S. Shirley, S. Barbone and L. Rice. Indiana: Hackett Publishing Company.

Stanley, J. and Williamson, T. (2001) 'Knowing-how'. *Journal of Philosophy*. 48 (4), pp. 411–444.

Steiner, H. (1994) *An Essay on Rights*. Oxford: Blackwell.

Stenhouse, L. (1967) *Culture and Education*. London: Nelson.

Tacitus (1948) *Tacitus on Britain and Germany*. Translated by H. Mattingly. London: Penguin Books.

Taylor, C. (1985a) *Philosophical Papers: Human Agency and Language*. New York: Cambridge University Press.

Taylor, C. (1985b) *Philosophical Papers: Philosophy and the Human Sciences*. New York: Cambridge University Press.

Tomlinson, S. (2005) *Education in a Post-Welfare Society*. Buckingham: Open University Press.

Tooley, J. (2007) 'From Adam Swift to Adam Smith: how the 'Invisible Hand' overcomes middle class hypocrisy'. *Journal of Philosophy of Education*. 41 (4), pp. 727–741.

Tuck, R. (1972) 'Why is Authority Such a Problem?', in P. Laslett, W.G. Runciman and Q. Skinner (eds) *Philosophy, Politics and Society, Fourth Series*. Oxford: Basil Blackwell, pp. 194–207.

Tuck, R. (1979) *Natural Rights*. Cambridge: Cambridge University Press.

Tuck, R. (1993) *Philosophy and Government 1572–1651*. Cambridge: Cambridge University Press.

United Nations (1948) *Universal Declaration of Human Rights*. [Online] available at: www.un.org/en/documents/udhr/ (accessed 25 March 2014).

Vygotsky, L. (1962) *Thought and Language*. Cambridge, MA: MIT Press.

Weber, M. (1948) *From Max Weber: Essays in Sociology*, eds H.H. Gerth and C. Wright Mills. London: Routledge, Kegan and Paul, pp. 196–240.

White, J. (2009) 'Why General Education? Peters, Hirst and History'. *Journal of Philosophy of Education*. 43 (1), pp. 123–141.

Wiggins, D. (2012) 'Practical knowledge: knowing how to and knowing that'. *Mind*. 121 (481), pp. 97–130.

Willis, P.E. (1977) *Learning to Labour: How Working Class Kids get Working Class Jobs*. Farnborough: Saxon House.

Wilson, T.S. (2010) 'Civil fragmentation or voluntary association?'. *Educational Theory*. 60 (6), pp. 643–664.

Winch, C. (2010) *Dimensions of Expertise*. London: Continuum.

Winch, C. (2013) 'Curriculum design and epistemic ascent'. *Journal of Philosophy of Education*. 47 (1), pp. 128–146.

Winch, P. (1967) 'Authority', in A. Quinton *Political Philosophy*. Oxford: Oxford University Press, p. 106.

Wirszubski, C.H. (1950) *Libertas*. Cambridge: Cambridge University Press.

Wittgenstein, L. (1958) *Philosophical Investigations*. Oxford: Blackwell.

Wooding, L. (2009) *Henry VIII*. London: Routledge.

Young, M. (ed.) (1971) *Knowledge and Control: New Directions for the Sociology of Education*. Buckingham: Open University.

Young, M. (2008) *Bringing Knowledge Back In: From Social Constructivism to Social Realism in the Sociology of Education*. London: Routledge.

Young, M. (2010) 'Why educators must differentiate knowledge from experience'. *Journal of the Pacific Circle Consortium for Education*. 2 (1), pp. 9–20.